P9-BYI-338

Visual Basic .Net
Core Language

Little Black Book

Steven Holzner

PARAGLYPH
PRESS

President
Keith Weiskamp

Editor-at-Large
Jeff Duntemann

Vice President, Sales, Marketing, and Distribution
Steve Sayre

Vice President, International Sales and Marketing
Cynthia Caldwell

Editorial Director
Sharon Linsenbach

Production Manager
Kim Eoff

Visual Basic.Net Core Language Little Black Book

Limits of Liability and Disclaimer of Warranty

The author and publisher of this book have used their best efforts in preparing the book and the programs contained in it. These efforts include the development, research, and testing of the theories and programs to determine their effectiveness. The author and publisher make no warranty of any kind, expressed or implied, with regard to these programs or the documentation contained in this book.

The author and publisher shall not be liable in the event of incidental or consequential damages in connection with, or arising out of, the furnishing, performance, or use of the programs, associated instructions, and/or claims of productivity gains.

Trademarks

Trademarked names appear throughout this book. Rather than list the names and entities that own the trademarks or insert a trademark symbol with each mention of the trademarked name, the publisher states that it is using the names for editorial purposes only and to the benefit of the trademark owner, with no intention of infringing upon that trademark.

Paraglyph Press, Inc.
2246 E. Myrtle Avenue
Phoenix, Arizona 85202
Phone: 602-749-8787

Paraglyph Press ISBN: 1-932111-68-9

Printed in the United States of America
10 9 8 7 6 5 4 3 2 1

PARAGLYPH PRESS

The Paraglyph Mission

This book you've purchased is a collaborative creation involving the work of many hands, from authors to editors to designers and to technical reviewers. At Paraglyph Press, we like to think that everything we create, develop, and publish is the result of one form creating another. And as this cycle continues on, we believe that your suggestions, ideas, feedback, and comments on how you've used our books is an important part of the process for us and our authors.

We've created Paraglyph Press with the sole mission of producing and publishing books that make a difference. The last thing we all need is yet another tech book on the same tired, old topic. So we ask our authors and all of the many creative hands who touch our publications to do a little extra, dig a little deeper, think a little harder, and create a better book. The founders of Paraglyph are dedicated to finding the best authors, developing the best books, and helping you find the solutions you need.

As you use this book, please take a moment to drop us a line at **feedback@paraglyphpress.com** and let us know how we are doing - and how we can keep producing and publishing the kinds of books that you can't live without.

Sincerely,

Keith Weiskamp & Jeff Duntemann
Paraglyph Press Founders

Paraglyph Press
2246 East Myrtle Ave.
Phoenix, AZ 85020

email:
feedback@paraglyphpress.com
Web: **www.paraglyphpress.com**
Phone: 602-749-8787
Fax: 602-861-1941

To Nancy, now and forever!

&

About the Author

Steven Holzner wrote the book on Visual Basic . . . a number of times. He co-authored with Peter Norton the bestseller *Peter Norton's Visual Basic for Windows* and *Peter Norton's Guide to Visual Basic*. He also wrote *Advanced Visual Basic Programming*, a 650-pager that came out in three editions, and *Internet Programming With Visual Basic*, as well as several other Visual Basic books. His most recent is the comprehensive *Visual Basic .NET Black Book*. All in all, this former contributing editor for *PC Magazine* has authored 71 books ranging in subjects from assembly language to Visual C++, but Visual Basic is his favorite topic. Holzner's books have sold over a million copies and have been translated into 16 languages around the world.

Steve Holzner was on the faculty of Cornell University for 10 years, where he earned his Ph.D. He's also been on the faculty at his undergraduate school, Massachusetts Institute of Technology. Steve loves to travel, and has been to over 30 countries, from Afghanistan to India, from Borneo to Iran, from Sweden to Thailand, with more to come. He and Nancy live in a small picturesque town on the New England coast and spend summers in their house in the Austrian Alps.

Contents at a Glance

Table of Contents

Introduction

Welcome to the Visual Basic .NET Little Black Book. There is as much Visual Basic .NET crammed into this book as possible, broken down into hundreds of easily-accessible topics, each short and to the point, and each with an example. The format here is like no other computer book series, and it's designed to give you exactly what you want, when you want it.

The task-based format we use in this book is the one many programmers appreciate, because programming is a task-based business. Rather than reading about subjects in the order I might think best, you can go directly to your topic of interest and find the bite-sized nugget of information you need.

And best of all, there's a working example in code for almost every programming topic in the book. The actual process of programming is not abstract, it's very applied, and so instead of vague generalities, we get down to the specifics—all the specifics—that give you everything you need to understand and use Visual Basic .NET.

In the old days, programming books used to be very top-down, with chapters on subjects like "Conditional Branching," "Loop Structures," "Variable Declarations," and so forth. But who sits down to program by saying, "I'm about to create a conditional program flow branch"?

Instead, programmers are more interested in performing useful tasks, like adding buttons, menus, list boxes, or toolbars to a windows; creating graphics animation; creating dialog boxes; creating setup programs, working with files, linking to Web pages, multi-threading, supporting online help, and so on. And this book is written for programmers.

Because this book is written for programmers, each chapter is broken up into dozens of practical programming tasks. After selecting the chapter you want, you can turn to the Table of Contents, or the first page in that chapter, to find the task you're interested in. Hundreds of tasks are covered in this book, chosen to be the ones that programmers want to see.

In addition, this book is filled with examples covering nearly every Visual Basic .NET programming area there is. These examples are bite-sized and to the point, so you don't have to wade through a dozen files trying to understand one simple topic.

What's in This Book

From an extensive language reference to ADO.NET database programming, from creating Web applications to dragging and dropping data adapters onto forms, from creating Windows and Web controls to setup programs, there's a great amount of information in this book. Note, however, that we can't fit everything into a book this size; if you can't find what you're looking for here, take a look at the Visual Basic .NET Black Book, which is the most complete book out there on the subject.

Here's some of what we'll see in this book:

- The Visual Basic Intgrated Development Environment (IDE)
- The complete Visual Basic syntax
- Using Structured Exception Handling
- Exception Filtering in the Catch Block
- Throwing Exceptions
- Creating Windows applications
- Creating Web applications
- Showing and Hiding Controls and Forms
- Working With Multiple Forms
- Creating Dialog Boxes
- Adding and Removing Controls at Run Time
- Using the core Windows and Web controls.
- Creating Menus
- Creating Submenus
- Creating Menu Access Keys
- Changing a Menu Item's Caption at Run Time

- Drawing Menu Items Yourself
- Creating Context Menus
- Object-oriented Programming (OOP)
- Creating Classes, Objects, OOP Structures, Modules, and Constructors
- Creating Data Members, Methods, Properties, and Events
- Overloading Methods
- Inheriting From a Base Class
- Overriding Base Class Members
- Overloading Base Class Members
- Forcing Event Handling in Web Forms
- Writing HTML to a Web Form at Run Time
- Detecting Browser Type and Capabilities
- Saving Program Data Across Server Round Trips
- Creating Web Form Validators
- Creating a New Data Connection
- Creating a Dataset
- Data Access Using Data Adapter Controls
- Adding Multiple Tables to a Dataset
- Simple and Complex Data Binding
- Navigating in Datasets
- Accessing Individual Data Items in a Dataset
- Writing Datasets to XML and Reading Datasets From XML
- Creating Multithreaded Applications
- Starting, Suspending, Resuming, Stopping, and Sleeping Threads
- Synchronizing Threads
- Joining Threads
- Creating a Windows Service
- Creating a Windows Service Installer
- Deploying Applications

That's just some of what's coming up—Visual Basic .NET is a big topic, and the topics we'll cover number in the hundreds. And if you have suggestions for more, please send them in!

Conventions

There are a few conventions in this book that you should know about. For example, when some code is new and should be especially pointed out, it'll appear shaded. And when there's more code that I'm not showing to save space, you'll see three dots arranged vertically like this:

```
Public Class Form1
    Inherits System.Windows.Forms.Form

#Region " Windows Form Designer generated code"

    Public Sub New()
        MyBase.New()
        .
        .
        .
```

Also, when we discuss the in-depth syntax of Visual Basic statements, there are a few conventions and terms you should be aware of. In the formal definition of each statement, you use brackets, [and], for optional items, and curly braces, { and }, to indicate that you select one of the enclosed items, like this for the **Dim** statement:

```
[{ Public | Protected | Friend | Protected Friend | Private | Static
}] [ Shared ] [ Shadows ] [ ReadOnly ] Dim [ WithEvents ] name[
(boundlist) ] [ As [ New ] type ] [ = initexpr ]
```

And I use the standard syntax for menu items—for example, the File | New item refers to the New item in the File menu. You'll also see many tips throughout the book, which are meant to give you something more—more insight and more behind-the-scenes data. Tips look like this one:

Tip: Needing a server roundtrip to access your data can slow things down considerably. The Internet Explorer actually does have a number of data source objects that you can use to work with recordsets directly with scripting languages in the browser. One of the data source objects built into the Internet Explorer, the Remote Data Service (RDS), even lets you use connection strings, SQL, and so on, to fill a recordset object.

And you'll also see notes, which are designed to give you some additional information, like this this note in Chapter 1:

Note: *In Visual Basic 6.0, coordinates for forms and controls were expressed in twips; in Visual Basic.NET, coordinates are expressed in pixels (and only pixels).*

What You'll Need

To use this book, you'll need Visual Basic .NET. In addition, if you want to create Web applications and services, you'll also need a Web server running the Microsoft Internet Information Server (IIS), as detailed in Chapter 13. IIS can be running on your local machine, and it comes with some Windows versions, such as Windows 2000 (note that although comes on the Windows 2000 CDs, it may not have been installed on your machine by your computer's manufacturer).

To work with databases, you'll need to use a data provider, as discussed in Chapter 15. I use SQL Server here, but you can use other providers. (However, note that most database examples that use a connection to a data provider use the pubs example database that comes with SQL Server.) Knowing some SQL will be a good idea to work with data applications.

Resources

Where can you go for additional Visual Basic support? You can find Visual Basic user groups all over, and more are appearing every day. Although the content varies in accuracy there are many usenet groups dedicated to Visual Basic as well, but be careful what you read there—there's no guarantee it's accurate. About three dozen of those groups are hosted by Microsoft, including:

- microsoft.public.dotnet.languages.vb
- microsoft.public.dotnet.languages.vb.upgrade
- microsoft.public.vb.bugs
- microsoft.public.vb.addins
- microsoft.public.vb.controls
- microsoft.public.vb.database
- microsoft.public.vb.installation
- microsoft.public.vb.syntax

Other, non-Microsoft groups include some of these usenet forums:

- comp.lang.basic.visual
- comp.lang.basic.visual.3rdparty

- comp.lang.basic.visual.announce
- comp.lang.basic.visual.database
- comp.lang.basic.visual.misc

And, of course, there are plenty of Web pages out there on Visual Basic. Here are a few starter pages from Microsoft:

- http://msdn.microsoft.com/vbasic/ The main Visual Basic page
- http://msdn.microsoft.com/vbasic/technical/articles.asp The tech page for Visual Basic
- www.microsoft.com/net/default.asp The home page for the .NET initiative

The Little Black Book Philosophy

Written by experienced professionals, Paraglyph's Little Black Books are terse, easily "thumb-able" question-answerers and problem solvers. The Little Black Book's unique two-part chapter format—brief technical overviews followed by practical immediate solutions—is structured to help you use your knowledge, solve problems, and quickly master complex technical issues to become an expert. By breaking down complex topics into easily manageable components, this format helps you quickly find what you need with the code you need to make it happen.

We welcome your feedback on this book. You can email us at Paraglyph at feedback@paraglyphpress.com.

And that's it, that's all the introduction we need—it's time to start digging into Visual Basic .NET now. As I said, this book has been designed to be your complete support package for Visual Basic .NET, so if you see something that should be covered and isn't—let me know. In the meantime, happy programming!

Chapter 1

Essential Visual Basic

Welcome to the Little Black Book on Visual Basic .NET! Visual Basic .NET has been almost three years in the making, and it's an entirely new direction for Visual Basic. Besides the biggest change—support for Web development—the very syntax of Visual Basic has undergone great change. And I'm going to take a look at as much of all of it as I can in this book.

If you already know previous versions of Visual Basic, a great number of techniques that you've probably learned carefully, such as data handling, are now completely different, and many controls, project types, and other aspects will no longer be available at all. All of this means that there's a terrific amount of material we need to cover—so I'm going to pack as much Visual Basic .NET into this book as will fit.

Even so, note that there's more Visual Basic .NET than I'm going to pack into the space I have here—if you need more complete coverage on a particular topic, take a look at the *Visual Basic .NET Black Book*.

This book's coverage isn't going to be like a lot of other books that hold their topic at an arm's length and just give you dry documentation. This book is written from the programmer's point of view, for programmers, and I'm going to try to give you as much of the good stuff as I can. I use Visual Basic .NET myself, and I know that to master this subject, nothing is better than an in-depth treatment with many examples and tips that will save you a lot of time.

Visual Basic has a long and, so far, glorious history. When it first appeared, it created a revolution in Windows programming. Never before had Windows programming been so easy—just build the program you want, right before your eyes, and then run it. Visual Basic introduced unheard-of ease to Windows programming and changed programming from a chore to something very much like fun.

In time, Visual Basic has gotten more complex as well as more powerful. Today, it's more complex than ever, and if you've used Visual Basic 6, you may be surprised at all the new additions. In this book on VB .NET, you're going to see how to use Visual Basic in a task-oriented way, which is the best way to write about programming. Instead of superimposing some abstract structure on the material in this book, I'll organize it the way programmers want it—task by task.

I'll start this book with an overview of Visual Basic, taking a look at topics common to the material in the rest of the book. In this chapter, we'll create the foundation we'll rely on later as we take a look at the basics of Visual Basic, including how to create Visual Basic projects, seeing what's in such projects, seeing what's new in Visual Basic .NET, and getting an overview of essential Visual Basic .NET concepts like Windows and Web forms, controls, events, properties, methods, and so on. Note, however, that I'll assume in this chapter that you have at least a little experience with Visual Basic and programming.

Before I start covering all the details in Visual Basic in depth, let's take a look at an example. Rather than getting lost in the details, let's see Visual Basic at work immediately. Because one has to master so many details, it's easy to forget that Visual Basic is there to make things as easy as possible for you. In fact, programming in Visual Basic can be as close to *fun* as programming gets.

Putting Visual Basic to Work

Start Visual Studio now. You'll see the Visual Studio Integrated Development Environment appear, as in Figure 1.1. I'm not going to go into the details here because I'll cover them in the next chapter—right now, let's just have a little fun.

Generally, Visual Basic has three types of applications—those based on Windows forms (such applications are usually local to your machine), Web forms (which come to you across the Internet), and console applications (which run in a DOS window). I'll take a look at Windows forms here first, which will be the most familiar to Visual Basic 6 programmers.

Creating a Windows Application

To create an application based on Windows forms, select the New item in the File menu, and then select the Project item in the submenu that appears. This brings up the New Project dialog box you see in Figure 1.2.

Select the folder labeled Visual Basic Projects in the Project Types box, as shown in Figure 1.2, and select the Windows Application project type in the Templates box. You can also name the new

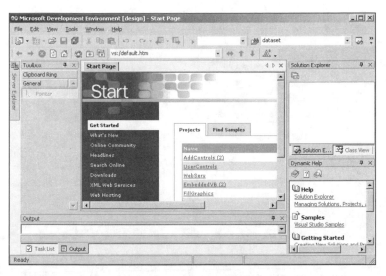

Figure 1.1   The Visual Basic Integrated Development Environment.

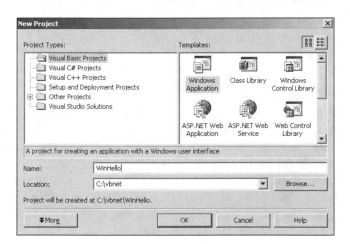

Figure 1.2   The Visual Basic New Project dialog box.

project—I'll name it WinHello—and specify where to store it—I'll store it in the c:\vbnet folder, as you see in Figure 1.2. Now click on OK to create this new Visual Basic project. Visual Basic creates a new Windows project and gives you the result you see in Figure 1.3.

The window you see at the center of Figure 1.3, labeled "Form1," is the window that will become our new Windows application; in Visual Basic, as you most likely know, these windows are called *forms*. The genius of Visual Basic has always been that it's *visual*, which means

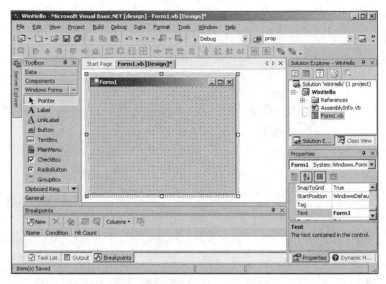

Figure 1.3   Designing a new Windows application.

that you can design your applications visually. In this case, I'll just add two Windows *controls* to this form—a text box and a button. When you click on the button, the application will display the text "Hello from Visual Basic" in the text box.

Controls are user-interface elements that you see in Windows all the time, such as list boxes, scrollbars, buttons, menus, and so on. To add a text box to Form1, first make sure that the Visual Basic *toolbox* is open. You can see the toolbox to the left of Form1 in Figure 1.3; if you don't see the toolbox, select the View|Toolbox menu item to display it. Now click the Windows Forms item in the toolbox so that the toolbox displays the possible controls you can use in Windows forms, such as text boxes, buttons, labels, link labels, and so on.

In a move that's very familiar to Visual Basic programmers, you can now simply *drag* a text box from the toolbox to Form1 or just double-click the ToolBox entry in the toolbox. This adds a text box to Form1; position and stretch it with the mouse until it appears roughly as you see it in Figure 1.4. (The boxes you see around the text box are *sizing handles*, and if you've used Visual Basic at all, you know that you can use them to change the size of the text box.)

Next, add a button to Form1 in the same manner, as you see in Figure 1.5. Visual Basic 6 programmers can already see many differences here—including the fact that the button is labeled **Button1**, not **Command1**, and that the text box is labeled **TextBox1**, not **Text1**.

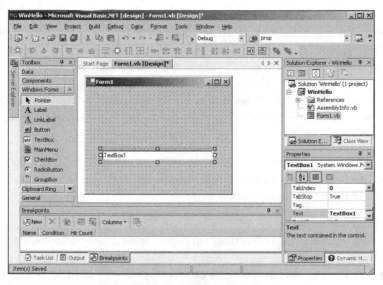

Figure 1.4   Adding a text box to a Windows application.

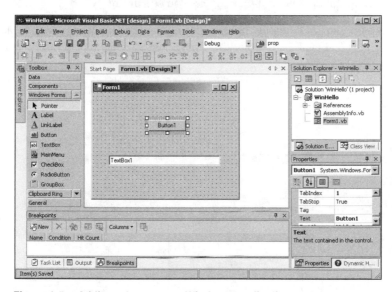

Figure 1.5   Adding a button to a Windows application.

These are the controls that will appear in our application. The next step is to customize them; in this case, I'll start by changing the caption of the button from "Button1" to "Click Me." To do that, click on the button in Form1 to select it so that the fuzzy outline you see in Figure 1.5 appears around it. Next, move to the Properties window at the lower right of the IDE, which lists the properties of the currently selected control or object (if you can't see the Properties window, select the View|Properties Window menu item). Click on the **Text** property (no longer the **Caption** property of Visual Basic 6) in the Properties window and change the text of the button from "Button1" to "Click Me", as you see in Figure 1.6. You set *properties* of objects like this button to customize them, and we'll be doing so throughout the book. The Properties window lists properties like the **Text** property on the left and their values on the right; to change a property's value, you only have to edit its setting and press Enter.

In the same way, erase the text in the text box by using its **Text** property in the Properties window, giving you the result you see in Figure 1.7, where the text in both controls is as we want it.

Visual Basic has done a lot of programming for us to get us to this point, but it can't do everything; in particular, it's up to us to add some code to place the message "Hello from Visual Basic" in the text box when the user clicks on the button. To associate code with the button, you just double-click on the button, as you would in Visual Basic 6, opening the corresponding code, as you see in Figure 1.8.

Find the part of the code that handles clicks of the button, which looks like this (this will also look different to Visual Basic 6 programmers):

```
Private Sub Button1_Click(ByVal sender As System.Object, _
    ByVal e As System.EventArgs) Handles Button1.Click

End Sub
```

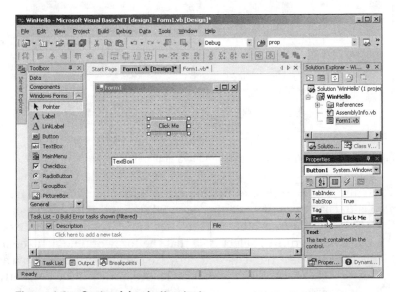

Figure 1.6   Customizing button text.

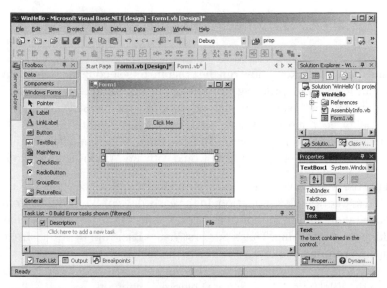

Figure 1.7   Customizing a text box's text.

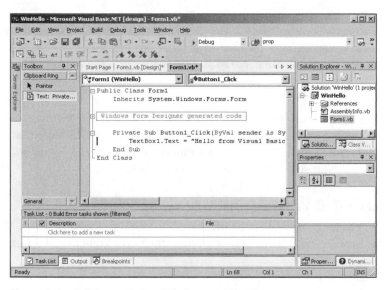

Figure 1.8   Editing code in a Windows application.

To place the text we want in the text box when the user clicks on the button, enter the following directly into the code, as you see in Figure 1.8; this sets the **Text** property of the text box, **TextBox1**, to "Hello from Visual Basic".

```
Private Sub Button1_Click(ByVal sender As System.Object, _
    ByVal e As System.EventArgs) Handles Button1.Click
```

```
     TextBox1.Text = "Hello from Visual Basic"
End Sub
```

And that's all it takes—now run the program by selecting the Debug|Start menu item or by pressing F5. The application starts, as you see in Figure 1.9—and when you click on Click Me, the message "Hello from Visual Basic" appears in the text box, as you see in Figure 1.9. That's it—our first program is a success. To close the application, click on the X button at the upper right, as you would with any Windows application.

This is the magic of Visual Basic—with one line of code, we've created a functioning application. In the early days of Windows, it would have taken a minimum of five pages of dense C or C++ code to have done the same thing. That's our first Visual Basic application, already up and running. Make sure you save the WinHello application (Visual Basic will save all files when it runs an application, but you can also use the File|Save All menu item) before moving on.

TIP: As Visual Basic programmers know, Visual Basic has a handy way of letting you know when a file has been changed and has not yet been saved—an asterisk (*) will appear after the name of the file. You can see this asterisk for the file Form1.vb, if you look in the IDE's title bar and in the tabs above the code window in Figure 1.8 because we've modified that file without saving it yet.

In fact, this is all pretty familiar to Visual Basic 6 programmers—so let's do something new: create a Web application. This application will do the same as the Windows application we've just seen, but it'll run on a Web server and appear in a browser.

Creating a Web Application

To create a new Web application in Visual Basic, select the File|New|Project menu item, opening the New Project dialog box as

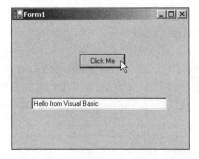

Figure 1.9   Running a Windows application.

before. This time, select the Visual Basic Projects folder in the Project Types box, also as before, but this time select ASP.NET Web Application in the Templates box.

Give this new application the name WebHello, as you see in Figure 1.10—and now comes the tricky part. To create a Web application, you need a Web server that uses the Microsoft Internet Information Server (IIS) version 5.0 or later (with FrontPage extensions installed), and that server must be running. You can enter the location of your server in the Location box in the New Project dialog box. If you have IIS running on your local machine, Visual Basic will find it and use that server by default, as you see in Figure 1.10, where Visual Basic has selected **http:// STEVE**, my local IIS server. (IIS comes with operating systems like Windows 2000 Server; it also comes with Windows 2000 Professional, although you have to install it from the Windows 2000 CDs.) When you click on OK, Visual Basic will create the new Web application, as you see in Figure 1.11.

As you can see, designing Web applications looks much like designing Windows applications. You can see a note in the Web form under design—called a page—at the center of the IDE that says that we're using the *grid layout mode*. In this mode, controls will stay where you position them, just as they did when we created our Windows application. The other layout mode is the *flow layout mode*; in this mode, the controls in your application will move around as they would in a standard Web page, depending on where the browser wants to put them. (If your

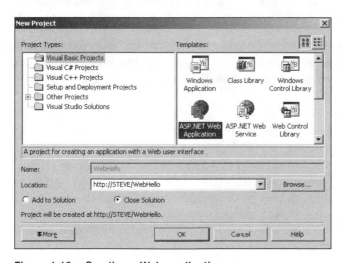

Figure 1.10   Creating a Web application.

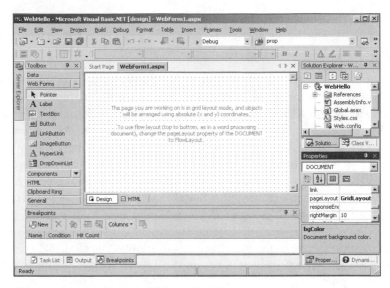

Figure 1.11   Designing a Web application.

Web application happens to start in flow layout mode, click on the Web form itself, and then set the **pageLayout** property in the Properties window at the lower right to **GridLayout**. If you've used Visual Basic before, you're already familiar with the Properties window; it's also covered in detail in the next chapter.)

Now we can design our new Web application just as we did the Windows application. Click the Web forms item in the toolbox and add both a text box and a button to the Web form, as you see in Figure 1.12.

And, as before, we can double-click the button to open its associated code, as you see in Figure 1.13. We can add the same code to handle the button click as before; find this code in the code window:

```
Private Sub Button1_Click(ByVal sender As System.Object, _
    ByVal e As System.EventArgs) Handles Button1.Click

End Sub
```

Then add this code, as we have before:

```
TextBox1.Text = "Hello from Visual Basic"
```

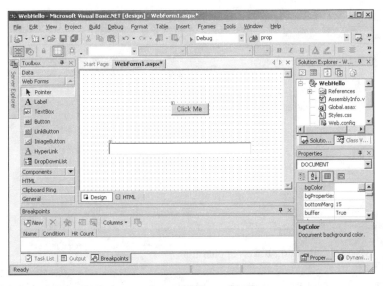

Figure 1.12   Adding controls to a Web application.

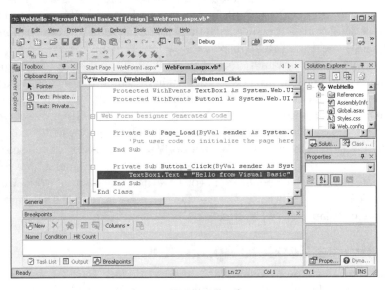

Figure 1.13   Adding code to a Web application.

That's all it takes—now run the application as we have before by selecting the Debug|Start menu item or by pressing F5. The application comes up in your browser, as shown in Figure 1.14, and when you click on the button, the message "Hello from Visual Basic" appears in the text box, just as it did in our Windows application.

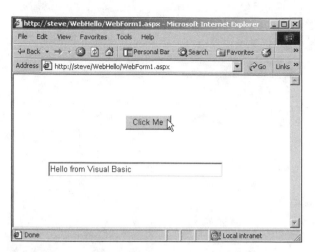

Figure 1.14   Running a Web application.

That's our first Web application. To close the application, just close the browser window. As you can see, this Web application is remarkably similar to our Windows application, and that's the primary inspiration behind VB .NET—bringing Visual Basic to the Internet. Web applications like this one use HTML to display their controls in a Web page, so those controls have more limitations than do Windows controls, but as you can see, the design process is very similar. Behind the scenes, Visual Basic .NET has been storing the application's files on the Web server automatically—no special uploading needed. Anyone with a browser can look at the application on the Internet simply by navigating to its URL (in this case, that's **http://steve/WebHello/WebForm1.aspx**, as you see in the browser's title bar in Figure 1.14). If you're like me, the first time you create and run a Web application, you'll feel a lot like saying, "Wow." Web applications like this will make Web development a great deal easier and more popular on IIS platforms.

Creating a Console Application

Another new type of Visual Basic application in VB .NET consists of console applications. These applications are command-line based and run in DOS windows. This gives one the feeling once again that VB .NET is following the lead of Java because Java applications run in DOS windows in Windows (and before this, Visual Basic itself hadn't interacted with DOS for years—not since the ancient and ill-fated VB DOS version). However, the change is a welcome one because it provides you with an option for very simple programming without worrying about user interface implementation and issues.

To see how console applications work, use the File|New|Project menu item to open the New Project menu item and select Console Application in the Templates box, as shown in Figure 1.15. Name this new project ConsoleHello as in Figure 1.15. Then click on OK to create the new project.

When you create this new project, you see the result in Figure 1.16. Note that in this case, because no user interface is present, Visual Basic opens the project directly to a code window.

The code here looks like this:

```
Module Module1

    Sub Main()

    End Sub

End Module
```

Console applications are based on Visual Basic *modules*, which are specifically designed to hold code that is not attached to any form or other such class. Notice also the **Sub Main()** procedure here. As we'll see in more depth in Chapter 5, a **Sub** procedure is a series of Visual Basic statements enclosed by the **Sub** and **End Sub** statements. When the console application is run, those statements are run automatically.

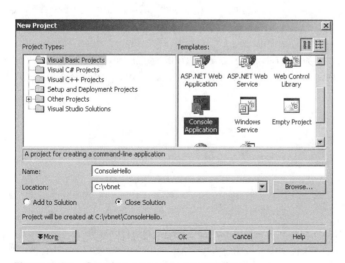

Figure 1.15   Creating a console application.

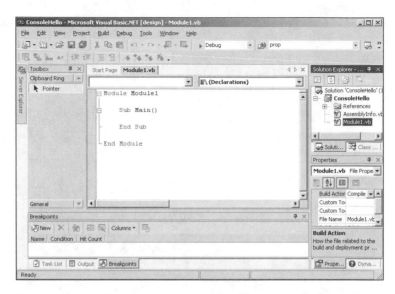

Figure 1.16   Coding a console application.

We can display our "Hello from Visual Basic" message in this console application using the **WriteLine** method, which is a prewritten procedure available to us in Visual Basic. This method is part of the **System.Console** class, which in turn is part of the **System** *namespace*. The **System.Console** class is part of the .NET framework class library, along with thousands of other classes. To organize all those classes, .NET uses namespaces, which give classes their own space and stop conflicts between the various names in such classes; for example, if two classes defined a **WriteLine** method, you could keep them from conflicting by placing them in different namespaces so that Visual Basic knows which one you mean. You'll become more familiar with namespaces later in the book; for now, we can use **WriteLine** to display our message like this:

```
Module Module1

    Sub Main()
        System.Console.WriteLine("Hello from Visual Basic")
    End Sub

End Module
```

You can run this program now by selecting the Debug|Start menu item; when the program runs, it displays both our message and the prompt about pressing any key, like this:

```
Hello from Visual Basic
Press any key to continue
```

You can see this result in Figure 1.17. There, the DOS window stays open until the user is ready to dismiss it by pressing Enter or by clicking on the X button at the upper right in the DOS window.

Windows applications are already familiar to Visual Basic 6 programmers, but Web applications and console applications like the examples we've developed are new. To understand how new things are in VB .NET, you have to understand a whole new programming philosophy— the .NET philosophy.

The .NET Framework and the Common Language Runtime

VB .NET is only one component of a revolution in Windows—the .NET framework. This framework provides the new support for software development and operating system support in Windows, and it's more extensive than anything we've seen in Windows before. The .NET framework wraps the operating system with its own code, and your VB .NET programs actually deal with .NET code instead of dealing with the operating system itself. And it is specially designed to make working with the Internet easy.

At the base of the .NET framework is the Common Language Runtime (CLR). The CLR is the module that actually runs your VB .NET applications. When you create a VB .NET application, what really happens is that your code is *compiled* into the CLR's *Internal Language* (named MSIL, or IL for short), much like byte codes in Java. When you run

Figure 1.17   Running a console application.

the application, that IL code is translated into the binary code your computer can understand by some special *compilers* built into the CLR. Compilers translate your code into something that your machine's hardware or other software can deal with directly. In this way, Microsoft one day will be able to create a CLR for other operating systems than Windows, and your VB .NET applications, compiled into IL, will run on them.

The second major part of the .NET framework is the .NET Framework class library. The class library holds an immense amount of prewritten code that all the applications you create with Visual Basic, Visual C++, C#, and other Visual Studio languages build on. The class library gives your program the support it needs; for example, your program may create several forms, and because a class for forms exists in the class library, your program doesn't have to perform all the details of creating those forms from scratch. All your code has to do is declare a new form, and the CLR compilers can get the actual code that supports forms from the .NET Framework class library itself. In this way, your programs can be very small compared to earlier Windows applications because you can rely on the millions of lines of code already written in the class library—not everything has to be in your application's executable (EXE) file.

All this assumes that you're working on a machine that has the .NET framework and, therefore, the CLR and the .NET framework class library installed. All the code for all the elements you use in a VB .NET application—forms, buttons, menus, and all the rest—comes from the class library. And other Visual Studio applications use the same class library, which makes it easy to mix languages in your programming, even in the same application. In addition, distributing applications is easier because all the support you need is already on the machine you're installing your application to.

As mentioned, the .NET framework organizes its classes into namespaces. For example, the .NET framework includes the namespaces **Microsoft.VisualBasic**, **Microsoft.JScript**, **Microsoft.CSharp**, and **Microsoft.Win32**. In fact, these namespaces contain relatively few classes; the real way we'll interact with the .NET framework class library in this book is through the **System** namespace.

The System Namespace

You can't build a VB .NET application without using classes from the .NET **System** namespace, as you'll see over and over again in this book. When you want to use a Windows form, for example, you must use the **System.Windows.Forms.Form** class. A button in a Windows form comes from the **System.Windows.Forms.Button** class, and so on. Many such classes exist and are organized into various namespaces, such as **System.Windows.Forms**. Here's an overview of some of those namespaces:

- **System**—Includes essential classes and base classes that define commonly used data types, events and event handlers, interfaces, attributes, exceptions, and so on.

- **System.Collections**—Includes interfaces and classes that define various collections of objects, including such collections as lists, queues, arrays, hash tables, and dictionaries.

- **System.Data**—Includes classes that make up ADO.NET. ADO.NET lets you build data-handling components that manage data from multiple distributed data sources.

- **System.Data.OleDb**—Includes classes that support the OLE DB .NET data provider.

- **System.Data.SqlClient**—Includes classes that support the SQL Server .NET data provider.

- **System.Diagnostics**—Includes classes that allow you to debug your application and to step through your code. Also includes code to start system processes, read and write to event logs, and monitor system performance.

- **System.Drawing**—Provides access to the GDI+ graphics packages that give you access to drawing methods.

- **System.Drawing.Drawing2D**—Includes classes that support advanced two-dimensional and vector graphics.

- **System.Drawing.Imaging**—Includes classes that support advanced GDI+ imaging.

- **System.Drawing.Printing**—Includes classes that allow you to customize and perform printing.

- **System.Drawing.Text**—Includes classes that support advanced GDI+ typography operations. The classes in this namespace allow users to create and use collections of fonts.

- **System.Globalization**—Includes classes that specify culture-related information, including the language, the country/region, calendars, the format patterns for dates, currency and numbers, the sort order for strings, and so on.

- **System.IO**—Includes types that support synchronous and asynchronous reading from and writing to both data streams and files.

- **System.Net**—Provides an interface to many of the protocols used on the Internet.

- **System.Net.Sockets**—Includes classes that support the Windows Sockets interface. If you've worked with the Winsock API, you should be able to develop applications using the **Socket** class.

- **System.Reflection**—Includes classes and interfaces that return information about types, methods, and fields and that have the ability to dynamically create and invoke types.

- **System.Security**—Includes classes that support the structure of the common language runtime security system.

- **System.Threading**—Includes classes and interfaces that enable multithreaded programming.

- **System.Web**—Includes classes and interfaces that support browser/server communication. Included in this namespace are the **HTTPRequest** class that provides information about HTTP requests, the **HTTPResponse** class that manages HTTP output to the client, and the **HTTPServerUtility** class that provides access to server-side utilities and processes. You can also use cookies, support file transfer, and more with these classes.

- **System.Web.Security**—Includes classes that are used to implement ASP.NET security in Web server applications.

- **System.Web.Services**—Includes classes that let you build and use Web Services, which are programmable entities on the Web server that code can communicate with using standard Internet protocols.

- **System.Windows.Forms**—Includes classes for creating Windows-based forms that make use of the user interface controls and other features available in the Windows operating system.

- **System.Xml**—Includes classes that support processing of XML.

These, along with the many other **System** classes, make up the foundation on which VB .NET applications rest. It's time now to start taking a look at how to build those applications.

Building VB .NET Applications

To build applications in VB .NET, you have to get some terminology under our belts because the .NET framework requires a new structure for applications. In particular, *assemblies* are now the building blocks of the .NET framework; they form the fundamental unit of deployment, version control, reuse, security permissions, and more.

An assembly provides the CLR with the information and compiled code it needs to know how to run your code, much as .EXE files did for Windows in VB6.

Assemblies

You combine assemblies to form .NET applications, and although you won't deal with them directly very often, you need to get the terminology down. An assembly holds the Intermediate Language modules for your application. When you create an application in VB .NET and run it, VB .NET creates one or more assemblies, which are run by the CLR. That is, assemblies are how your applications interact with the .NET framework instead of the EXE or DLL files of VB6.

Here's what's in a .NET assembly: First is the *manifest*, which is sort of like a table of contents, giving the name and version of the assembly. The manifest also lists what other assemblies are needed to support this one and how to handle security issues. The actual meat of the assembly is made up of *modules*, which are internal files of IL code, ready to run. That's how VB .NET stores the IL it creates—in modules inside assemblies. Each module, in turn, contains *types*, which are the classes and interfaces that your code has defined and which the assembly has to know about to let the various modules interact with each other.

You won't often deal with assemblies directly because all that's needed happens behind the scenes with the CLR and the .NET framework—but you do have to know the terminology because you'll hear these terms frequently when dealing with VB .NET. For example, to set the version of a Visual Basic project, you edit its AssemblyInfo.vb file in the Visual Basic IDE.

Solutions and Projects

When you created applications in Visual Basic 6, you created *projects*. Each project held the code and data for an application, ActiveX control, or whatever else you wanted to build. If you wanted to combine projects, you created a *project group*. In VB.NET, however, project groups have become far more integral to the development process, and now they're called *solutions*.

By default, when you create a new project in VB .NET, Visual Basic will create a new solution first and then add a project to that solution. For example, look at the Solution Explorer window at the right in Figure 1.8 above the Properties window. In that case, we've created our Visual Basic project called WinHello, and you can see that project in the Solutions Explorer—but note that Visual Basic has also placed that project inside a solution with the same name, WinHello. If we were to add new projects to the current solution (which you can do with the New Project dialog box), those new projects would appear in the Solution Explorer as part of the current solution. This is a change from VB6, where you created projects by default, not project groups. It's also worth noting that Microsoft calls the files in each project, such as the files for a form, *items*. So the terminology here is that solutions contain projects, which in turn contain items.

File Extensions Used in VB .NET

When you save a solution, it's given the file extension .sln (such as WinHello.sln), and all the projects in the solution are saved with the extension .vbproj. Here's a list of the types of file extensions you'll see in files in VB .NET and the kinds of files they correspond to; the most popular file extension is .vb. This is a useful list because if VB .NET has added files that you haven't expected to your solution, you can often figure them out by their file extensions:

- **.vb**—Can be a basic Windows form, a code file, a module file for storing functions, a user control, a data form, a custom control, an inherited form, a Web custom control, an inherited user control, a Windows service, a custom setup file, an image file for creating a custom icon, or an AssemblyInfo file used to store assembly information such as versioning and assembly name

- **.xsd**—An XML schema provided to create typed data sets

- **.xml**—An XML document file

- **.htm**—An HTML document

- **.txt**—A text file

- **.xslt**—An XSLT style-sheet file used to transform XML documents and XML schemas

- **.css**—A cascading style-sheet file

- **.rpt**—A Crystal Report

- **.bmp**—A bitmap file

- **.js**—A JScript file (Microsoft's version of JavaScript)

- **.vbs**—A VBScript file

- **.wsf**—A Windows scripting file

- **.aspx**—A Web form

- **.asp**—An Active Server Page

- **.asmx**—A Web service class

- **.vsdisco**—A dynamic discovery project that provides a means to enumerate all Web services and all schemas in a Web project

- **.web**—A Web configuration file that configures Web settings for a Web project

- **.asax**—A global application class used to handle global ASP.NET application-level events

- **.resx**—A resource file used to store resource information

Debug and Release Versions

Note that you've started our programs so far from the Debug menu's Start item, which causes Visual Basic to launch the program while staying in the background; if a problem arises, Visual Basic will reappear to let you debug the program's code. That's useful for development, but when your program is ready to go and to be used by others, you hardly want them to have to launch your program from Visual Basic.

That's where the difference between *debug* and *release* versions of your program comes in. In a debug version of your program, Visual Basic stores a great deal of data needed to interface with the debugger in your program when it runs, which makes the corresponding assembly not only larger but also slower. In the release version of your program, the program doesn't have all that added data and can run as a standalone program, without needing to be launched from Visual Basic (although it still needs the .NET framework).

When you create a new solution, Visual Basic creates it in debug mode, which means that you launch it from the Debug menu as we've been doing. However, you can switch to release mode in several ways (like many things in VB .NET, there's more than one way to do it):

- Select the Configuration Manager item in the Build menu, and then select Release in the Active Solution Configuration list box and click on OK.

- Select the solution you want to set the mode for by clicking on it in the Solution Explorer and find its **Active Config** property in the properties window. When you click the right-hand column in the Properties window next to this property, a drop-down list box will appear; select Release in that list box.

- Select the solution you want to set the mode for by clicking it in the Solution Explorer and select the Properties item in the Project menu, opening the solution's property pages. Select the

Configuration Properties folder in the box at the left and the Configuration item in that folder. Then select Release from the drop-down list box in the configuration column of the table that appears and click OK.

- Probably the easiest way to set the solution mode to Release or Debug is simply to use the drop-down list box that appears in the Visual Basic .NET standard toolbar at the top of the IDE. When you create a new solution or project, this list box displays the word "Debug." To switch to release mode, simply select Release instead.

When you've set the mode for a solution to Release, you build it using the Build menu's Build item. The Build menu item causes Visual Basic to compile only items it thinks have been newly changed; to force it to compile all items in the solution, choose the Rebuild All item instead of Build. This builds the solution in a way that others can use it, and you can deploy your program this way (usually with the help of a deployment project that you build in Visual Basic, as you'll do later in the book).

That gives you the background you need on VB .NET solutions and projects as you head into the following chapters, where I'll assume this knowledge and put it to work. I'll also take for granted that you know your way around Visual Basic .NET itself, so in the next chapter, I'll take a look at the Visual Basic Integrated Development Environment—the VB IDE.

Chapter 2

The Visual Basic Integrated Development Environment

In this chapter, we're going to take a look at the Integrated Development Environment, (IDE), which you use in Visual Basic to develop your applications. The IDE, which appears in Figure 2.1, has become more complex than in previous versions of Visual Basic, and being able to use it, or at least knowing what the various parts are called, is a skill you'll need in the coming chapters. Part of the reason it's become more complex is that the same IDE is now shared by all Visual Studio languages, such as VB and C# (something Microsoft has promised for many years but has implemented only now). You've already seen the IDE at work, but now it's time to take a more systematic look.

The IDE has so many independent windows that it's easy to misplace or rearrange them inadvertently. The IDE windows are docking windows, which means that you can use the mouse to move windows around as you like; when the windows are near an edge, they'll "dock"—adhere—to that edge

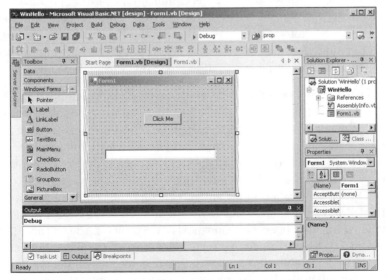

Figure 2.1   The Visual Basic Integrated Development Environment.

23

so that you can reconfigure the IDE windows as you like. If you move IDE windows inadvertently, don't panic; just use the mouse to move them back.

TIP: You can also restore the default window layout by selecting the Tools/Options item, and then selecting the General item in the Environment folder and clicking on Reset Window Layout. That's really good to know because sooner or later Visual Basic will dock some window you didn't want to dock, such as the Edit Replace window, to the IDE; this will rearrange all your other windows and it might take a long time to try to fix that manually.

Also note that the windows in the IDE come with an X button at the upper right, which means that you can close them. I don't know about you, but I sometimes click on these when I don't mean to, and a window I wanted disappears. It's easy to panic: The toolbox is gone, and I'll have to reinstall everything. In fact, you only have to find that window in the View menu again (such as View|Toolbox) to make it reappear. Make note: Some windows are hidden in the View|Other Windows menu item, which opens a submenu of additional windows—simply too many windows exist to fit them all into one menu without needing to use a submenu.

So much is packed into the IDE that Microsoft has started to make windows share space, and you can keep them separate using tabs, such as those you can see above the form at the center of Figure 2.1. If you click on the Form1.vb[Design] tab, you see the form itself as it'll appear when the program runs; if you click on the Form1.vb tab, you'll see the form's code; and if you click on the Start Page tab, you'll see the Start page, which lets you select from among recent solutions to open. Also note at the lower right that the Properties window and the Dynamic Help window—a new VB .NET feature—are sharing the same space, and you can select between them using buttons.

The IDE is a very crowded place, and in an effort to unclutter it, VB .NET adds a new button in dockable IDE windows—a little thumbtack button at the upper right—as you see in various windows in Figure 2.1—next to the X close button. This is the "auto hide" feature, which lets you reduce a window to a tab connected to the edge it's docked on. For example, in Figure 2.1, the Server Explorer window (which lets you explore data sources on servers) is hidden and has become a tab at the upper left in the IDE. If I let the mouse move over that tab, the full Server Explorer window will glide open, covering most of the toolbox. You can auto hide most windows like this; for example, if I were to click on the thumbtack button in the toolbox, it would close and become a tab under the Server Explorer tab in the IDE. To restore a window to stay-open status, just click on the thumbtack again.

You can customize the IDE as well. For example, to customize IDE options such as the fonts and colors used to display code, select the Tools|Options menu item and use the various items in the Environment folder. To customize menus and toolbars, such as specifying which toolbars to display (you can choose from 27 toolbars), or what buttons go on what toolbars, use the Tools|Customize menu item.

That's it for general discussion—it's time to get to the IDE itself, starting with the Start page.

The Start Page

You've already seen the Start page, which is what you see when you first start Visual Basic and which appears outlined in Figure 2.2. You can use the Start page to select from recent projects; by default, the Get Started item is selected in the Start page at the upper left. You can also create a new project here by clicking on New Project.

The Start page has other useful aspects as well. For example, because you use the same IDE for all Visual Studio languages, it'll also search through all those languages when you search the help files. To make it search only pertinent help files, you can select the My Profile item in the Start page and select either Visual Basic or Visual Basic And Related (which is my preference) in the Help Filter drop-down list box.

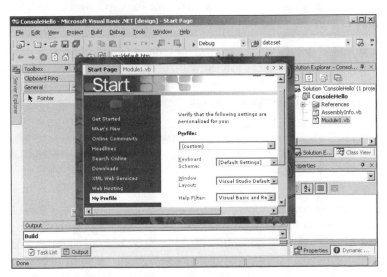

Figure 2.2   The Visual Basic IDE Start page.

*TIP: The Start page is actually being displayed in a browser. Its URL is **vs:/default.htm**, as you can see in a drop-down list box above the Start page. Entering a new URL in that drop-down list box and pressing Enter navigates to that new URL, replacing the Start page. And if you have a URL in your code (a quoted string that begins with "http://"), VB .NET will turn that text into a hyperlink, underline it, and allow you to click on that URL to bring up the corresponding Web page in place of the Start page.*

The Menu System

After you've started Visual Basic and have seen the Start page, you often turn to the menu system to proceed, as when you want to create a new project and use the File|New|Project menu item to bring up the New Project dialog box (you can do the same thing by clicking on New Project in the Start page).

The IDE menu system is very involved, with many items to choose from—and you don't even see it all at once. The menu system changes as you make selections in the rest of the IDE. For example, the Project menu will display 16 items if you first select a project in the Solution Explorer but only four if you've selected a solution, not a project. In fact, even more dramatic changes take place. For example, try clicking on a form under design, and you'll see a Data menu in the menu bar, which is used to generate data sets. However, if you then select not at the form but at the form's code (for example, double-click the form to open the code window), the Data menu disappears.

Hundreds of menu items are here, and many useful ones will quickly become favorites, such as File|New|Project, or the most recently used (MRU) list of files and projects that you can access from the Recent Files or Recent Projects items near the bottom of the File menu.

TIP: You can set the number of items that appear in MRU lists by selecting the Tools|Options menu item, clicking on the Environment folder and selecting the General item, and entering a value in the Most Recently Used Lists text box.

The menu system also allows you to switch from debug to release modes if you use the Build|Configuration Manager item, lets you configure the IDE with the Tools|Options and Tools|Customize items, and so on. I'll introduce more menu items throughout the book as appropriate.

Toolbars

Toolbars are another handy aspect of the IDE and appear near the top of the IDE, as shown in Figure 2.3. You can choose from a variety of toolbars, and sometimes VB .NET will choose them for you, as when it displays the Debug toolbar when you've launched a program with the Start item in the Debug menu.

Because the IDE displays tool tips (those small yellow windows with explanatory text that appear when you let the mouse rest over a control such as a button in a toolbar), it's easy to get to know what the buttons in the toolbars do. As mentioned, you can customize the toolbars in the IDE, selecting which toolbars to display or customizing which buttons appear in which toolbars with the Tools|Customize menu item. In addition, you can right-click on a toolbar itself to get a menu of the possible toolbars to display (the bottom item in this popup menu is Customize, which lets you customize which buttons go where), or you can open the Toolbars submenu in the View menu to do the same thing (as is often the case in Visual Basic, there's more than one way to do it).

Toolbars present a quick way to select menu items, and although often I personally stick to using the menu system, toolbar buttons no doubt can be quicker; for example, to save the file you're currently working on, you need only click on the diskette button in the standard toolbar (as you see in Figure 2.3) or on the stacked diskettes to save all the files in the solution.

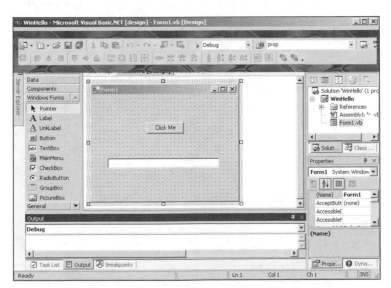

Figure 2.3   Visual Basic IDE toolbars.

The New Project Dialog Box

When you want to create a new project, you turn to the New Project dialog box, which we've already used quite a bit and which you can see in Figure 2.4.

Besides letting you select from all the possible types of projects you can create in Visual Basic, you can also set the name of the project and its location; for Windows projects, the location is a folder on disk, but for Web projects, you specify a server running Internet Information Server (IIS).

Note also that you can add projects to the current solution using the New Project dialog box; just click on the Add To Solution radio button instead of the Close Solution one (the default). If your project is entirely new, VB .NET will create an enclosing solution for the new project if one doesn't already exist.

Finally, note the Setup And Deployment Projects folder, which you use to create projects to deploy your program, as we'll do near the end of the book, in Chapter 20.

Graphical Designers

When you're working on a project that has user interface elements like forms, VB. NET can display what those elements will look like at runtime—that's what makes Visual Basic *visual*. For example, when you're looking at a Windows form, you're actually looking at a *Windows form designer*, as you see in Figure 2.5, and you can manipulate the form, add controls to it, and so on.

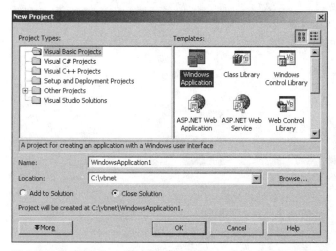

Figure 2.4   The New Project dialog box.

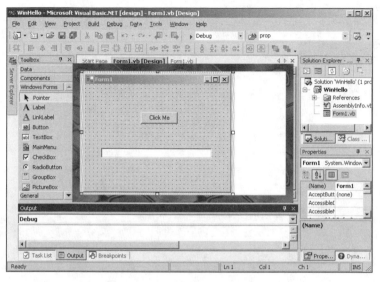

Figure 2.5   A Visual Basic Application graphical designer.

The different types of graphical designers include the following:

- Windows form designers
- Web form designers
- Component designers
- XML designers

You may have noticed (or already know from VB6) that Windows forms display a grid of dots, which you can see in Figure 2.5. To set the grid spacing and specify whether controls should "snap" to the grid (that is, position their corners on grid points), you can use the Tools|Options menu item to open the Options dialog box and select the Windows Forms Designers folder, displaying the possible options for you to set.

NOTE: *In Visual Basic 6, coordinates for forms and controls were expressed in twips; in Visual Basic .NET, coordinates are expressed only in pixels.*

Code Designers

Unlike graphical designers, code designers let you edit the code for a component; Figure 2.6 shows an example of a code designer. You can use the tabs at the top center of the IDE to switch between graphical designers (such as the Form1.vb[Design] tab, which displays a graphical designer, and the Form1.vb tab, which displays the corresponding code designer). You can also switch between graphical and code designers

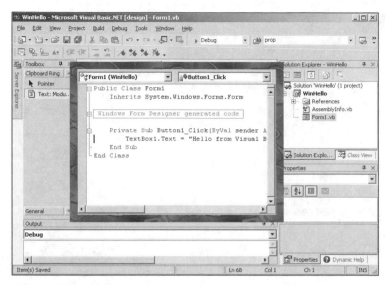

Figure 2.6   A code designer.

using the Designer and Code items in the View menu, or you can use the top two buttons at the left in the Solution Explorer.

Note the two drop-down list boxes at the top of the code designer; the one on the left lets you select what object's code you're working with, and the one on the right lets you select the part of the code that you want to work on, letting you select between the declarations area, functions, **Sub** procedures, and methods (all of which you'll see starting in the coming chapters). The declarations area, which you select by selecting the **(Declarations)** item in the right-hand list box, is where you can put declarations of module-level objects, as you'll see in Chapter 5 (see the section "Understanding Scope" in that chapter).

TIP: *When you double-click a control in a graphical designer, its code designer will open, and Visual Basic creates an event handler (see the section "Handling Events" in Chapter 7) for its default event (such as the **Click** event for buttons), which is a procedure that is called when the event occurs, as you'll see in Chapter 7. To add code to a different event handler, select the object you want to work with in the left-hand drop-down list box in the code designer and select the event you want to add code to in the right-hand drop-down list box; Visual Basic will create an event handler for that event.*

Also note the + and - boxes in the code designer's text area at the left. Those are new in VB. NET and were introduced because VB. NET now writes a great deal of code for your forms and components automatically. You can use the + and - buttons to show or hide that code. For example, here's what that code looks like for a typical Windows form:

```
#Region " Windows Form Designer generated code "

    Public Sub New()
        MyBase.New()

        'This call is required by the Windows Form Designer.
        InitializeComponent()

        'Add any initialization after the InitializeComponent()
            call

    End Sub

    'Form overrides dispose to clean up the component list.
    Protected Overloads Overrides Sub Dispose(ByVal disposing As
Boolean)
        If disposing Then
            If Not (components Is Nothing) Then
                components.Dispose()
            End If
        End If
        MyBase.Dispose(disposing)
    End Sub
    Friend WithEvents TextBox1 As System.Windows.Forms.TextBox
    Friend WithEvents Button1 As System.Windows.Forms.Button

    'Required by the Windows Form Designer
    Private components As System.ComponentModel.Container

    'NOTE: The following procedure is required by the Windows Form
Designer
    'It can be modified using the Windows Form Designer.
    'Do not modify it using the code editor.
    <System.Diagnostics.DebuggerStepThrough()> Private Sub _
        InitializeComponent()
        Me.TextBox1 = New System.Windows.Forms.TextBox()
        Me.Button1 = New System.Windows.Forms.Button()
        Me.SuspendLayout()
        '
        'TextBox1
        '
        Me.TextBox1.Location = New System.Drawing.Point(32, 128)
        Me.TextBox1.Name = "TextBox1"
        Me.TextBox1.Size = New System.Drawing.Size(224, 20)
        Me.TextBox1.TabIndex = 0
        Me.TextBox1.Text = ""
        '
        'Button1
        '
```

```
Me.Button1.Location = New System.Drawing.Point(112, 56)
Me.Button1.Name = "Button1"
Me.Button1.TabIndex = 1
Me.Button1.Text = "Click Me"
'
'Form1
'
Me.AutoScaleBaseSize = New System.Drawing.Size(5, 13)
Me.ClientSize = New System.Drawing.Size(292, 213)
Me.Controls.AddRange(New System.Windows.Forms.Control() _
    {Me.Button1, Me.TextBox1})
Me.Name = "Form1"
Me.Text = "Form1"
Me.ResumeLayout(False)

End Sub

#End Region
```

We'll dissect what this code means when we start working with Windows applications in depth in Chapter 7; for now, note the **#Region** and **#End Region** directives at the top and bottom of this code—those are how the code designer knows that this region of code can be collapsed or expanded with a + or - button. Visual Basic also automatically adds those + or - buttons for other programming constructions, such as procedures, enumerations, and so on, allowing you to hide the parts of your code you don't want to see. The IDE is cluttered enough, and this helps unclutter it somewhat.

TIP: *You can use the **#Region** and **#End Region** directives in your own code as well, allowing you to expand and contract whole sections of code at once.*

As with the rest of the IDE, many features are packed into code designers. For example, right-clicking on a symbol lets you go to its definition, its declaration, and so on.

IntelliSense

One useful feature of VB. NET code designers is Microsoft's *IntelliSense*. IntelliSense is what's responsible for those boxes that open as you write your code, listing all the possible options and even completing your typing for you. IntelliSense is one of the first things you encounter when you use VB .NET; you can see an example in Figure 2.7, where I'm looking at all the members of a text box object.

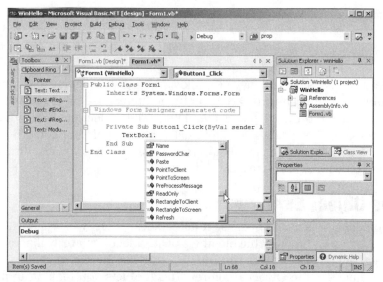

Figure 2.7   Using IntelliSense.

TIP: *If you enter some code that VB .NET considers a syntax error, it will underline the error with a wavy red line, and you can rest the mouse over the underlined text to see a tool tip explaining what VB .NET thinks is wrong. That's not part of the IntelliSense package, although it is useful.*

IntelliSense is made up of a number of options, including the following:

- *List Members*—Lists the members of an object

- *Parameter Info*—Lists the arguments of procedure calls

- *Quick Info*—Displays information in tool tips as the mouse rests on elements in your code

- *Complete Word*—Completes typed words

- *Automatic Brace Matching*—Adds parentheses or braces as needed

A Visual Basic–specific IntelliSense offers syntax tips that display the syntax of the statement you're typing. This is great if you know what statement you want to use but don't recall its exact syntax because its syntax is automatically displayed.

TIP: *IntelliSense is particularly useful when you can't remember what arguments a built-in Visual Basic procedure accepts (if these terms are not familiar to you, note that they're coming up in Chapter 5) because it'll display those arguments as you type in the call to the procedure. Such procedures can also be overloaded, which means they have several forms*

---

that take different arguments—in such cases, IntelliSense will display an up and down arrow in its tool tip with the text "1 of n," where n is the number of overloaded forms, and you can use the arrows to select the overloaded form of the procedure you want prompts for.

IntelliSense is something you quickly get used to and come to rely on. However, you can turn various parts of IntelliSense off if you want; just select the Tools|Options menu item. Then select the Text Editor folder, the Basic subfolder, and finally the General item in the Basic subfolder. You'll see a number of IntelliSense options you can turn on and off with checkboxes.

The Object Explorer

IntelliSense is useful because it automatically tells you what syntax is correct or it lists all the members of an object that are available. In fact, another tool that's too often overlooked by Visual Basic programmers is the Object Explorer. This tool lets you look at all the members of an object at once, which is invaluable when you want to pry into the heart of objects you've added to your code. The Object Explorer helps open up any mysterious objects that Visual Basic has added to your code so that you can see what's going on inside.

To open the Object Explorer, select View|Other Windows|Object Explorer, which opens this tool, as you can see in Figure 2.8. The Object Explorer shows all the objects in your program and gives you access to what's going on in all of them. For example, I'm looking at a Windows form, Form1, in Figure 2.8, and all its internal members and the parameters they require are made visible. To close the Object Explorer, just click on the X button at its upper right.

The Toolbox

The toolbox is something that all veteran Visual Basic developers are familiar with, and you can see it in Figure 2.9. Microsoft has crammed more and more into the toolbox with each successive version of Visual Basic, and now the toolbox uses tabs to divide its contents into categories; you can see these tabs, marked Data, Components, Windows Forms, and General, in Figure 2.9; which tabs are available, as you might surmise, depends on the type of project you're working on—and even what type of designer you're working with. The Data, Components, Windows Forms, and General tabs appear when you're working with a Windows form in a Windows form designer, but when you switch to a code designer in the same project, all you'll see are General and Clipboard Ring (which displays recent items stored in the clipboard and allows you to select from among them) in the

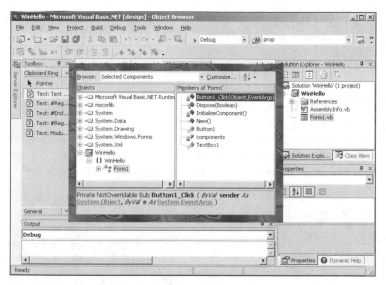

Figure 2.8   The Object Explorer.

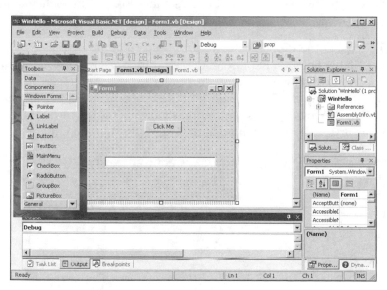

Figure 2.9   The Visual Basic toolbox.

toolbox. When you're working on a Web form, you'll see Data, Web Forms, Components, HTML, Clipboard Ring, General, and so on.

The Data tab displays tools for creating data sets and making data connections, the Windows Forms tab displays tools for adding controls to Windows forms, the Web Forms tab displays tools for adding server controls to Web forms, and so on. The General tab is empty by default and is a place to store general components, controls, and fragments of code (you can even add more tabs to the toolbox by right-clicking the toolbox and selecting the Add Tab item). In fact, so many controls are available that even when you click a tab in the toolbox, you'll still most likely get a list that you have to scroll in order to see everything that's available.

TIP: *When you're adding controls to forms using the toolbox, note that you can use the items in the Format menu and the Layout toolbar to align, make the same size, and set the spacing for controls. You can also select multiple controls and move and resize them all at once.*

The Solution Explorer

I've already discussed the Solution Explorer quite a bit; this window gives you an overview of the solution you're working with, including all the projects in it and the items in those projects. You can see the Solution Explorer in Figure 2.10; this tool displays a hierarchy, with the solution at the top of the hierarchy, the projects one step down in the hierarchy, and the items in each project also a step down in the hierarchy.

You can set the properties of various items in a project by selecting them in the Solution Explorer and then setting their properties in the properties window. And you can set properties of solutions and projects by right-clicking them and selecting the Properties item in the menu that appears, or you can select an item and click the properties button, which is the right-most button at the top of the Solution Explorer.

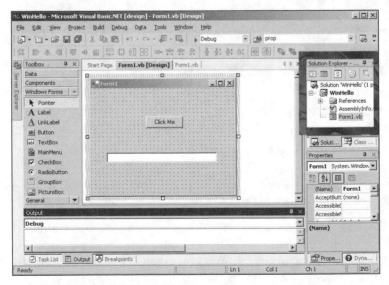

Figure 2.10   The Solution Explorer.

If you're working on an object that has both a user interface and code, you can switch between graphical and code designers by using the buttons that appear at the top left in the Solution Explorer when that object has been selected. You can right-click a solution and add a new project to it by selecting the Add|New Project menu item in the pop-up menu that appears. And you can specify which of multiple projects runs first—that is, the startup project or projects—by right-clicking the project and selecting the Set As Startup Object item or by right-clicking the solution and selecting the Set Startup Projects item.

Much of what goes on in the VB .NET IDE depends on which solution or project is the current one, and you set that by selecting it in the Solution Explorer. For example, you can specify what icon you want an application to use in Windows if you don't like the plain default one; to do that, you select its project in the Solution Explorer, select Properties in the Project menu, then open the Common Properties|Build folder, browse to the ICO (icon) file you want, and click OK.

The Solution Explorer tracks the items in your projects; to add new items, you can use the menu items in the Project menu, such as Add Windows Form and Add User Control. To add new empty modules and classes to a project (we'll see what these terms mean in detail soon), you can use the Project|Add New Items menu item.

The Solution Explorer sees things in terms of files, as you can see in Figure 2.10. There, the References folder holds the currently *referenced* items (such as namespaces) in a project—more on that soon—AssemblyInfo.vb is the file that holds information about the assembly you're creating, and Form1.vb is the file that holds the code for the form under design. However, object-oriented programs can be looked at another way—in terms of classes—and the Class View window does that.

TIP: *The data in AssemblyInfo.vb gives all kinds of information about the assembly, such as its version number. To set the version number of the assembly you're creating, open AssemblyInfo.vb and edit the line* **<Assembly: AssemblyVersion("1.0.*")>** *according to the directions you'll find directly above this line. Windows will be able to display this version number to the user in Windows tools like the Windows Explorer.*

The Class View Window

If you click on the Class View tab under the Solution Explorer, you'll see the Class View window, as shown in Figure 2.11. This view presents solutions and projects in terms of the classes they contain and the members of these classes.

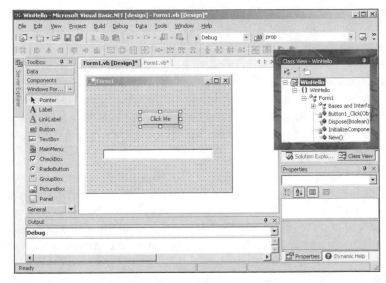

Figure 2.11   The Class View window.

Using the Class View window gives you an easy way to jump to a member of a class that you want to get to fast—just find it in the Class View window and double-click it to bring it up in a code designer.

The Properties Window

The Properties window is another old favorite in Visual Basic, although now it shares its space with the Dynamic Help window. The Properties window appears in Figure 2.12.

You set properties of various objects in Visual Basic to customize them. For example, I've set the **Text** property of a button in the WinHello project to "Click Me" to make that text appear in the button. To set an object's properties when you're designing your program in Visual Basic—called *design time* (as opposed to runtime)—you select that object (by clicking a control, form, project, or solution) and then set the new property values you want in the Properties window.

The Properties window is divided into two columns of text, with the properties on the left and their settings on the right. The object you're setting properties for appears in the drop-down list box at the top of the Properties window, and you can select from all the available objects using that list box. When you select a property, Visual Basic will give you an explanation of the property in the panel at the bottom of the properties window, as you see in Figure 2.12. You can display the Properties alphabetically by clicking on the second button from the left at the top of the Properties window, or you can display categories by clicking the left-most button.

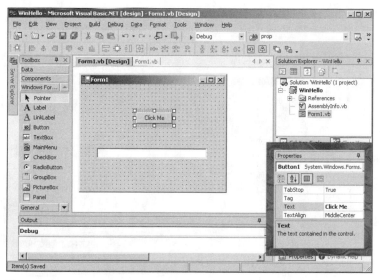

Figure 2.12 The Properties window.

To change a property's setting, you need only click the right-hand column next to the name of the property and enter the new setting. Often, properties can have only a few specific values, in which case Visual Basic will display a drop-down list box next to the property's name when you click the right-hand column, and you can select values from that list. Sometimes, Visual Basic requires more information, as when you create data connections, and instead of a list box, a button with an ellipsis ("...") appears; when you click that button, Visual Basic will usually walk you through the steps it needs to get that information. Note also that, as usual with properties and methods in Visual Basic, not all properties of a form or control will be available at design time in the Properties window when you're designing your code—some will be available only at runtime.

In fact, not many changes have been made in the Properties window since VB6 (something VB6 programmers might be pleased to hear), so if you've used it before, you're all set.

The Dynamic Help Window

The window that shares the Properties window's space—the Dynamic Help window—is new. Visual Basic .NET includes the usual Help menu with Contents, Index, and Search items, but now it also supports dynamic help, which looks things up for you automatically. You can see the Dynamic Help window by clicking the Dynamic Help tab under the Properties window; see Figure 2.13.

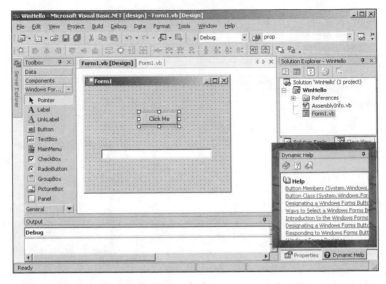

Figure 2.13   The Dynamic Help window.

VB .NET automatically looks up all kinds of help topics on the element you've selected. For example, in Figure 2.13, I've selected a button on a Windows form, and dynamic help has responded by displaying all kinds of helpful links to information on buttons. This is more helpful than simply searching the whole help system for the word "button" because dynamic help will typically select introductory and overview help topics, not all the hundreds of topics with the word "button" in their text. If you click on a help link in the dynamic help window, the corresponding help topic is opened in the central space of the IDE where the designers appear (and you can switch between designers and help topics using tabs).

TIP: *If you're like me, you'll find it too cramped in the IDE to display help topics effectively. If you wish, you can have VB .NET display help in an external IDE-independent window instead—select Tools|Options, select the Help item in the Environment folder, click on the External Help radio button, and click on OK.*

Component Trays

In VB6, when you added a component, such as a timer control, to a form and that component wasn't visible at runtime, the timer would still appear on the form at design time. That's changed in VB .NET; now, when you add components that are invisible at runtime, they'll appear in a *component tray*, which will appear automatically in the designer, as you see in Figure 2.14.

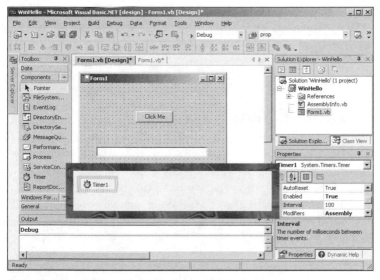

Figure 2.14   Adding a timer to an application in a component tray.

The Server Explorer

You use the Server Explorer, which appears in Figure 2.15, to explore
what's going on in a server. It's a great tool to help make distant sev-
ers feel less distant because you can see everything you need in an
easy graphical environment.

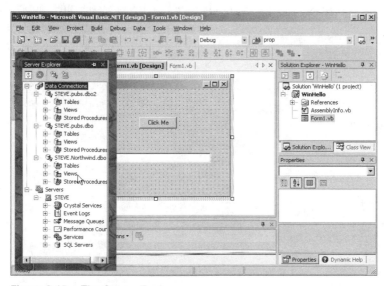

Figure 2.15   The Server Explorer.

You can do more than just look using the Server Explorer—you can also drag and drop whole items onto Windows forms or Web forms from the Server Explorer. For example, if you dragged a database table onto a form, VB .NET would create the connection and command objects you need to access that table from code.

The Output Window

If you look at the bottom of the IDE, you'll see two tabs for the Output and Breakpoints windows. We'll see the Breakpoints window when we discuss debugging because it lets you manage the breakpoints at which program execution halts when you're debugging your code. On the other hand, the Output window, which you see in Figure 2.16, gives you the results of building and running programs, as you can also see in the figure.

You can also send messages to the Output window yourself if you use the **System.Diagnostics.Debug.Write** method like this: **System. Diagnostics.Debug.Write("Hello from the Output window!")**.

The Task List

The Task List is another useful window that not many Visual Basic programmers know about. To see it, select View|Show Tasks|All; this window appears in Figure 2.17. As its name implies, the Task List displays tasks that VB .NET assumes you still have to take care of, and when you click on a task, the corresponding location in a code designer appears.

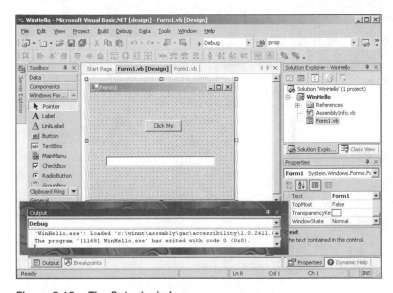

Figure 2.16   The Output window.

ualal Basic
Integrated Development
Environment

2. The Visual Basic Integrated Development Environment

In Brief

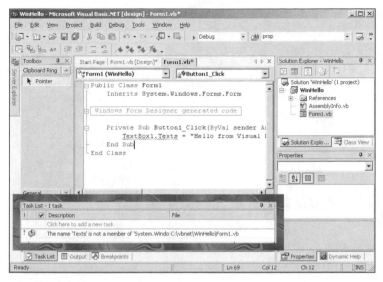

Figure 2.17   The Task List.

A number of such tasks exist. For example, if VB .NET has detected a syntax error with a wavy underline, as shown in Figure 2.17, that error will appear in the Task List. If you've used a wizard, such as the Upgrade Wizard where VB .NET still wants you to take care of certain issues, it'll put a "TODO" comment into the code:

```
If blnDrawFlag Then
    'UPGRADE_ISSUE: Graphics statements can't be migrated.
    'Click for more: ms-help://MS.MSDNVS/vbcon/html/vbup2034.htm
    Line(X,Y)
End If
```

TODO comments like this will appear in the Task List.

TIP: In fact, you can create your own custom comments that the Task List will track. To do that, select the Tools|Options menu item, then select the Task List item in the Environment folder and enter the name of your custom comments in the Comment Token area. For example, if I enter "STEVE", any comments beginning with "STEVE" will be tracked in the Task List.

The Command Window

Plenty of other windows are available. For example, selecting View|Other Windows|Command Window opens the Command Window, as you see in Figure 2.18.

43

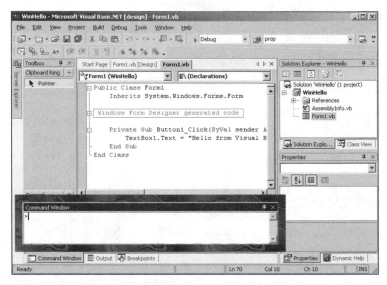

Figure 2.18   The Command Window.

This window is somewhat like the Immediate window in VB6 because you can enter commands like **File.AddNewProject** here, and VB .NET will display the Add New Project dialog box. This window is not exactly like the Immediate window, however, because you can't enter Visual Basic code and have it executed.

We'll look at other windows as needed.

Another new aspect of the IDE bears mention: macros. You can use macros to execute a series of commands in the Visual Studio environment. If you want to give macros a try, take a look at the Macros submenu in the Tools menu.

There's more to the IDE than we've been able to cover here, but now we've gotten the foundation we'll need in the coming chapters. I'll end this chapter by taking a look at coding practices in VB .NET; if you're not thoroughly familiar with Visual Basic yet, some of this might not make sense, so treat it as a section to refer back to later.

Coding to Get the Most from Visual Basic

In this section, we'll discuss some best-practices coding for Visual Basic. All these practices come from professional programmers, but whether you implement them is up to you. Here we go.

Avoid "magic numbers" when you can. A magic number is a number (excluding 0 or 1) that's hardwired right into your code like this:

```
Function blnCheckSize(dblParameter As Double) As Boolean

    If dblParameter > 1024 Then
        blnCheckSize = True

    Else
        blnCheckSize = False

    End If
End Function
```

Here, 1024 is a magic number. It's better to declare such a number as a constant, especially if you have several. When it's time to change your code, you need only change the constant declaration in one place, not try to find all the magic numbers scattered around your code.

Be modular. Putting code and data together into modules and classes hides it from the rest of the program, makes it easier to debug, makes it easier to work with conceptually, and even makes load time of procedures in the same module quicker. Being modular, also called information hiding or encapsulation in object-oriented programming, is the backbone of working with larger programs. "Divide and conquer" is the idea here.

Program defensively. For example, check data that is passed to you in a procedure before using it. This can save a bug from propagating throughout your program and help pinpoint its source. Make no assumptions.

Ideally, Visual Basic procedures should have only one purpose. This is also an aid in larger programs when things start to get complex. Certainly, if a procedure has two distinct tasks, consider breaking it up.

Avoid deep nesting of conditionals or loops because debugging them visually is very inefficient. If you need to, place some of the inner loops or conditionals in new procedures and call them. Three levels of nesting should be about the maximum.

Use property procedures to protect sensitive data (this is part of programming defensively). Property procedures are called by the rest of the program when you want to work with sensitive data, and they provide an interface to that data.

Ideally, variables should always be defined with the smallest scope possible. Global variables can create enormously complex conditions.

Don't pass global variables to procedures; if you do, the procedure you pass that variable to might give it one name (as a passed parameter) and also reference it as a global variable, which can lead to some serious bugs because now the procedure has two different names for the variable.

When you create a long string, use the underscore line-continuation character to create multiple lines of code so that you can read or debug the string easily. For example,

```
Dim Msg As String
Msg = "Well, there is a problem " _
& "with your program. I am not sure " _
& "what the problem is, but there is " _
& "definitely something wrong."
```

Microsoft recommends that you indent your code with four spaces (believe it or not, serious studies have been undertaken on this issue, and two to four spaces were found to be best). But at least be consistent.

If you work in teams, use version control. Several well-known utilities can help programmers work in teams, and you can integrate such utilities into VB .NET. The enterprise edition of Visual Basic comes with Visual SourceSafe, which is perfect for this purpose.

That's enough overview—it's time to start creating Visual Basic programs and seeing what goes into the process. Let's get to some working programs now in Chapter 3.

The Visual Basic Language: Handling Data

In Brief

This and the next few chapters are all about the glue that holds the various parts of a Visual Basic program together: the Visual Basic language itself. In this chapter, we'll take a look at the elements of the Visual Basic language that let you store data: how to declare variables, arrays, and text strings and how to use those elements. We'll also see how to handle special Visual Basic formats like dates and financial data.

We'll see a lot of code in this and the next few chapters on the Visual Basic syntax, and to keep things simple, I'll use console applications because they're the simplest to code and will keep extraneous details from getting in the way. Here's the console application we developed in Chapter 1 that displayed the words "Hello from Visual Basic" in a DOS window:

```
Module Module1
    Sub Main()
        System.Console.WriteLine("Hello from Visual Basic")
    End Sub
End Module
```

Here, we're creating a Visual Basic *module*, and modules are designed to hold code. **Sub Main** indicates the entry point of the program—the part that will be executed first. And we're using the **WriteLine** *method* of the **System.Console** class to write to the console (that is, DOS window). Methods are procedures that are built into classes—note the syntax here; to call a method, you specify the class or object the method is part of, followed by a dot (.) and the method name. This tells Visual Basic where to look to find the method you want to use. We'll become familiar with syntax like this in this chapter and Chapter 5. As you can see, all kinds of terms here have special meaning in Visual Basic, such as **Sub**, **Module**, **End**, and so on, and those are Visual Basic *keywords*.

The Visual Basic Keywords

As with all programming languages, Visual Basic is built using keywords, which you'll find in Table 3.1. These keywords are reserved for use by Visual Basic, and you use them to build your programs.

TIP: *Although the keywords in Table 3.1 are reserved for use by VB .NET, it turns out that you can use them if you surround them with square brackets: [and]. For example, if you wanted to name a text string **Error**, you could actually use the term **[Error]** as a variable.*

Table 3.1   The Visual Basic keywords.

#Const	#If…Then…#	Else
&	&	=
*	*=	/
/=	\	\=
^	^=	+
+=	=	-=
Add	AddHandler	AddressOf
Alias	And	AndAlso
Ansi	AppActivate	As
Asc	AscW	Assembly
Auto	Beep	Boolean
ByRef	Byte	ByVal
Call	CallByName	Case
Catch	CBool	CByte
CChar	CDate	CDbl
CDec	Char	ChDir
ChDrive	Choose	Chr
CInt	Class	Clear
CLng	Close	CObj
Command	Const Count	CreateObject
CShort	CSng	CStr
CType	CurDir	Date
DateAdd	DateDiff	DatePart
DateSerial	DateString	DateValue
Day	DDB	Decimal
Declare	Default	Delegate
DeleteSetting	Description	Dim
Dir	Do	Double
Each	Else	ElseIf
End	Enum	Environ
EOF	Erase	Erl
Err	Error	ErrorToString
Event	Exit	ExternalSource
False	FileAttr	FileCopy
FileDateTime	FileGet	FileLen
FileOpen	FilePut	FileWidth
Filter	Finally	Fix
For	FormatCurrency	FormatDateTime
FormatNumber	FormatPercent	FreeFile
Friend	Function	FV
Get	GetAllSettings	GetAttr
GetChar	GetException	GetObject
GetSetting	GetType	GoTo

continued

Table 3.1   The Visual Basic keywords (continued).

Handles	HelpContext	HelpFile
Hex	Hour	If
IIf	Implements	Imports
In	Inherits	Input
InputBox	InputString	InStr
InStrRev	Int	Integer
Interface	IPmt	IRR
Is	IsArray	IsDate
IsDBNull	IsError	IsNothing
IsNumeric	IsReference	Item
Join	Kill	LastDllError
LBound	LCase	Left
Len	Let	Lib
Like	LineInput	Loc
Lock	LOF	Long
Loop	LSet	LTrim
Me	Mid	Minute
MIRR	MkDir	Mod
Module	Month	MonthName
MsgBox	MustInherit	MustOverride
MyBase	MyClass	Namespace
New	Next	Not
Nothing	NotInheritable	NotOverridable
Now	NPer	NPV
Number	Object	Oct
On	Option	Optional
Or	OrElse	Overloads
Overridable	Overrides	ParamArray
Partition	Pmt	PPmt
Preserve	Print	PrintLine
Private	Property	Protected
Public	PV	QBColor
Raise	RaiseEvent	Randomize
Rate	ReadOnly	ReDim
Region	Rem	Remove
RemoveHandler	Rename	Replace
Reset	Resume	Return
RGB	RmDir	Rnd
RSet	RTrim	SaveSetting
ScriptEngine	ScriptEngine	BuildVersion

continued

Table 3.1   The Visual Basic keywords (continued).

ScriptEngineMajorVersion	ScriptEngineMinorVersion	Second
Seek	Select	Set
SetAttr	Shadows	Shared
Shell	Short	Single
SLN	Source	Space
Spc	Split	Static
Step	Stop	Str
StrComp	StrConv	StrDup
String	StrReverse	Structure
Sub	Switch	SYD
SyncLock	SystemType	Name
Tab	Then	Throw
TimeOfDay	Timer	TimeSerial
TimeString	TimeValue	To
Today	Trim	True
Try	TypeName	TypeOf
UBound	UCase	Unicode
Unlock	Until	Val
Variant	VarType	VbTypeName
WeekDay	WeekDayName	When
While	With	WithEvents
Write	WriteLine	WriteOnly
Xor	Year	

A number of keywords and phrases in VB6 are now obsolete in VB .NET. These are shown in Table 3.2

In general, Visual Basic programs are made up line by line of code, and these lines of code are called *statements*.

Table 3.2   Visual Basic 6 keywords and phrases that are now obsolete.

As	Any	Atn	Calendar	Circle
Currency	Date$	Debug.Assert	Debug.Print	Deftype
DoEvents	Empty	Eqv	GoSub	Imp
Initialize	Instancing	IsEmpty	IsMissing	IsNull
IsObject	LetLine	LSet	MsgBox	Now
Null	On...GoSub	On...GoTo	Option Base	Option
Private Module	Property Get	Property Let	Property Set	PSet
Rnd	Round	RSet	Scale	Set
Sgn	Sqr	Terminate	Time	Time$
Type	Variant	VarType	Wend	

Visual Basic Statements

A Visual Basic statement is a complete instruction and can contain the following:

- *Keywords*—Words reserved for Visual Basic's use.

- *Operators*—Symbols used to perform operations, like **+**, which performs addition operations; **-**, which performs subtraction operations; and so on.

- *Variables*—Symbolic names given to values stored in memory and declared with the **Dim** keyword. For example, if you've declared a variable named **temperature** as an **Integer** type, you can store integer values like 72 or 83 in it.

- *Literal values*—These are simple values, like 5 or "Hello".

- *Constants*—The same as variables, except that constants are assigned a value that cannot then be altered.

- *Expressions*—Combinations of terms and/or keywords that yield a value. For example, if the variable **temperature** holds the value 72, the expression **temperature + 3** yields the value 75.

Each statement is one of the following:

- A declaration statement, which can name and create a variable, constant, or procedure and can also specify a *data type*. The data type can be **Boolean**, **Byte**, **Char**, **Date**, **Decimal**, **Double**, **Integer**, **Long**, **Object**, **Short**, **Single**, or **String** or the name of an enumeration (a series of constants defined at the same time), structure, class, or interface.

- An executable statement, which can perform an action. These statements can execute a method or function, or they can loop through code using one of the Visual Basic loops we'll see in the next chapter, which execute a series of statements repetitively, or they can be an *assignment statement*, which assigns a value or expression to a variable or constant like this: **temperature = 72**, and so on.

Besides having single statements in your code, statements can also be grouped into *blocks*, as we'll see when we discuss conditions like the **If** statement, which might look like this, where I'm testing the value in the variable **BankBalance** to see whether it's less than 0:

```
Module Module1

    Sub Main()
        Dim BankBalance As Single = 500.01
```

```
        If (BankBalance < 0) Then
            Dim strError As String
            strError = "Hey, your bank balance is negative!"
            System.Console.WriteLine(strError)
        End If
    End Sub

End Module
```

In this case, I've surrounded three statements inside an **If** statement (which we'll see in depth in the next chapter). This **If** statement starts with **If (BankBalance < 0) Then** and ends with **End If**, creating a block of statements. The statement that uses the **Dim** keyword is a declaration statement that creates the variable **BankBalance** and gives it the value 500.01; when you create a variable like this, you can also set its *data type*, selecting **Boolean**, **Byte**, **Char**, **Date**, **Decimal**, **Double**, **Integer**, **Long**, **Object**, **Short**, **Single**, or **String** or the name of an enumeration, structure, class, or interface (more on these options later in this chapter).

Statements like **System.Console.WriteLine("Press Enter to continue...")** are execution statements that perform actions. Note also the statement **strError = "Hey, your bank balance is negative!"**—this is an assignment statement (a type of execution statement) where I'm assigning the text "Hey, your bank balance is negative!" to the variable **strError**. To be able to handle text strings this way, I've declared **strError** as a variable of type **String**. After I've declared **strError**, I can assign strings to this variable using the = *assignment operator*.

You can also have multiple statements on the same line in VB .NET if you separate them with a colon (:), as I'm doing here, where I'm declaring a variable named **temperature** (you need to declare variables before using them) and giving it a value of 72:

```
Dim temperature As Integer : temperature = 72
```

Conversely, you can also break up long statements over several lines if you want, as long as you use an underscore (_) at the end of each line, like this, where I'm assigning a value to the **temperature** variable:

```
Dim temperature As Integer
temperature = 1 + 2 + 3 _
+ 4 + 5 + 6 _
+ 7 + 8 + 9 + 10
```

However, you have to be careful about strings of text, which are enclosed in quotation marks in Visual Basic .NET. If you want to break a statement in the middle of a string, you must divide the string into two or more strings, using the **&** *string concatenation operator* (**+** can also function as a concatenation operator) to tell Visual Basic that you want multiple strings joined together into one, like this:

```
System.Console.WriteLine("This is a very long sentence that I " _
& "want to display to the user")
```

All About Statement Syntax

Each statement has its own syntax, and you should be aware of a few conventions and terms before starting. In the formal definition of each statement, you use square brackets, [and], for optional items and curly braces, { and }, to indicate that you need to select one of the enclosed items, like this for the **Dim** statement:

```
[ <attrlist> ] [{ Public | Protected | Friend |
Protected Friend | Private | Static }] [ Shared ]
[ Shadows ] [ ReadOnly ] Dim [ WithEvents ]
name[ (boundlist) ] [ As [ New ] type ] [ = initexpr ]
```

Here, all the items in square brackets are optional, and you choose one of the items in curly braces only if you want to use the keyword **Public**, **Protected**, **Friend**, **Protected Friend**, **Private**, or **Static**. I'll explain the keywords used in each statement like this:

- *attrlist*—A list of attributes that apply to the variables you're declaring in this statement. You separate multiple attributes with commas.

- **Public**—Gives variables public access, which means that no restrictions are placed on their accessibility. You can use **Public** only at the module, namespace, or file level (which means that you can't use it inside a procedure). Note that if you specify **Public**, you can omit the **Dim** keyword if you want to.

NOTE: *Keywords like **Public**, **Protected**, **Friend**, **Protected Friend**, and **Private** will really make sense only when you've mastered object-oriented programming (OOP), which we'll discuss later in the book.*

Overview: Procedures, Classes, Modules, Methods, and More

The previously mentioned terms *module* and *class* are important in the definition of the **Dim** statement. If you've programmed in Visual Basic before, you're familiar with terms like these. However, if these terms are unfamiliar to you, they can present a barrier in your study of Visual Basic because, as with so many aspects of Visual Basic .NET, you need some preliminary understanding of such terms to get anywhere. Here's an overview of terms that will come up a great deal. If you're already familiar with Visual Basic programming, feel free to skip this list; if some of these are unfamiliar to you, don't worry—you'll see all of them in detail in this book. This is just an overview so we can get started:

- *Block*—As you've seen, a block of statements is made up of a number of statements enclosed inside another statement designed for that purpose.

- *File*—Code contained in the same file.

- *Variable*—A named memory location of a specific data type (such as **Integer**) that stores data. You can assign data to a variable with the assignment operator; for example, if you have a variable named **temperature**, you can assign it a value of 72 like this: **temperature = 72**.

- *Procedure*—A callable series of statements that may or may not return a value. You can pass data to the procedure in the form of *parameters* in a procedure call like **addem(2, 3)**, where **2** and **3** are parameters I'm passing to a procedure named **addem**. When the series of statements terminates, control returns to the statement that called the procedure.

- *Sub procedure*—A procedure that does not return a value.

- *Function*—A procedure that returns a value.

- *Method*—A procedure that is built into a class.

- *Constructor*—A special method that is automatically called when you create an object from a class. This is used to initialize and customize the object. You can pass data to constructor methods just like other methods.

- *Module*—Visual Basic modules are designed to hold code, that is, to separate the code in them from other, possibly conflicting code. Their main purpose is to make your code more modular, and if your program is a long one, you should consider breaking it up into modules.

- *Class*—This is an OOP class, which can contain both code and data; you use classes to create objects. A class can have *members*, which are elements that can be accessible from outside the class if you so specify. Data members are called *fields*, and procedure members are called *methods*.

- *Object*—This is an *instance* of a class, much like a variable is an instance of a data type.

- *Shared or static members and instance members*—Fields and methods that apply to a class and are invoked with the class name are called *shared* or *static* fields and methods; the fields and methods that apply to objects created from the class are called *instance* fields and methods.

- *Structure*—Also an OOP element, just like a class but with some additional restrictions. You used to use structures to create user-defined types in VB6 and earlier; now they are another form of OOP classes.

Note also the term ***attrlist*** in the description of the parts of the previously mentioned **Dim** statement. This term corresponds to a list of attributes; attributes are new to VB .NET, so I'll take a look at them here.

Understanding Attributes

Attributes are items that let you specify information about the items you're using in VB .NET. You enclose attributes in angle brackets, **<** and **>**, and you use them when VB .NET needs to know more than standard syntax can specify. For example, if you want to call one of the functions that make up the Windows Application Programming Interface (API), you have to specify which of the Windows dynamic link libraries (DLLs) that the function you're calling resides in, which you can do with the **DllImport** attribute like this:

```
Public Shared Function <DllImport("user32.dll")> MessageBox(ByVal_
Hwnd...
```

As you need to use various attributes, I'll discuss how they work. You can use an attribute like this: **<theAttribute>**; or you can pass it values as parameters as you do to a procedure, like this: **<theAttribute("Watch out!")>**. Some attributes require the use of named parameters, which you must list specifically when you assign a value to them with the **:=** operator like this: **<theAttribute(Warning := "Watch out!")>**. We won't be using attributes in these early chapters.

The Option and Imports Statements

Two additional statements that are very important to know about when constructing programs are the **Option** and **Imports** statements. The **Option** statement sets a number of options for the rest of your code, and the **Imports** statement imports namespaces into your code, making them more readily available.

Option Statements

You use **Option** statements to set the "ground rules" for your code, helping prevent syntax and logic errors. Here are the possibilities:

- **Option Explicit**—Set to **On** or **Off**. **On** is the default. This requires declaration of all variables before they are used. (This is the default statement.)

- **Option Compare**—Set to **Binary** or **Text**. This specifies whether strings are compared using binary or text comparison operations.

- **Option Strict**—Set to **On** or **Off**. **Off** is the default. When you assign a value of one type to a variable of another type, Visual Basic will consider that an error if this option is on and any possibility of data loss exists, as when you're trying to assign the value in a variable to a variable of less precise data storage capacity. In that case, you must use explicit conversion functions of the kind we'll see in this chapter, like **CLng**.

You use **Option** statements as the first element in code, like this, where I'm turning **Option Strict** off:

```
Option Strict Off
Module Module1
    Sub Main()
        System.Console.WriteLine("Hello from Visual Basic")
    End Sub

End Module
```

Imports Statements

You use **Imports** statements to import a namespace, so you don't have to qualify items in that namespace by listing the entire namespace when you refer to them. For example, here's what our code might look like; the **WriteLine** procedure is built into the **System.Console** namespace, so it is a method of that namespace. To use it, I qualify its name with the namespace it belongs to:

```
Option Strict Off
Module Module1

    Sub Main()
        System.Console.WriteLine("Hello from Visual Basic")
    End Sub

End Module
```

On the other hand, if I import the **System.Console** namespace, that makes that namespace immediately available, so I don't have to qualify the **WriteLine** method name anymore (note that **Option** statements, if any exist, must still come first):

```
Option Strict Off
Imports System.Console
Module Module1

    Sub Main()
        WriteLine("Hello from Visual Basic")
    End Sub

End Module
```

TIP: *Each project has its own root namespace. By default, Visual Basic uses the name of the project for the root namespace. If you prefer, you can set another namespace—just right-click on the project in the Solution Explorer, select the Properties menu item, open the Common Properties folder, select the General item, and enter the new namespace name in the Root Namespace box.*

That completes the introductory material we need. It's time to turn to the Immediate Solutions, where we'll take a look at data handling in the Visual Basic language.

Immediate Solutions

Declaring Constants

You've filled your code with numeric values—and now it's time to change them all as you start work on the new version of the software. What a pain to have to track down and change all the numeric values throughout all the code. Isn't there a better way?

There is—use constants and declare them all in one place, then refer to the constants by name throughout the code instead of hardwiring numeric values in the code. When it's time to change those values, you just change the constants, all in one well-defined part of the code.

How do you use constants? You declare constants in Visual Basic with the **Const** statement, which you can use at the module, class, structure, procedure, or block level to declare constants for use in place of literal values:

```
[ <attrlist> ] [{ Public | Protected | Friend |
  Protected Friend | Private }] [ Shadows ] Const name
  [ As type ] = initexpr
```

Here are the various parts of this statement:

- *attrlist*—A list of attributes that apply to the constants you're declaring in this statement. You separate multiple attributes with commas.

- **Public**—Gives constants public access, which means that no restrictions are made on their accessibility. You can use **Public** only at the module, namespace, or file level (which means that you can't use it inside a procedure). Note that if you specify **Public**, you can omit the **Dim** keyword if you want to.

- **Protected**—Gives constants protected access, which means that they are accessible only from within their own class or from a class derived from that class. You can use **Protected** only at the class level (which means that you can't use it inside a procedure) because you use it to declare members of a class. Note that if you specify **Protected**, you can omit the **Dim** keyword if you want to.

- **Friend**—Gives constants friend access, which means that they are accessible from within the program that contains their declaration as well as from anywhere else in the same assembly. You can use **Friend** only at the module, namespace, or file level (which means that you can't use it inside a procedure). Note that if you specify **Friend**, you can omit the **Dim** keyword if you want to.

- **Protected Friend**—Gives constants both protected and friend access, which means that they can be used by code in the same assembly as well as by code in derived classes.

- **Private**—Gives constants private access, which means that they are accessible only from within their declaration context (usually a class), including any nested procedures. You can use **Private** only at the module, namespace, or file level (which means that you can't use it inside a procedure). Note that if you specify **Private**, you can omit the **Dim** keyword if you want to.

- **Shadows**—Makes this constant a shadow of an identically named programming element in a base class. A shadowed element is unavailable in the derived class that shadows it. You can use **Shadows** only at the module, namespace, or file level (but not inside a procedure). This means that you can declare shadowing variables in a source file or inside a module, class, or structure but not inside a procedure. Note that if you specify **Shadows**, you can omit the **Dim** keyword if you want to.

- *name*—The name of the constant. You can declare as many constants as you like in the same declaration statement, specifying the *name* and *initexpr* parts for each one. You separate multiple constants with commas.

- *type*—The data type of the constant. This can be **Boolean**, **Byte**, **Char**, **Date**, **Decimal**, **Double**, **Integer**, **Long**, **Object**, **Short**, **Single**, **String**, or the name of an enumeration. Note that you must use a separate **As** clause for each constant being defined. Note also that if *type* is **Object**, *initexpr* must be set to **Nothing**.

- *initexpr*—An initialization expression. This can consist of a literal, another constant, a member of an enumeration, or any combination of literals, constants, and enumeration members.

Each attribute in the *attrlist* list must use this syntax:

```
<attrname [({ attrargs | attrinit })]>
```

Here are the parts of the *attrlist* list:

- *attrname*—Name of the attribute.
- *attrargs*—List of arguments for this attribute. You separate multiple arguments with commas.
- *attrinit*—List of field or property initializers for this attribute. You separate multiple arguments with commas.

Here's an example showing how to declare and use a constant. In this case, I'm creating a constant named **Pi**, as well as **Area** and **Radius** variables, using the * (multiplication) operator to find the area of a circle, converting that area from a number to a string with the Visual Basic **Str** function, and then displaying the result:

```
Imports System.Console
Module Module1

    Sub Main()
        Const Pi = 3.14159
        Dim Radius, Area As Single
        Radius = 1
        Area = Pi * Radius * Radius
        WriteLine("Area = " & Str(Area))
    End Sub

End Module
```

Creating Enumerations

You have a hundred constants to declare and would like to break them up into functional groups—isn't there an easy way to handle this? There is—you can create an *enumeration*, which is a related set of constants. You create enumerations with the **Enum** statement at the module, class, structure, procedure, or block level:

```
[ <attrlist> ] [{ Public | Protected | Friend | Protected
Friend | Private }] [ Shadows ] Enum name [ As type ]
   [<attrlist1>] membname1 [ = initexpr1 ]
   [<attrlist2>] membname2 [ = initexpr2 ]
      .
      .
      .
   [<attrlistn>] membnamen [ = initexprn ]
End Enum
```

The parts of this statement are the same as for constants (see the previous topic). Here's an example to show how this works; in this case, I'm setting up an enumeration that assigns a constant to every day of the week:

```
Module Module1
    Enum Days
        Sunday = 1
        Monday = 2
        Tuesday = 3
        Wednesday = 4
        Thursday = 5
        Friday = 6
        Saturday = 7
    End Enum

    Sub Main()
        System.Console.WriteLine("Friday is day " & Days.Friday)
    End Sub

End Module
```

To use a constant in the enumeration, you refer to it like this: **Days.Friday**, **Days.Monday**, and so on. Here's the result of this code:

```
Friday is day 6
Press any key to continue
```

Declaring Variables

You need to store some data in your program—so you need to declare some variables. How does that work? Unlike VB6 and earlier versions of Visual Basic, by default you must declare all variables before using them in VB .NET. You can declare variables with the **Dim** statement (which originally stood for "dimension," as when you set the dimensions of an array); this statement is used at the module, class, structure, procedure, or block level:

```
[ <attrlist> ] [{ Public | Protected | Friend |
Protected Friend | Private | Static }] [ Shared ]
[ Shadows ] [ ReadOnly ] Dim [ WithEvents ]
name[ (boundlist) ] [ As [ New ] type ] [ = initexpr ]
```

Here are the parts of this statement:

- ***attrlist***—A list of attributes that apply to the variables you're declaring in this statement. You separate multiple attributes with commas.

- **Public**—Gives variables public access, which means that no restrictions are made on their accessibility. You can use **Public** only at the module, namespace, or file level (which means that you can't use it inside a procedure). Note that if you specify **Public**, you can omit the **Dim** keyword if you want to.

- **Protected**—Gives variables protected access, which means that they are accessible only from within their own class or from a class derived from that class. You can use **Protected** only at the class level (which means that you can't use it inside a procedure) because you use it to declare members of a class. Note that if you specify **Protected**, you can omit the **Dim** keyword if you want to.

- **Friend**—Gives variables friend access, which means that they are accessible from within the program that contains their declaration as well as from anywhere else in the same assembly. You can use **Friend** only at the module, namespace, or file level (which means that you can't use it inside a procedure). Note that if you specify **Friend**, you can omit the **Dim** keyword if you want to.

- **Protected Friend**—Gives variables both protected and friend access, which means that they can be used by code in the same assembly as well as by code in derived classes.

- **Private**—Gives variables private access, which means that they are accessible only from within their declaration context (usually a class), including any nested procedures. You can use **Private** only at the module, namespace, or file level (which means that you can't use it inside a procedure). Note that if you specify **Private**, you can omit the **Dim** keyword if you want to.

- **Static**—Makes variables static, which means that they'll retain their values, even after the procedure in which they're declared ends. You can declare static variables inside a procedure or a block within a procedure but not at the class or module level. Note that if you specify **Static**, you can omit the **Dim** keyword if you want to, but you cannot use either **Shadows** or **Shared**.

- **Shared**—Declares a shared variable, which means that it is not associated with a specific instance of a class or structure but can be shared across many instances. You access a shared variable by referring to it either with its class or structure name or with the variable name of an instance of the class or structure. You can use **Shared** only at the module, namespace, or file level (but not at the procedure level). Note that if you specify **Shared**, you can omit the **Dim** keyword if you want to.

- **Shadows**—Makes this variable a shadow of an identically named programming element in a base class. A shadowed element is unavailable in the derived class that shadows it. You can use **Shadows** only at the module, namespace, or file level (but not inside a procedure). This means that you can declare shadowing variables in a source file or inside a module, class, or structure but not inside a procedure. Note that if you specify **Shadows**, you can omit the **Dim** keyword if you want to.

- **ReadOnly**—Means that this variable can be only read and not written. This can be useful for creating constant members of reference types, such as an object variable with preset data members. You can use **ReadOnly** only at the module, namespace, or file level (but not inside procedures). Note that if you specify **Shadows**, you can omit the **ReadOnly** keyword if you want to.

- **WithEvents**—Specifies that this variable is used to respond to events caused by the instance that was assigned to the variable. Note that you cannot specify both **WithEvents** and **New** in the same variable declaration.

- *name*—Specifies the name of the variable. You separate multiple variables by commas. If you specify multiple variables, each variable is declared of the data type given in the first **As** clause encountered after its *name* part.

- *boundlist*—Declares arrays; this gives the upper bounds of the dimensions of an array variable. Multiple upper bounds are separated by commas. An array can have up to 60 dimensions.

- **New**—Means that you want to create a new object immediately. If you use **New** when declaring an object variable, a new instance of the object is created. Note that you cannot use both **WithEvents** and **New** in the same declaration.

- *type*—The data type of the variable. Can be **Boolean**, **Byte**, **Char**, **Date**, **Decimal**, **Double**, **Integer**, **Long**, **Object**, **Short**, **Single**, or **String** or the name of an enumeration, structure, class, or interface. To specify the type, you use a separate **As** clause for each variable, or you can declare a number of variables of the same type by using common **As** clauses. If you do not specify *type*, the variable takes the data type of *initexpr*. Note that if you don't specify either *type* or *initexpr*, the data type is set to **Object**.

- *initexpr*—An initialization expression that is evaluated and the result assigned to the variable when it is created. Note that if you declare more than one variable with the same **As** clause, you cannot supply *initexpr* for those variables.

Each attribute in the *attrlist* list must use this syntax:

```
<attrname [({ attrargs | attrinit })]>
```

Here are the parts of the *attrlist* list:

- *attrname*—Name of the attribute.

- *attrargs*—List of arguments for this attribute. You separate multiple arguments with commas.

- *attrinit*—List of field or property initializers for this attribute. You separate multiple arguments with commas.

Here are a few examples where I'm declaring variables. Note in particular that you can initialize the value in a variable when you declare it by using the = sign and assigning it a value, as here, where I'm initializing the first variable to the value 1 and the second one to "Bob Owens":

```
Dim EmployeeID As Integer = 1
Dim EmployeeName As String = "Bob Owens"
Dim EmployeeAddress As String
```

If you do not specify a data type, the default is **Object** (not **Variant**, as in VB6, because **Variant** no longer exists). Note also that if you do not specify an initialization value for a variable, Visual Basic will initialize it to a default value for its data type:

- 0 for all numeric types (including **Byte**).

- Binary 0 for **Char**.

- **Nothing** for all reference types (including **Object**, **String**, and all arrays). **Nothing** means that no object is associated with the reference.

- **False** for **Boolean**.

- 12:00 AM of January 1 of the year 1 for **Date**.

To create a new object, you use the **New** keyword, as in this case, where I'm creating a new VB .NET **LinkLabel** control (which works like a hyperlink):

```
Dim LinkLabel1 As New LinkLabel
```

Note that you do not have to create a new object using **New** when you declare it—you can create it later using **New**, after it's been declared:

```
Dim LinkLabel1 As LinkLabel
    .
    .
    .
LinkLabel1 = New LinkLabel()
```

In VB6, you could also declare an object with the **New** keyword to create that object—but although it seemed that doing this would create the new object immediately, the object wasn't actually created until used in code, which created some hard-to-find bugs. This has been fixed in VB .NET, where the new object is created immediately if you declare it with the **New** keyword.

Also in Visual Basic 6, you could declare variables of different types in the same statement, but you had to specify the data type of each variable or it defaulted to **Variant** (which no longer exists). Here's an example:

```
Dim count1, count2 As Integer
    'count1 is a Variant, count2 is an Integer.
```

In Visual Basic .NET, on the other hand, you can declare multiple variables of the same data type without having to repeat the type keyword:

```
Dim count1, count2 As Integer
    'count1 is an Integer, count2 is an Integer.
```

Determining What Data Types Are Available

It's time to create a new variable—but what type should you use? For that matter, exactly what variable types exist, and what do they do? Even if you remember what types exist, you probably won't remember the range of possible values that each variable type allows.

A wide range of data types exist, so we'll use a table to display them. The Visual Basic variable types appear in Table 3.3 for reference, making selecting the right type a little easier. Note that the **Single** and **Double** types handle floating point values, which the **Integer** types (such as **Short**, **Integer**, and **Long**) do not; these names are short for *single-precision floating point* and *double-precision floating point*. You might also notice that some new types are available in VB .NET that weren't in VB6, like **Char**, and that some other types, like **Currency** or **Variant**, are gone. Note in particular the **Boolean** data type, which takes values like **True** or **False** only, also called *logical* values.

Table 3.3   Visual Basic .NET data types.

Type	Storage size	Value range
Boolean	2 bytes	**True** or **False**
Byte	1 byte	0 to 255 (unsigned)
Char	2 bytes	0 to 65535 (unsigned)
Date	8 bytes	January 1, 0001, to December 31, 9999
Decimal	16 bytes	+ 79,228,162,514,264,337,593,543,950,335 with no decimal point; +/− 7.9228162514264337593543950335 with 28 places to the right of the decimal; smallest nonzero number is +/− 0.0000000000000000000000000001
Double	8 bytes	−1.79769313486231E+308 to −4.94065645841247E−324 for negative values; 4.94065645841247E−324 to 1.79769313486231E+308 for positive values
Integer	4 bytes	−2,147,483,648 to 2,147,483,647
Long	8 bytes	−9,223,372,036,854,775,808 to 9,223,372,036,854,775,807
Object	4 bytes	Any type can be stored in a variable of type **Object**
Short	2 bytes	−32,768 to 32,767
Single	4 bytes	−3.402823E+38 to −1.401298E−45 for negative values; 1.401298E−45 to 3.402823E+38 for positive values
String	Depends on implementing platform	0 to approximately 2 billion Unicode characters
User-defined type (structure)		Sum of the sizes of its members Each member of the structure has a range determined by its data type and independent of the ranges of the other members

Related solution:	*Found on page:*
Handling Dates and Times	94

Converting between Data Types

Take a look at this code:

```
Option Strict On
Module Module1
    Sub Main()
        Dim dblData As Double
        Dim intData As Integer
        dblData = 3.14159
        intData = dblData
        System.Console.WriteLine("intData = " & Str(intData))
    End Sub

End Module
```

3. The Visual Basic Language: Handling Data

TIP: *Note how I'm using **WriteLine** to display text and the value in a variable by passing it the expression "**intData = " & Str(intData)**. You can also embed codes like {0}, {1}, and so on into a text string, which will then be replaced by successive values passed to **WriteLine**. For example, the code **System.Console.WriteLine("The time is: {0} hours {1} minutes",** 10, 2)* displays the text "The time is: 10 hours 2 minutes".*

In this case, I've turned **Option Strict** on, which means that Visual Basic will not automatically convert data types when you assign a value of one type to a variable of another; thus, it'll have problems with the previously highlighted statement, where I assign a double-precision floating point variable to an integer variable. To fix this problem, I have to do a specific type conversion, which I do with the **CInt** function, which converts its argument to type **Integer**:

```
Option Strict On
Module Module1
    Sub Main()
        Dim dblData As Double
        Dim intData As Integer
        dblData = 3.14159
        intData = CInt(dblData)
        System.Console.WriteLine("intData = " & Str(intData))
    End Sub

End Module
```

When I run this code, I get this result—notice that the decimal places have been removed to make the value of pi into an integer:

```
intData =   3
Press any key to continue
```

Here's the list of conversion functions you can use:

- **CBool**—Convert to **Bool** data type
- **CByte**—Convert to **Byte** data type
- **CChar**—Convert to **Char** data type
- **CDate**—Convert to **Date** data type
- **CDbl**—Convert to **Double** data type
- **CDec**—Convert to **Decimal** data type
- **CInt**—Convert to **Int** data type
- **CLng**—Convert to **Long** data type
- **CObj**—Convert to **Object** type
- **CShort**—Convert to **Short** data type
- **CSng**—Convert to **Single** data type
- **CStr**—Convert to **String** type

If you can't remember the name of a particular conversion function, you can also use the **CType** function, which lets you specify a type to convert to (which is useful if you're converting to a type that is not one of the simple types in the previous list):

```
Option Strict On
Module Module1
    Sub Main()
        Dim dblData As Double
        Dim intData As Integer
        dblData = 3.14159
        intData = CType(dblData, Integer)
        System.Console.WriteLine("intData = " & Str(intData))
    End Sub
End Module
```

TIP: CType is compiled inline, meaning that the conversion code is part of the code that evaluates the expression. Execution is faster because no call is made to a procedure to perform the conversion.

Visual Basic supports a number of ways of converting from one type of variable to another—in fact, that's one of the strengths of the language. You can also use the conversion statements and procedures shown in Table 3.4.

Table 3.4   Visual Basic data conversion functions.

To convert	Use this
Character code to character	**Chr**
String to lowercase or uppercase	**Format, LCase, UCase, String.ToUpper, String.ToLower, String.Format**
Date to a number	**DateSerial, DateValue**
Decimal number to other bases	**Hex, Oct**
Number to string	**Format, Str**
One data type to another	**CBool, CByte, CDate, CDbl, CDec, CInt, CLng, CObj, CSng, CShort, CStr, Fix, Int**
Character to character code	**Asc**
String to number	**Val**
Time to serial number	**TimeSerial, TimeValue**

Checking Data Types

Visual Basic has a number of data verification functions, shown in Table 3.5. You can use these functions to interrogate objects and determine their types.

Table 3.5   Type-checking functions.

Function	Does this
IsArray()	Returns **True** if passed an array
IsDate()	Returns **True** if passed a date
IsDBNull()	Returns **True** if passed a database **NULL** value, that is, a **System.DBNull** value
IsError()	Returns **True** if passed an error value
IsNumeric()	Returns **True** if passed an numeric value
IsReference()	Returns **True** if passed an **Object** variable that has no object assigned to it; otherwise, returns **False**

*TIP: You can also use the **TypeOf** keyword to get the type of an object like this: **If (TypeOf Err.GetException() Is OverflowException) Then...** See "Making Decisions with **If...Else** Statements" in Chapter 4 for more details.*

Related solution:	Found on page:
Making Decisions with **If...Else** Statements	86

Declaring Arrays and Dynamic Arrays

It's time to start coding the database program. But wait a moment—how are you going to handle the data? It's just a simple program, so you don't want to start tangling with the full database techniques. An array would be perfect; how do you set them up?

Arrays are programming constructs that let you access your data by numeric index. To dimension arrays, you can use **Dim** (standard arrays), **ReDim** (dynamic arrays), **Static** (arrays that don't change when between calls to the procedure they're in), **Private** (arrays private to the form or module they're declared in), **Protected** (arrays restricted to a class or classes derived from that class), **Public** (arrays global to the whole program), and more, as discussed in the section "Declaring Variables" earlier in the chapter. I'll start with standard arrays.

Standard Arrays

You usually use the **Dim** statement to declare a standard array; here are a few examples of standard array declarations:

```
Dim Data(30)
Dim Strings(10) As String
Dim TwoDArray(20, 40) As Integer
Dim Bounds(10, 100)
```

The **Data** array now has 30 elements, starting from **Data(0)**, which is how you refer to the first element, up to **Data(29)**; 0 is the *lower bound* of this array, and 29 is the *upper bound*. (Following the lead of Java, in VB .NET, the lower bound of every array index is 0, and you can no longer use the **Option Base** statement or **To** keyword that used to be available in VB to set custom lower bounds.) The **Bounds** array has two indices, one of which runs from 0 to 9 and the other of which runs from 0 to 99.

I can treat an array as a set of variables accessible with the array index, as here, where I'm storing a string in **Strings(3)** (that is, the fourth element in the array) and then displaying that string on the console:

```
Dim Data(30)
Dim Strings(10) As String
Dim TwoDArray(20, 40) As Integer
Dim Bounds(10, 100)
Strings(3) = "Here's a string!"
System.Console.WriteLine(Strings(3))
```

You can also initialize the data in an array if you don't give an array an explicit size; here's the syntax to use, where I'm initializing an array with the values 10, 3, and 2:

```
Dim Data() = {10, 3, 2}
```

Dynamic Arrays

You can use the **Dim** statement to declare an array with empty parentheses to declare a *dynamic array*. Dynamic arrays can be dimensioned or redimensioned as you need them with the **ReDim** statement (which you must also use the first time you want to use a dynamic array). Here's how you use **ReDim**:

```
ReDim [Preserve] varname(subscripts)
```

You use the **Preserve** keyword to preserve the data in an existing array when you change the size of the last dimension. The *varname* argument holds the name of the array to (re)dimension. The *subscripts* term specifies the new dimension of the array.

This is one of those topics that are made easier with an example, so here's an example using dynamic arrays, where I declare an array, dimension it, and the redimension it, like this:

```
Dim DynaStrings() As String
ReDim DynaStrings(10)
DynaStrings(0) = "String 0"
'Need more data space!
ReDim DynaStrings(100)
DynaStrings(50) = "String 50"
```

TIP: *You can find the upper bound of an array with the **UBound** function.*

Handling Strings

You've decided to lead the way into the future by letting your users type in sentences as commands to your program. Unfortunately, this means that you have to *parse* (that is, break down to individual words) what they type. So what was that string function that lets you break a string into smaller strings again? We'll get an overview of string handling in this section. Strings are supported by the .NET **String** class in Visual Basic. You declare a string this way:

```
Dim strText As String
```

As with other types of variables, you can also initialize a string when you declare it, like this:

```
Dim myString As String = "Welcome to Visual Basic"
```

A string can contain up to approximately 2 billion Unicode characters, and it can grow or shrink to match the data you place in it. A number of string-handling functions are built into Visual Basic .NET. For example, you use **Left**, **Mid**, and **Right** to divide a string into substrings; you find the length of a string with **Len**; and so on.

Besides the string-handling functions that are built into VB .NET, many .NET framework functions are built into the **String** class that VB .NET uses. For example, the Visual Basic **UCase** function will convert strings to uppercase, and so will the **String** class's **ToUpper** method. That means that I can convert a text string to uppercase by using either the VB .NET **UCase** function or the **String** class's **ToUpper** method:

```
Option Strict On
Module Module1
    Sub Main()
        Dim strText1 As String = "welcome to visual basic"
        Dim strText2 As String
        Dim strText3 As String
        strText2 = UCase(strText1)
        strText3 = strText1.ToUpper
        System.Console.WriteLine(strText2)
        System.Console.WriteLine(strText3)
    End Sub

End Module
```

In this example, I'm changing some text to uppercase, and you can see the result in Figure 3.1.

Here's another example—I can use the **Mid** function to get a substring from the middle of another string if I pass it that string, the location to start extracting the substring from (starting at position 1), and the length of the substring. I can do the same thing with the **String** class's **Substring** method if I pass it the location to start extracting the substring from (starting at position 0 this time) and the length of the substring. In this case, I'll extract "look" from "Hey, look here!":

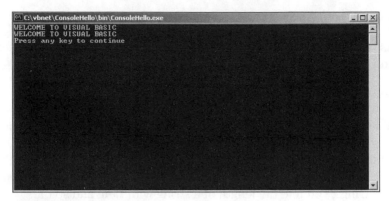

Figure 3.1   Working with strings in Visual Basic.

```
Module Module1
    Sub Main()
        Dim strText1 As String = "Hey, look here!"
        Dim strText2 As String
        Dim strText3 As String
        strText2 = Mid(strText1, 6, 4)
        strText3 = strText1.Substring(5, 4)
        System.Console.WriteLine(strText2)
        System.Console.WriteLine(strText3)
    End Sub
End Module
```

Here's what you see when you execute this example:

```
look
look
Press any key to continue
```

For reference, the popular Visual Basic string-handling functions and methods appear in Table 3.6, organized by task (new in VB .NET). Note that you now cannot use **LSet** and **RSet** to assign one data type to another. Note especially the string-trimming functions, which are very handy and can trim leading or trailing spaces or other characters.

Table 3.6   String-handling functions and methods.

To do this	Use this
Concatenate two strings	**&, +, String.Concat, String.Join**
Compare two strings	**StrComp, String.Compare, String.Equals, String.CompareTo**
Convert strings	**StrConv, CStr, String.ToString**

continued

3. The Visual Basic Language: Handling Data

Table 3.6   String-handling functions and methods (continued).

To do this	Use this
Copy strings	**=, String.Copy**
Convert to lowercase or uppercase	**Format, Lcase, Ucase, String.Format, String.ToUpper, String.ToLower**
Convert to and from numbers	**Str, Val.Format, String.Format**
Create a string of a repeating character	**Space, String, String.String**
Create an array of strings from one string	**String.Split**
Find the length of a string	**Len, String.Length**
Format a string	**Format, String.Format**
Get a substring	**Mid, String.SubString**
Insert a substring	**String.Insert**
Justify a string with padding	**LSet, Rset, String.PadLeft, PadRight**
Manipulate strings	**InStr, Left, LTrim, Mid, Right, RTrim, Trim, String.Trim, String.TrimEnd, String.TrimStart**
Remove text	**Mid, String.Remove**
Replace text	**Mid, String.Replace**
Set string comparison rules	**Option Compare**
Search strings	**InStr, String.Chars, String.IndexOf, String.IndexOfAny, String.LastIndexOf, String.LastIndexOfAny**
Trim leading or trailing spaces	**LTrim, RTrim, Trim, String.Trim, String.TrimEnd, String.TrimStart**
Work with character codes	**Asc, AscW, Chr**

Here's another point you should know—to concatenate (join) strings together, you can use the **&** or **+** operators or the **String** class's **Concat** method. Here's an example we saw in Chapter 2, breaking a long string up over several lines:

```
Dim Msg As String
Msg = "Well, there is a problem " _
& "with your program. I am not sure " _
& "what the problem is, but there is " _
& "definitely something wrong."
```

Fixed-Length Strings

Visual Basic 6 and earlier supported fixed-length strings, where you can specify a nonchanging length for a string, but that's changed in VB .NET to match the .NET framework. However, a special class in VB .NET, **VB6.FixedLengthString**, supports fixed-length strings. For example, this declaration in VB6, which declares a string of 1,000 characters,

```
Dim strString1 As String * 1000
```

now becomes

```
Dim strString1 As New VB6.FixedLengthString(1000)
```

TIP: *If you're going to use fixed-length strings in structures (that is, user-defined types), you should know that the fixed-length string is not automatically created when the structure is created.*

TIP: *You can also create strings of spaces with the SPC function or insert tabs into strings with the **TAB** function.*

Converting Strings to Numbers and Back Again

You're all set to write your calculator program, SuperDuperDeluxeCalc, in Visual Basic—but suddenly you realize that the user will be entering numbers in text form, not in numeric form. How can you translate text into numbers and then numbers into text to display your results?

It's common in Visual Basic to have to convert values from numbers to strings or from strings to numbers, and it's easy to do. You can use **Str** to return a string representation of a number, and you use **Val** to convert a string to a number. That's all there is to it, but it's easy to forget those two functions, so I'm including them here for reference. Here's an example that converts a string into a number and then back into a string:

```
Module Module1
    Sub Main()
        Dim strText1 As String = "1234"
        Dim intValue1 As Integer
        intValue1 = Val(strText1)
        strText1 = Str(intValue1)
        System.Console.WriteLine(strText1)
    End Sub
End Module
```

Besides **Str** and **Val**, you can also use **Format** and **String.Format**, which let you format expressions and convert them to string form.

Converting between Characters and Character Codes

The characters a program stores internally are stored using Unicode character codes; for example, the character code 65 stands for "A". How can you convert back and forth between characters and character codes? You can use the **Asc** and **Chr** functions:

- **Asc**—Takes a character and returns its character code. For example, **Asc("A")** returns 65.

- **Chr**—Takes a character code and returns the corresponding character. For example, **Chr(65)** returns "A".

Chapter 4

The Visual Basic Language: Operators, Conditionals, and Loops

In Brief

The previous chapter was all about storing your data; this chapter is all about putting that data to *work*. For example, what if you wanted to add two values and display the result? You can do that with the Visual Basic **+** operator like this:

```
Module Module1
    Sub Main()
        Dim intVariable1 As Integer = 1234
        Dim intVariable2 As Integer = 2345
        Dim intVariable3 As Integer
        intVariable3 = intVariable1 + intVariable2
        System.Console.WriteLine(intVariable3)
    End Sub
End Module
```

Or what if you wanted to read integers the user types in? You can read those integers with the **System.Console.ReadLine** method and then test their values with an **If** statement, which allows you to execute the code you choose, depending on what those values are, as we'll see in this chapter:

```
Module Module1
    Sub Main()
        Dim intInput As Integer
        System.Console.WriteLine("Enter an integer...")
        intInput = Val(System.Console.ReadLine())
        If intInput = 1 Then
            System.Console.WriteLine("Thank you.")
        ElseIf intInput = 2 Then
            System.Console.WriteLine("That's fine.")
        ElseIf intInput = 3 Then
            System.Console.WriteLine("Too big.")
        Else
            System.Console.WriteLine("Not a number I know.")
        End If
    End Sub
End Module
```

We'll see all kinds of Visual Basic syntax in this chapter—operators that let you add, subtract, multiply, and divide your data; **If** statements that let you test your data and take appropriate action; and loop statements that let you execute code over and over on your data—even how to end a program at any time. Now it's time to turn to the Immediate Solutions to see all this in action.

Immediate Solutions

Using Visual Basic Operators

You've seen all kinds of ways of setting up variables and strings, but what about doing something with that data? Visual Basic comes with plenty of built-in operators that let you manipulate your data. For example, here I'm adding the values in **intVariable1** and **intVariable2** with the addition operator, **+**, and storing the result in **intVariable3** with the assignment operator, **=**:

```
Module Module1
    Sub Main()
        Dim intVariable1 As Integer = 1234
        Dim intVariable2 As Integer = 2345
        Dim intVariable3 As Integer
        intVariable3 = intVariable1 + intVariable2
        System.Console.WriteLine(intVariable3)
    End Sub
End Module
```

This code prints out the result of adding 1234 and 2345, which is 3579. An operator works on *operands*; for example, in the expression 5 + 4, 5 is *operand1*, + is the *operator*, and 4 is *operand2*. Some operators in Visual Basic take two operands, and some take one.

Various types of operators are used in Visual Basic, and I'll go over all of them here. Here are the arithmetic operators (for example, the expression 5 + 4 yields a value of 9):

- ^—Exponentiation
- *—Multiplication
- /—Division
- \—Integer division
- **Mod**—Modulus
- **+**—Addition
- -—Subtraction

These are the assignment operators (for example, **temperature = 72** stores the value 72 in the variable **temperature**):

- **=**—Assignment
- **^=**—Exponentiation followed by assignment
- ***=**—Multiplication followed by assignment
- **/=**—Division followed by assignment
- **\=**—Integer division followed by assignment
- **+=**—Addition followed by assignment
- **-=**—Subtraction followed by assignment
- **&=**—Concatenation followed by assignment

Here are the comparison operators, which we'll use later in this chapter—see the section "Making Decisions with **If...Else** Statements" (these values yield true or false values—for example, 5 > 4 yields a value of **True**):

- **<**—Less than; true if *operand1* is less than *operand2*
- **<=**—Less than or equal to; true if *operand1* is less than or equal to *operand2*
- **>**—Greater than; true if *operand1* is greater than *operand2*
- **>=**—Greater than or equal to; true if *operand1* is greater than or equal to *operand2*
- **=**—Equal to; true if *operand1* equals *operand2*
- **<>**—Not equal to; true if *operand1* is not equal to *operand2*
- **Is**—True if two object references refer to the same object
- **Like**—Performs string pattern matching

These are the string concatenation operators (for example, **"Hi " & "there"** yields the string **"Hi there"**):

- **&**—String concatenation
- **+**—String concatenation

These are the logical/bitwise operators, where "bitwise" means working bit by bit with numerical values. These types of operators can work on logical values (for example, if **blnValue1** is set to **True** and **blnValue2** is set to **False**, **blnValue1 Or blnValue2** returns a value of **True**) or numbers for bitwise operations, which work on their operands bit by bit (for example, if **intValue1** is set to 2 and **intValue2** is set to 1, **intValue1 Or intValue2** yields 3):

- **And**—Performs an **And** operation. (For logical operations, true if both operands are true, false otherwise; the same for bit-by-bit operations where you treat 0 as false and 1 as true.)

- **Not**—Reverses the logical value of its operand, from true to false and false to true; for bitwise operations, turns 0 into 1 and 1 into 0.

- **Or**—Performs an **Or** operation. (For logical operations, true if either operand is true, false otherwise; the same for bit-by-bit operations where you treat 0 as false and 1 as true.)

- **Xor**—Performs an exclusive **Or** operation. (For logical operations, true if either operand, but not both, is true and false otherwise; the same for bit-by-bit operations where you treat 0 as false and 1 as true.)

- **AndAlso**—A "short-circuited" **And** operator; if the first operand is false, the second operand is not tested.

- **OrElse**—A "short-circuited" **Or** operator; if the first operand is true, the second is not tested.

Here are other, miscellaneous operators:

- **AddressOf**—Gets the address of a procedure

- **GetType**—Gets information about a type

In Visual Basic .NET, if the first operand of an **And** operator evaluates to **False**, the remainder of the logical expression is not evaluated. Similarly, if the first operand of an **Or** operator evaluates to **True**, the remainder of the logical expression is not evaluated. This is called *short-circuiting*.

Understanding Visual Basic Operator Precedence

When expressions contain operators from more than one category, they are evaluated according to the following rules:

- The arithmetic and concatenation operators have an order of precedence that is described in the following list, and all have higher precedence than the comparison and logical operators.

- Comparison operators have higher precedence than the logical operators but lower precedence than the arithmetic and concatenation operators. All comparison operators have equal precedence; that is, they are evaluated in the order, left to right, in which they appear.

The arithmetic operators have the highest precedence and are arranged this way, from highest precedence to lowest:

- Exponentiation (^)
- Negation (-) (for example, -**intValue** reverses the sign of the value in **intValue**)
- Multiplication and division (*, /)
- Integer division (\)
- Modulus arithmetic (**Mod**)
- Addition and subtraction (**+, -**)

Next come the concatenation operators:

- String concatenation (**+**)
- String concatenation (**&**)

Next come the comparison operators, all of which have the same precedence and are evaluated left to right as Visual Basic encounters them:

- Equality (=)
- Inequality (<>)
- Less than, greater than (<, >)
- Greater than or equal to (>=)
- Less than or equal to (<=)
- **Like**
- **Is**

Finally come the logical/bitwise operators, which have this precedence order, from highest to lowest:

- Negation (**Not**)
- Conjunction (**And, AndAlso**)
- Disjunction (**Or, OrElse, Xor**)

Commenting Your Code

In general, you should add comments to your code when you can to make it clearer what's going on. Comments in Visual Basic start with an apostrophe (') and make Visual Basic ignore whatever follows the apostrophe on the line. Here's an example, where I'm adding comments to code to make it easier to read:

```
Module Module1
    Sub Main()
        'Declare the variables we will use
        Dim intGrade1, intGrade2, intGrade3, _
        NumberStudents As Integer
        'Fill the variables with data
        intGrade1 = 60
        intGrade2 = 70
        intGrade3 = 80
        NumberStudents = 3        'Three students
        'Display the average value
        System.Console.WriteLine("Average grade = " & _
        Str((intGrade1 + intGrade2 + intGrade3) / NumberStudents))
    End Sub
End Module
```

Making Decisions with **If...Else** Statements

How can you make choices in your code, deciding what to do next depending on the values in your variables? You can use the **If** statement, which is the bread and butter of Visual Basic conditionals and lets you evaluate your data and execute appropriate code. Here's how this statement works:

```
If condition Then
    [statements]
[ElseIf condition-n Then
    [elseifstatements] ...]
[Else
    [elsestatements]]
End If
```

You use comparison operators in the condition here to generate a logical result that's true or false; for example, if *condition* is **intVariable > 5**, then *condition* will be true if the value in **intVariable** is greater than 5.

If *condition* is true, the statements immediately following the **Then** keyword in the body of the **If** statement will be executed, and the **If** statement will terminate before the code in any **ElseIf** or **Else** statement is executed. If *condition* is false, the following **ElseIf** statements are evaluated, if there are any; this statement lets you test additional conditions, and if any are true, the corresponding code (*elseifstatements*) is executed and the **If** statement terminates. If there are no **ElseIf** statements, or if none of their conditions is true, the code in the **Else** statement (*elsestatements*), if there is one, is executed automatically.

Here's an example showing how to use the various parts of this popular statement—in this case, I'm reading an integer that the user types at the console using the **System.Console.ReadLine** method and checking it against various values:

```
Module Module1
    Sub Main()
        Dim intInput As Integer
        System.Console.WriteLine("Enter an integer...")
        intInput = Val(System.Console.ReadLine())
        If intInput = 1 Then
            System.Console.WriteLine("Thank you.")
        ElseIf intInput = 2 Then
            System.Console.WriteLine("That's fine.")
        ElseIf intInput = 3 Then
            System.Console.WriteLine("Too big.")
        Else
            System.Console.WriteLine("Not a number I know.")
        End If
    End Sub
End Module
```

Note that when you compare strings, not numbers, in *condition*, the string expressions are evaluated on the basis of their alphabetical sort order by default. The sort order for strings is evaluated on the basis of the **Option Compare** setting (see the In Brief section of Chapter 3). You can also use the **String.Compare** method to compare strings.

Note that you can also use the **TypeOf** and **Is** keywords to check the type of an object in an **If** statement like this:

```
If (TypeOf Err.GetException() Is OverflowException) Then
    System.Console.WriteLine("Overflow error!")
End If
```

Using Select Case

You have to get a value from the user and respond in several different ways, but don't look forward to a long and tangled series of **If...Then...Else** statements. What can you do?

If your program can handle multiple values of a particular variable and you don't want to stack up a lot of **If...Else** statements to handle them, you should consider **Select Case**. You use **Select Case** to test an expression, seeing which of several cases it matches, and execute the corresponding code. Here's the syntax:

```
Select Case testexpression
[Case expressionlist-n
    [statements-n]] ...
[Case Else
    [elsestatements]]
End Select
```

You use multiple **Case** statements in a **Select** statement, each specifying a different value to test against *textexpression*, and the code in the **Case** statement that matches is executed.

Here's an example using **Select Case**. In this example, I'm modifying the code from the previous topic to use **Select Case** instead of **If...Then**. Note that I'm also using the **Select Is** keyword, which you can use like this: **Case Is** *condition*, allowing you to test *testexpression* against some condition (such as **Case Is > 7**). You can also test *testexpression* against a range of values with the **To** keyword (such as **Case 4 To 7**). And **Case Else** can handle values you don't explicitly provide code for—it's just like the **Else** statement in an **If...Then** statement because the code in it is executed if no other case matches. Here's the code:

```
Module Module1
    Sub Main()
        Dim intInput As Integer
        System.Console.WriteLine("Enter an integer...")
        intInput = Val(System.Console.ReadLine())
        Select Case intInput
            Case 1
                System.Console.WriteLine("Thank you.")
            Case 2
                System.Console.WriteLine("That's fine.")
            Case 3
                System.Console.WriteLine("OK.")
            Case 4 To 7
                System.Console.WriteLine("In the range 4 to 7.")
            Case Is > 7
                System.Console.WriteLine("Definitely too big.")
```

```
                    Case Else
                        System.Console.WriteLine("Not a number I know.")
                End Select
        End Sub
End Module
```

Making Selections with **Switch** and **Choose**

For some reason, few books on Visual Basic cover the **Switch** and **Choose** functions, but they certainly have their uses, and we'll take a look at them here.

The **Switch** Function

The **Switch** function evaluates a list of expressions and returns an **Object** value or an expression associated with the first expression in the list that is **true**. Here's the syntax:

```
Switch(expr-1, value-1[, expr-2, value-2 … [, expr-n, value-n]])
```

In this case, *expr-1* is the first expression to evaluate; if true, **Switch** returns *value-1*. If *expr-1* is not true but *expr-2* is, **Switch** returns *value-2*, and so on. Here's an example showing how to use **Switch**. In this case, I'm using **Switch** to calculate the absolute value of the variable **intValue** (having temporarily forgotten how to use the built-in Visual Basic absolute value function, **Abs**):

```
intAbsValue = Switch(intValue < 0, -1 * intValue, _
    intValue >= 0, intValue)
```

TIP: *Using the negation operator, -, you can write* **-1 * intValue** *simply as* **-intValue***.*

The **Choose** Function

You use the **Choose** function to return one of a number of choices based on an index. Here's the syntax:

```
Choose(index, choice-1[, choice-2, ... [, choice-n]])
```

If the **index** value is 1, the first choice is returned; if **index** equals 2, the second choice is returned; and so on. Here's an example using **Choose**. In this case, we have three employees, Bob, Denise, and Ted, with employee IDs 1, 2, and 3. This code uses an ID value to assign the corresponding employee name to **strEmployeeName**:

```
strEmployeeName = Choose(intID, "Bob", "Denise", "Ted")
```

Using the **Do** Loop

The **Do** loop keeps executing its enclosed statements while or until (depending on which keyword you use, **While** or **Until**) *condition* is true. You can also terminate a **Do** loop at any time with an **Exit Do** statement. The **Do** loop has two versions; you can either evaluate a condition at the beginning,

```
Do [{While | Until} condition]
    [statements]
    [Exit Do]
    [statements]
Loop
```

or at the end,

```
Do
    [statements]
    [Exit Do]
    [statements]
Loop [{While | Until} condition]
```

---

*TIP: Note that the second form of the **Do** loop ensures that the body of the loop is executed at least once.*

Here's an example where the code keeps displaying the message "What should I do?" until the user types "Stop." (Note that I'm using **UCase** to uppercase what the user types and comparing it to "STOP" to let them use any combination of case when they type "Stop."):

```
Module Module1
    Sub Main()
        Dim strInput As String
        Do Until UCase(strInput) = "STOP"
            System.Console.WriteLine("What should I do?")
            strInput = System.Console.ReadLine()
```

```
        Loop
    End Sub
End Module
```

Using the **For** Loop

The **For** loop is probably the most popular of all Visual Basic loops.
The **Do** loop doesn't need a *loop index*, but the **For** loop does. A loop
index counts the number of loop iterations as the loop executes. Here's
the syntax for the **For** loop—note that you can terminate a **For** loop
at any time with **Exit For**:

```
For index = start To end [Step step]
    [statements]
    [Exit For]
    [statements]
Next [index]
```

The ***index*** variable is originally set to ***start*** automatically when the
loop begins. Each time through the loop, ***index*** is incremented by
step (***step*** is set to a default of 1 if you don't specify a value), and
when ***index*** equals ***end***, the loop ends.

Here's how to put this loop to work; in this case, I'm displaying "Hello
from Visual Basic" four times (that is, **intLoopIndex** will hold 0 the
first time, 1 the next time, followed by 2, and then 3, at which point
the loop terminates):

```
Module Module1
    Sub Main()
        Dim intLoopIndex As Integer
        For intLoopIndex = 0 To 3
            System.Console.WriteLine("Hello from Visual Basic")
        Next intLoopIndex
    End Sub
End Module
```

Here's what you see when you run this code:

```
Hello from Visual Basic
Hello from Visual Basic
Hello from Visual Basic
```

```
Hello from Visual Basic
Press any key to continue
```

The following example uses a step size of 2:

```
For intLoopIndex = 0 To 3 Step 2
    System.Console.WriteLine("Hello from Visual Basic")
Next intLoopIndex
```

You'd see this result:

```
Hello from Visual Basic
Hello from Visual Basic
Press any key to continue
```

TIP: Although it's been common practice to use a loop index after a loop completes (to see how many loop iterations were executed), that practice is now discouraged by people who make it their business to write about good and bad programming practices.

We'll see **For** loops throughout the book.

Using the **For Each...Next** Loop

You use the **For Each...Next** loop to loop over elements in an array or a Visual Basic collection. This loop is great because it automatically loops over all the elements in the array or collection—you don't have to worry about getting the loop indices just right to make sure you get all elements, as you do with a **For** loop. Here's the syntax of this loop:

```
For Each element In group
    [statements]
    [Exit For]
    [statements]
Next [element]
```

You can get a look at this loop in action with an example like this, where I'm displaying all the elements of an array:

```
Module Module1
    Sub Main()
        Dim intIDArray(3), intArrayItem As Integer
        intIDArray(0) = 0
        intIDArray(1) = 1
```

```
        intIDArray(2) = 2
        intIDArray(3) = 3

        For Each intArrayItem In intIDArray
            System.Console.WriteLine(intArrayItem)
        Next intArrayItem
    End Sub
End Module
```

Here's the results of this code:

```
0
1
2
3
Press any key to continue
```

Using the **While** Loop

While loops keep looping while the condition they test remains true, so you use a **While** loop if you have a condition that will become false when you want to stop looping. Here's the **While** loop's syntax (note that you used to end this loop with **Wend** in VB6 and before—that's changed to **End While** now):

```
While condition
    [statements]
End While
```

Here's an example putting **While** to work:

```
Sub CheckWhile()
    Dim intCounter As Integer = 0
    Dim intNumber As Integer = 10
    While intNumber > 6
        intNumber -= 1
        intCounter += 1
    End While
    MsgBox("The loop ran " & intCounter & " times.")
End Sub
```

Here's what you see when you run this code:

```
The loop ran 4 times.
Press any key to continue
```

> **TIP:** Many Visual Basic functions, like **EOF**, which is true when you've reached the end of a file while reading from it, are explicitly constructed to return values of **True** or **False** so that you can use them to control loops, such as **Do** and **While**.

Using the **With** Statement

The **With** statement is not a loop, properly speaking, but it can be as useful as a loop—and, in fact, many programmers actually think of it as a loop. You use the **With** statement to execute statements using a particular object. Here's the syntax:

```
With object
    [statements]
End With
```

Here's an example showing how to put **With** to work. Here, I'm using a text box, **Text1**, in a Windows form program and setting its **Height**, **Width**, and **Text** properties in the **With** statement:

```
With TextBox1
    .Height = 1000
    .Width = 3000
    .Text = "Welcome to Visual Basic"
End With
```

Handling Dates and Times

One of the biggest headaches a programmer can have is working with dates and times. Handling hours, minutes, and seconds can be as bad as working with shillings, pence, and pounds. Fortunately, Visual Basic has a number of date- and time-handling functions, which appear in Table 4.1—you can even add or subtract dates using those functions. VB6 programmers will notice a number of new properties in this table.

Table 4.1   Visual Basic .NET date and time properties.

To Do This	Use This
Get the current date or time	**Today**, **Now**, **TimeofDay**, **DateString**, **TimeString**
Perform date calculations	**DateAdd**, **DateDiff**, **DatePart**

continued

Table 4.1   Visual Basic .NET date and time properties (continued).

To Do This	Use This
Return a date	**DateSerial, DateValue**
Return a time	**TimeSerial, TimeValue**
Set the date or time	**Today, TimeofDay**
Time a process	**Timer**

Here's an example where I'm adding 22 months to 12/31/2002 using **DateAdd**—you might note in particular that you can assign dates of the format 12/31/2002 to variables of the **Date** type if you enclose them inside **#** symbols:

```
Imports System.Math
Module Module1
    Sub Main()
        Dim FirstDate As Date
        FirstDate = #12/31/2002#
        System.Console.WriteLine("New date: " & _
        DateAdd(DateInterval.Month, _
        22, FirstDate))
    End Sub
End Module
```

Here's what you see when you run this code:

```
New date: 10/31/2004
Press any key to continue
```

There's something else you should know—the **Format** function makes it easy to format dates into strings, including times. For easy reference, see Table 4.2, which shows some ways to display the date and time in a string—note how many ways there are to do this.

Table 4.2   Using Format to display dates and times.

Format Expression	Yields This
Format*(Now, "M-d-yy")*	"1-1-03"
Format*(Now, "M/d/yy")*	"1/1/03"
Format*(Now, "MM - dd - yy")*	"01 /01 / 03"
Format*(Now, "ddd, MMMM d, yyy")*	"Friday, January 1, 2003"
Format*(Now, "d MMMM, yyy")*	"1 Jan, 2003"
Format*(Now, "hh:mm:ss MM/dd/yy")*	"01:00:00 01/01/03"
Format*(Now, "hh:mm:ss tt MM-dd-yy")*	"01:00:00 AM 01-01-03"

You can also compare dates and times directly. For example, here's how you loop until the current time (returned as a string by **TimeString**) exceeds a certain time; when the time is up, the code beeps using the Visual Basic **Beep** function:

```
While TimeString < "15:45:00"
End While
Beep()
```

TIP: *Don't use the previous code snippet for more than an example of how to compare times. The eternal looping while waiting for something to happen is a bad idea in Windows because your program monopolizes a lot of resources that way. Instead, set up a Visual Basic Timer and have a procedure called, say, every second.*

Ending a Program at Any Time

Our last topic in this chapter will be about ending programs. At times you'll want to end a program without any further ado—for example, to make an Exit menu item active. How do you do that?

You use the **End** statement. This statement stops execution of your program; here's an example in which I end the program when the user types "Stop" (or "stop" or "STOP" and so on):

```
Module Module1
    Sub Main()
        Dim strInput As String
        Do Until UCase(strInput) = "STOP"
            System.Console.WriteLine("What should I do?")
            strInput = System.Console.ReadLine()
        Loop
        End
    End Sub
End Module
```

TIP: *The **Stop** statement is similar to **End**, except that it puts the program in a break state. Executing a **Stop** statement, therefore, will make the Visual Basic debugger come up.*

If you're thinking of stopping a program just because an error occurs, take a look at the error-handling discussion in Chapter 6.

Related solution:	Found on page:
Using Structured Exception Handling	130

Chapter 5

The Visual Basic Language: Procedures And Scope

In Brief

In this chapter, we'll take a look at a very important part of the Visual Basic language: *procedures*. Dividing your code into procedures allows you to break it up into more modular units. This is invaluable as your programs become longer because it stops everything from becoming too cluttered. In Visual Basic, all executable code must be in procedures. The two types of procedures are *Sub procedures* and *functions*. In Visual Basic, **Sub** procedures do not return values when they terminate, but functions do.

As your code gets longer, it also becomes more important to know what parts of your code are accessible from other parts of your code; this issue is known as *scope*. We'll take a look at the idea of scope in this chapter.

Sub Procedures and Functions

Procedures are made up of a series of Visual Basic statements that, when called, are executed. After the call is finished, control returns to the statement that called the procedure. In this way, procedures make it simple for you to package your code into discrete units. Ideally, each Visual Basic procedure should handle one—and only one—task to make this easy to remember. You can pass data to procedures, and the code in the procedures can work on that data. As mentioned previously, **Sub** procedures do not return a value, whereas functions do.

Let's take a look at creating a **Sub** procedure first. We've already placed all our executable code in the **Sub** procedure named **Main**, so this will be easy to do:

```
Module Module1
    Sub Main()
        System.Console.WriteLine("Hello from Visual Basic")
    End Sub
End Module
```

When this console application starts, control is transferred to the **Main Sub** procedure automatically, and the code in it runs. However, we can create our own **Sub** procedures as well. Here I'm creating a **Sub** procedure named **DisplayMessage** to display the same message that the previous code does:

```
Module Module1
    Sub Main()
    End Sub

    Sub DisplayMessage()
        System.Console.WriteLine("Hello from Visual Basic")
    End Sub
End Module
```

To execute the code in **DisplayMessage**, you must call that **Sub** procedure, which looks like this:

```
Module Module1
    Sub Main()
        DisplayMessage()
    End Sub

    Sub DisplayMessage()
        System.Console.WriteLine("Hello from Visual Basic")
    End Sub
End Module
```

TIP: *Optionally, you can also use the **Call** statement to call a **Sub** procedure like this: **Call DisplayMessage**. Although this usage is considered old-fashioned, it can make your code more readable.*

This produces the same results as before, displaying the message "Hello from Visual Basic"; when you call **DisplayMessage**, the code in that **Sub** procedure is executed. Note the parentheses following **DisplayMessage** in the previous code; you use these to enclose data that you pass to the procedure, which are called *arguments*. For example, to pass to **DisplayMessage** the text string we want to display, you can indicate that it accepts a text-string argument, like this:

```
Module Module1
    Sub Main()
    End Sub

    Sub DisplayMessage(ByVal strText As String)
        .
        .
        .
    End Sub
End Module
```

Here, the keyword **ByVal** indicates that the text string is passed *by value*, which means that a copy of the string is passed. This is the default in VB .NET. The other possibility is **ByRef**, which means that the argument will be passed *by reference*. When you pass a variable by reference (which was the default in VB6 and earlier), the *location* of the variable is passed to the procedure, which means that you have direct access to that variable back in the calling code. Changing the value in that variable (as by assigning it a new value like this: **intArgument1 = 5**) actually changes its value back in the code that called the procedure. In this way, if you pass variables by reference (but not by value) to a procedure, the code in that procedure can change the value in those variables.

Now that I've given the argument passed to **DisplayMessage** a name (**strText**), I can refer to that argument by name in the body of **DisplayMessage**:

```
Module Module1
    Sub Main()
    End Sub

    Sub DisplayMessage(ByVal strText As String)
        System.Console.WriteLine(strText)
    End Sub
End Module
```

And I can pass data to **DisplayMessage** when I call it. This string, "Hello from Visual Basic", will be stored in **strText** in **DisplayMessage**:

```
Module Module1
    Sub Main()
        DisplayMessage("Hello from Visual Basic")
    End Sub

    Sub DisplayMessage(ByVal strText As String)
        System.Console.WriteLine(strText)
    End Sub
End Module
```

This code displays our message as before.

TIP: *In VB6 and earlier versions, using parentheses to enclose the arguments you're passing to a procedure was optional under certain circumstances (as when you called **Sub** procedures). In VB .NET, that's no longer true; now you must always use parentheses, unless you're not passing any arguments to the procedure, in which case you can either use empty parentheses or omit them altogether.*

You can also create functions, which return values. For example, I might create a function named **Addem** that accepts two integer arguments and returns their sum. Declaring a function is much like declaring a **Sub** procedure, except that you use the keyword **Function** instead of **Sub** and specify the return type of the function, like this (note that you separate multiple arguments in the declaration of a procedure with commas):

```
Module Module1
    Sub Main()
    End Sub

    Function Addem(ByVal int1 As Integer, _
        ByVal int2 As Integer) As Long
        Return int1 + int2
    End Function
End Module
```

You return a value from a function with the **Return** statement, as I have here, where I'm returning the sum of the two arguments passed to the code. You also can avoid using the **Return** statement if you simply assign a value to the name of a function, as in this example, where the **Always5** function always returns a value of 5:

```
Private Sub Form1_Load(ByVal sender As System.Object, _
ByVal e As System.EventArgs) Handles MyBase.Load
    MsgBox(Always5())
End Sub

Private Function Always5() As Integer
    Always5 = 5
End Function
```

TIP: In Visual Basic 6, you could use the **Return** statement only to branch back to the code following a **GoSub** statement. In Visual Basic .NET, the **GoSub** statement is not supported, and you can use the **Return** statement to return control to the calling program from a **Function** or **Sub** procedure.

When you call a function by using its name and an argument list enclosed in parentheses, that name is replaced by the value returned by the function. For example, the call **Addem(2, 2)** is replaced by the value **4**, in the following code:

```
Module Module1
    Sub Main()
```

5. The Visual Basic Language: Procedures and Scope

```
            Dim intValue As Integer = 2
            System.Console.WriteLine("{0}+{1}={2}", _
                intValue, intValue, Addem(intValue, intValue))
    End Sub

    Function Addem(ByVal int1 As Integer, _
        ByVal int2 As Integer) As Long
        Return int1 + int2
    End Function
End Module
```

TIP: *Note that I'm using syntax in **WriteLine** that we've seen in the previous chapters, passing it a text string with terms like {0} and {1}. {0} will be replaced with the first argument following the text string, {1} with the second, and so on.*

When you run this code, you see this result:

```
2+2=4
```

Understanding Scope

The *scope* of an element in your code is all the code that can refer to it without qualifying its name (or making it available through an **Imports** statement). In other words, an element's scope is its *accessibility* in your code. As you write larger programs, scope will become more important because you'll be dividing code into classes, modules, procedures, and so on. You can make the elements in those programming constructs private, which means that they are tightly restricted in scope.

In VB .NET, where you declare an element determines its scope, and an element can have scope at one of the following levels:

- *Block scope*—Available only within the code block in which it is declared

- *Procedure scope*—Available only within the procedure in which it is declared

- *Module scope*—Available to all code within the module, class, or structure in which it is declared

- *Namespace scope*—Available to all code in the namespace

For example, if you declare a variable in a module outside any procedure, it has module scope, as in this case, where I'm declaring and creating a **LinkLabel** control that has module scope:

```
Dim LinkLabel1 As LinkLabel

Private Sub Button1_Click(ByVal sender As System.Object, _
    ByVal e As System.EventArgs) Handles Button1.Click
    LinkLabel1 = New LinkLabel()
    LinkLabel1.AutoSize = True
    LinkLabel1.Location = New Point(15, 15)
        .
        .
        .
```

TIP: *When you want to declare module-level variables, you can place the declaration outside any procedure in the module. You also can select the module in the left-hand drop-down list box in the code designer and the (Declarations) item in the right-hand drop-down list box, which will take you to a location at the very beginning of the module, outside any procedure.*

Declaring a variable in a procedure gives it procedure scope, and so on. Inside these levels of scope, you can also specify the scope of an element when you declare it. Here are the possibilities in VB .NET, which you'll become familiar with throughout the book:

- **Public**—The **Public** statement declares elements to be accessible from anywhere within the same project, from other projects that reference the project, and from an assembly built from the project. You can use **Public** only at the module, namespace, or file level. This means that you can declare a **Public** element in a source file or inside a module, class, or structure but not within a procedure.

- **Protected**—The **Protected** statement declares elements to be accessible only from within the same class or from a class derived from this class. You can use **Protected** only at the class level and only when declaring a member of a class.

- **Friend**—The **Friend** statement declares elements to be accessible from within the same project but not from outside the project. You can use **Friend** only at the module, namespace, or file level. This means that you can declare a **Friend** element in a source file or inside a module, class, or structure but not within a procedure.

- **Protected Friend**—The **Protected** statement with the **Friend** keyword declares elements to be accessible either from derived classes or from within the same project or both. You can use **Protected Friend** only at the class level and only when declaring a member of a class.

- **Private**—The **Private** statement declares elements to be accessible only from within the same module, class, or structure. You can use **Private** only at the module, namespace, or file level. This means that you can declare a **Private** element in a source file or inside a module, class, or structure but not within a procedure.

Let's take a look at an example. Here's what block scope looks like—in this case, I'll declare a variable, **strText**, in an **If** statement. That variable can be used inside the **If** statement's block but not outside. (VB .NET will tag the second use here as a syntax error.)

```
Module Module1
    Sub Main()
        Dim intValue As Integer = 1
        If intValue = 1 Then
            Dim strText As String = "No worries."
            System.Console.WriteLine(strText)
        End If
            System.Console.WriteLine(strText)          'Will not work!
    End Sub
End Module
```

Here's another example. In this case, I've created a second module, **Module2**, and defined a function, **Function1**, in that module. To make it clear that I want to be able to access **Function1** outside **Module2** (as when I call it as **Module2.Function1** in the **Main** procedure), I declare **Function1** public:

```
Module Module1
    Sub Main()
        System.Console.WriteLine(Module2.Function1())
    End Sub
End Module

Module Module2
    Public Function Function1() As String 'OK
        Return "Hello from Visual Basic"
    End Function
End Module
```

TIP: *Note that in this case, I've put **Module2** into the same file as **Module1**. You can also create a new file for **Module2** if you prefer—just select Project|Add New Item and then select Module in the Templates box of the Add New Item dialog box that opens.*

However, if I declared **Function1** as private to **Module2**, it's inaccessible in **Module1** (and VB .NET will tag **Module2.Function1** in the following as a syntax error):

```
Module Module1
    Sub Main()
        System.Console.WriteLine(Module2.Function1())
        'Will not work!
    End Sub
End Module

Module Module2
    Private Function Function1() As String
        Return "Hello from Visual Basic"
    End Function
End Module
```

Besides procedures, you also can make other elements, such as variables, public or private. Now it's time to turn to the Immediate Solutions to see the details on creating procedures, setting scope, and handling exceptions.

Immediate Solutions

Creating **Sub** Procedures

We know all about **Sub** procedures: They're the handy blocks of code that can organize your code into single-purpose sections to make programming easier. Unlike functions, **Sub** procedures do not return values, but like functions, you can pass values to **Sub** procedures in an argument list.

You declare **Sub** procedures with the **Sub** statement:

```
[ <attrlist> ] [{ Overloads | Overrides | Overridable |
  NotOverridable | MustOverride | Shadows | Shared }]
[{ Public | Protected | Friend | Protected Friend | Private }]
Sub name [(arglist)]
    [ statements ]
    [ Exit Sub ]
    [ statements ]
End Sub
```

Here are the parts of this statement:

- *attrlist*—List of attributes for this procedure. You separate multiple attributes with commas.

- **Overloads**—Specifies that this **Sub** procedure overloads one (or more) procedures defined with the same name in a base class. In this case, the argument list must be different from the argument list of every procedure that is to be overloaded (that is, the lists must differ in the number of arguments, their data types, or both). You cannot specify both **Overloads** and **Shadows** in the same procedure declaration.

- **Overrides**—Specifies that this **Sub** procedure overrides a procedure with the same name in a base class. Note that the number and data types of the arguments must match those of the procedure in the base class.

- **Overridable**—Specifies that this **Sub** procedure can be overridden by a procedure with the same name in a derived class.

- **NotOverridable**—Specifies that this **Sub** procedure may not be overridden in a derived class.

- **MustOverride**—Specifies that this **Sub** procedure is not implemented. Instead, this procedure must be implemented in a derived class. If it is not, that class will not be creatable.

- **Shadows**—Makes this **Sub** procedure a shadow of an identically named programming element in a base class. A shadowed element is unavailable in the derived class that shadows it. You can use **Shadows** only at the module, namespace, or file level (but not inside a procedure). This means that you can declare shadowing variables in a source file or inside a module, class, or structure but not inside a procedure. Note that you cannot specify both **Overloads** and **Shadows** in the same procedure declaration.

- **Shared**—Specifies that this **Sub** procedure is a shared procedure. As a shared procedure, it is not associated with a specific instance of a class or structure, and you can call it by qualifying it either with the class or structure name or with the variable name of a specific instance of the class or structure.

- **Public**—Procedures declared **Public** have public access. No restrictions are made on the accessibility of public procedures.

- **Protected**—Procedures declared **Protected** have protected access. They are accessible only from within their own class or from a derived class. Protected access can be specified only on members of classes.

- **Friend**—Procedures declared **Friend** have friend access. They are accessible from within the program that contains their declaration and from anywhere else in the same assembly.

- **Protected Friend**—Procedures declared **Protected Friend** have both protected and friend accessibility. They can be used by code in the same assembly as well as by code in derived classes.

- **Private**—Procedures declared **Private** have private access. They are accessible only within their declaration context, including from any nested procedures.

- *name*—Name of the **Sub** procedure.

- *arglist*—List of expressions (which can be single variables or simple values) representing arguments that are passed to the **Sub** procedure when it is called. Multiple arguments are separated by commas. Note that in VB .NET, if you supply an argument list, you must enclose it in parentheses.

- *statements*—The block of statements to be executed within the **Sub** procedure.

Each argument in the *arglist* part has the following syntax and parts:

```
[ <attrlist> ] [ Optional ] [{ ByVal | ByRef }]
[ ParamArray ] argname[( )]
[ As argtype ] [ = defaultvalue ]
```

Here are the parts of the *arglist*:

- *attrlist*—List of attributes that apply to this argument. Multiple attributes are separated by commas.

- **Optional**—Specifies that this argument is not required when the procedure is called. Note that if you use this keyword, all following arguments in *arglist* must also be optional and be declared using the **Optional** keyword. Every optional argument declaration must supply a *defaultvalue*. Also, **Optional** cannot be used for any argument if you also use **ParamArray**.

- **ByVal**—Specifies passing by value. In this case, the procedure cannot replace or reassign the underlying variable element in the calling code (unless the argument is a reference type). **ByVal** is the default in Visual Basic.

- **ByRef**—Specifies passing by reference. In this case, the procedure can modify the underlying variable in the calling code the same way the calling code itself can.

- **ParamArray**—Used as the last argument in *arglist* to indicate that the final argument is an optional array of elements of the specified type. The **ParamArray** keyword allows you to pass an arbitrary number of arguments to the procedure. A **ParamArray** argument is always passed **ByVal**.

- *argname*—Name of the variable representing the argument.

- *argtype*—This part is optional, unless **Option Strict** is set to **On**, and holds the data type of the argument passed to the procedure. Can be **Boolean**, **Byte**, **Char**, **Date**, **Decimal**, **Double**, **Integer**, **Long**, **Object**, **Short**, **Single**, or **String** or the name of an enumeration, structure, class, or interface.

- *defaultvalue*—Required for **Optional** arguments. Any constant or constant expression that evaluates to the data type of the argument. Note that if the type is **Object** or a class, interface, array, or structure, the default value can be only **Nothing**.

Each attribute in the *attrlist* part has the following syntax and parts:

```
<attrname [({ attrargs | attrinit })]>
```

Here are the parts of *attrlist*:

- *attrname*—Name of the attribute.

- *attrargs*—List of positional arguments for this attribute. Multiple arguments are separated by commas.

- *attrinit*—List of field or property initializers for this attribute. Multiple initializers are separated by commas.

---

*TIP: When you use **ByVal** (the default in VB .NET), you pass a copy of a variable to a procedure; when you use **ByRef**, you pass a reference to the variable, and if you make changes to that reference, the original variable is changed.*

You call a **Sub** procedure using the procedure name followed by the argument list. The **Exit Sub** keywords cause an immediate exit from a **Sub** procedure. Finally, **End Sub** ends the procedure definition. Here's an example we saw in the In Depth section of this chapter where I'm passing a text string, "Hello from Visual Basic", to the **DisplayMessage Sub** procedure, which displays that message in a console application:

```
Module Module1
    Sub Main()
        DisplayMessage("Hello from Visual Basic")
    End Sub

    Sub DisplayMessage(ByVal strText As String)
        System.Console.WriteLine(strText)
    End Sub
End Module
```

Creating Functions

Unlike **Sub** procedures, functions can return values, as discussed in the In Depth section of this chapter. You use the **Function** statement to create a function:

```
[ <attrlist> ] [{ Overloads | Overrides | Overridable |
  NotOverridable | MustOverride | Shadows | Shared }]
[{ Public | Protected | Friend | Protected Friend | Private }]
  Function name[(arglist)] [ As type ]
    [ statements ]
    [ Exit Function ]
    [ statements ]
  End Function
```

The various parts of this statement are the same as for **Sub** procedures except for the **As** *type* clause, which specifies the type of the return value from the function. *type* is optional unless **Option Strict** is **On**. The data type of the value returned by the **Function** procedure can be **Boolean, Byte, Char, Date, Decimal, Double, Integer, Long, Object, Short, Single**, or **String** or the name of an enumeration, structure, class, or interface.

TIP: *If you use* **Exit Function** *without assigning a value to* **name***, the function returns the default value appropriate to* **argtype***. This is* **0** *for* **Byte, Char, Decimal, Double, Integer, Long, Short***, and* **Single***;* **Nothing** *for* **Object, String***, and all arrays;* **False** *for* **Boolean***; and* **#1/1/0001 12:00 AM#** *for* **Date***.*

The **Return** statement simultaneously assigns the return value and exits the function; any number of **Return** statements can appear anywhere in the procedure. (You also can mix **Exit Function** and **Return** statements.) Here's an example function—**Addem**—we saw in the In Depth section of this chapter that adds two integer values passed to it:

```
Module Module1
    Sub Main()
        Dim intValue As Integer = 2
        System.Console.WriteLine("{0}+{1}={2}", _
            intValue, intValue, Addem(intValue, intValue))
    End Sub

    Function Addem(ByVal int1 As Integer, _
        ByVal int2 As Integer) As Long
        Return int1 + int2
    End Function
End Module
```

Specifying Optional Procedure Arguments

You can make arguments *optional* in VB .NET procedures if you use the **Optional** keyword when declaring those arguments. Note that if you make one argument optional, all the following arguments must also be optional, and you have to specify a *default value* for each optional argument (although you can set them to the keyword **Nothing** if you wish). You specify a default value with = *default_value* in the procedure's argument list. Here's an example where I'm making the string argument you pass to a **Sub** procedure named **DisplayMessage** optional and giving that argument the default value **"Hello from Visual Basic"**:

```
Module Module1
    Sub Main()
        DisplayMessage()
    End Sub

    Sub DisplayMessage(Optional ByVal strText As String = _
        "Hello from Visual Basic")
        System.Console.WriteLine(strText)
    End Sub
End Module
```

Now when I call **DisplayMessage** with no arguments, as in the previous code, the default value is used, and this code displays:

```
Hello from Visual Basic
```

TIP: *VB6 had a function named **IsMissing** that would test whether an optional argument had been given a value, but now that all optional arguments have default values, **IsMissing** has been removed. You can, however, use the **IsNothing** function to check whether an argument has been set to **Nothing**.*

Preserving the Values of Variables between Procedure Calls

You've written a function named **Counter** to keep track of the number of times the user clicks a particular button. Each time through a loop, you call the **Counter** function to increment the count, but when the program ends, it just displays 0 counts. Why? Let's look at the code:

```
Module Module1
    Sub Main()
        Dim intLoopIndex As Integer, intValue = 0
        For intLoopIndex = 0 To 4
            intValue = Counter()
        Next intLoopIndex
```

```
            System.Console.WriteLine(intValue)
        End Sub

        Function Counter() As Integer
            Dim intCountValue As Integer
            intCountValue += 1
            Return intCountValue
        End Function
    End Module
```

The problem here is that the counter variable, **intCountValue**, in the **Counter** function is reinitialized each time the **Counter** function is called (because a new copy of all the variables local to procedures is allocated each time you call that procedure). The solution is to declare **intCountValue** as *static*. This means that it will retain its value between calls to the **Counter** function. Here's the working code:

```
Module Module1
    Sub Main()
        Dim intLoopIndex As Integer, intValue = 0
        For intLoopIndex = 0 To 4
            intValue = Counter()
        Next intLoopIndex
        System.Console.WriteLine(intValue)
    End Sub

    Function Counter() As Integer
        Static intCountValue As Integer
        intCountValue += 1
        Return intCountValue
    End Function
End Module
```

Running this code displays a value of 5, as it should.

TIP: *You can also make **intCountValue** preserve its value between procedure calls by making it a module-level variable—just declare it outside any procedure. But note that you should restrict the scope of your variables as much as possible (to avoid inadvertent conflicts with variables of the same name), so making this variable a static variable in a procedure is probably a better choice.*

NOTE: *You were able to declare a whole function static in VB6, which meant that all the variables in it would be static, but you can't do that in VB .NET.*

Related solution:	*Found on page:*
Declaring Variables	62

Creating Procedure Delegates

Sometimes it's useful to be able to pass the *location* of a procedure to other procedures. That location is the address of the procedure in memory, and it's used in VB .NET to create the callback procedures we'll see later in the book. To work with the address of procedures, you use delegates in VB .NET.

Here's an example; in this case, I'll create a delegate for a **Sub** procedure named **DisplayMessage**:

```
Module Module1
    Sub Main()
        .
        .
        .
    End Sub

    Sub DisplayMessage(ByVal strText As String)
        System.Console.WriteLine(strText)
    End Sub
End Module
```

I start by declaring the delegate type, which I'll call **SubDelegate1**, and creating a delegate called **Messager**:

```
Module Module1
    Delegate Sub SubDelegate1(ByVal strText As String)

    Sub Main()
        Dim Messager As SubDelegate1
        .
        .
        .
    End Sub

    Sub DisplayMessage(ByVal strText As String)
        System.Console.WriteLine(strText)
    End Sub
End Module
```

5. The Visual Basic Language: Procedures and Scope

Now I use the **AddressOf** operator to assign the address of **DisplayMessage** to **Messager** and then use **Messager's Invoke** method to call **DisplayMessage** and display a message:

```
Module Module1
    Delegate Sub SubDelegate1(ByVal strText As String)

    Sub Main()
        Dim Messager As SubDelegate1
        Messager = AddressOf DisplayMessage
        Messager.Invoke("Hello from Visual Basic")
    End Sub

    Sub DisplayMessage(ByVal strText As String)
        System.Console.WriteLine(strText)
    End Sub
End Module
```

And that's all it takes—this code will display the message "Hello from Visual Basic", as it should.

Creating Properties

Visual Basic objects can have methods, fields, and *properties*. If you've worked with Visual Basic before, you're familiar with properties, which you use to set configuration data for objects, such as the text in a text box or the width of a list box. Using properties provides you with an interface to set or get the value of data internal to an object. You declare properties using **Get** and **Set** procedures in a **Property** statement (and, as you might expect, the syntax has changed from VB6):

```
[ <attrlist> ] [ Default ] [ Public | Private | Protected |
Friend | Protected Friend ] [ ReadOnly | WriteOnly ]
[Overloads | Overrides ] [Overridable | NotOverridable] |
MustOverride | Shadows | Shared]
Property varname([ parameter list ]) [ As typename ]
    [ Implements interfacemember ]
    [ <attrlist> ] Get
      [ block ]
    End Get
    [ <attrlist> ] Set(ByVal Value As typename )
      [ block ]
    End Set
End Property
```

Here are the parts of this statement that are different from the keywords used in the **Sub** statement (see the section "Creating **Sub** Procedures" earlier in this chapter):

- **Default**—Makes this a default property. Default properties can be set and retrieved without specifying the property name and must accept parameters.

- **ReadOnly**—Specifies that a property's value can be retrieved, but it cannot be modified. **ReadOnly** properties contain **Get** blocks but no **Set** blocks.

- **WriteOnly**—Specifies that a property can be set, but its value cannot be retrieved. **WriteOnly** properties contain **Set** blocks but no **Get** blocks.

- *varname*—A name that identifies the property.

- *parameter list*—The parameters you use with the property. The list default is **ByVal**.

- *typename*—The type of the property. If you don't specify a data type, the default type is **Object**.

- *interfacemember*—When a property is part of a class that implements an interface, this is the name of the property being implemented.

- **Get**—Starts a **Get** property procedure used to return the value of a property. **Get** blocks are optional unless the property is **ReadOnly**.

- **End Get**—Ends a **Get** property procedure.

- **Set**—Starts a **Set** property procedure used to set the value of a property. **Set** blocks are optional unless the property is **WriteOnly**. Note that the new value of the property is passed to the **Set** property procedure in a parameter named **Value** when the value of the property changes.

- **End Set**—Ends a **Set** property procedure.

Visual Basic passes a parameter named **Value** to the **Set** block during property assignments, and the **Value** parameter contains the value that was assigned to the property when the **Set** block was called. Here's an example where I'm creating a read/write property named **Prop1** in **Module2** and storing the property's value in a private text string named **PropertyValue** in **Module2**:

```
Module Module1
    Sub Main()
        .
        .
        .
```

```
        End Sub
End Module

Module Module2
    Private PropertyValue As String
    Public Property Prop1() As String
        Get
            Return PropertyValue
        End Get
        Set(ByVal Value As String)
            PropertyValue = Value
        End Set
    End Property
End Module
```

TIP: When you type the first line of a property procedure, such as **Public Property Prop1( ) As String** here, VB .NET will add a skeleton for the **Get** and **Set** procedures automatically.

Now I can refer to **Prop1** of **Module2**, setting it and reading its value, like this:

```
Module Module1
    Sub Main()
        Module2.Prop1 = 2
        System.Console.WriteLine("Prop1 = " & Module2.Prop1)
        System.Console.WriteLine("Press Enter to continue...")
    End Sub
End Module

Module Module2
    Private PropertyValue As String
    Public Property Prop1() As String
        Get
            Return PropertyValue
        End Get
        Set(ByVal Value As String)
            PropertyValue = Value
        End Set
    End Property
End Module
```

This console application displays this text in a DOS window:

```
Prop1 = 2
Press Enter to continue...
```

You also can index properties by passing an index value when refer-ring to a property. Here's an example; in this case, I'm creating a prop-erty array by adding an index value that you must specify each time you use the property:

```
Public Module Module1
    Private Data(200) As Integer

    Public Property Property1(ByVal Index As Integer) As Integer
        Get
            Return Data(Index)
        End Get
        Set(ByVal Value As Integer)
            Data(Index) = Value
        End Set
    End Property
End Module
```

Now instead of referring to the property simply as **Property1**, I must use an index value, such as **Property1(5)**, which refers to a particu-lar element in the property array:

```
Private Sub Form1_Load(ByVal sender As System.Object, _
    ByVal e As System.EventArgs) Handles MyBase.Load
    Module1.Property1(5) = 1
    MsgBox(Module1.Property1(5))
End Sub
```

5. The Visual Basic Language: Procedures and Scope

Chapter 6

The Visual Basic Language: Exception Handling

In Brief

Exceptions are runtime errors. They occur when a program is running (as opposed to syntax errors, which will prevent VB .NET from running your program at all). You can trap such exceptions and recover from them rather than letting them bring your program to an inglorious end. Errors that occur at runtime in VB .NET can be handled in two ways: unstructured exception handling and structured exception handling.

TIP: *In Visual Basic (unlike some other languages), the terms "exception handling" and "error handling" have become interchangeable.*

Unstructured Exception Handling

The old error-handling mechanism in VB6 and earlier is now called unstructured exception handling, and it revolves around the **On Error Goto** statement. You use this statement to tell VB .NET where to transfer control in case an exception has occurred, as in this case, where I'm telling Visual Basic to jump to the label "Handler" if there's been an exception. You create labels in your code with the label name followed by a colon, and the exception-handling code will follow that label:

```
Module Module1
    Sub Main()
        On Error Goto Handler
        .
        .
        .
        Exit Sub
Handler:
        .
        .
        .
    End Sub
End Module
```

NOTE: *I've added an Exit Sub statement to make sure that the code in the exception handler is not executed by mistake as part of normal program execution.*

Now I can execute some code that may cause an exception, as here, where the code performs a division by zero, which causes an exception. When the exception occurs, control will jump to the exception handler, where I'll display a message and then use the **Resume Next** statement to transfer control back to the statement immediately after the statement that caused the exception:

```
Module Module1
    Sub Main()
        Dim int1 = 0, int2 = 1, int3 As Integer
        On Error Goto Handler
        int3 = int2 / int1
        System.Console.WriteLine("The answer is {0}", int3)
Handler:
        System.Console.WriteLine("Divide by zero error")
        Resume Next
    End Sub
End Module
```

When you run this code, you see this message:

```
Divide by zero error
```

Structured Exception Handling

Visual Basic also supports structured exception handling. In particular, Visual Basic uses an enhanced version of the **Try . . . Catch . . . Finally** syntax already supported by other languages, such as Java. Here's an example that follows our previous example handling a division-by-zero exception; I start by creating a **Try** block—you put the exception-prone code in the **Try** section and the exception-handling code in the **Catch** section:

```
Module Module1
    Sub Main()
        Try
            .
            .
            .
        Catch e As Exception
            .
            .
        End Try
    End Sub
End Module
```

Note the syntax of the **Catch** statement, which catches an **Exception** object that I'm naming **e**. When the code in the **Try** block causes an exception, I can use the **e.ToString** method to display a message:

```
Module Module1
    Sub Main()
        Dim int1 = 0, int2 = 1, int3 As Integer
        Try
            int3 = int2 / int1
            System.Console.WriteLine("The answer is {0}", int3)
        Catch e As Exception
            System.Console.WriteLine(e.ToString)
        End Try
    End Sub
End Module
```

Here's what you see when you run this code:

```
System.OverflowException: Exception of type
  System.OverflowException was thrown.

    at Microsoft.VisualBasic.Helpers.IntegerType
    .FromObject(Object Value)
    at ConsoleHello.Module1.Main() in
    C:\vbnet\ConsoleHello\Module1.vb:line 5
```

Besides using the **e.ToString** method, you can also use the **e.message** field, which contains this message:

```
Exception of type System.OverflowException was thrown.
```

Now it's time to turn to the Immediate Solutions to see the details on creating procedures, setting scope, and handling exceptions.

Immediate Solutions

Using Unstructured Exception Handling

As discussed in the In Brief section of this chapter, runtime errors in Visual Basic can be handled with either unstructured or structured exception handling (exceptions are runtime errors). Unstructured exception handling revolves around the **On Error GoTo** statement, and structured exception handling uses the **Try . . . Catch . . . Finally** statement. Without an **On Error GoTo** or **Try . . . Catch . . . Finally** statement, any exception that occurs is fatal, and your program will stop.

I'll take a look at the **On Error GoTo** statement first in this and the next few sections. Although one gets the impression that Microsoft would rather you use **Try . . . Catch . . . Finally**, some things can be done with **On Error GoTo** that can't be with **Try . . . Catch . . . Finally**, such as resuming execution with a **Resume** statement.

The **On Error GoTo** statement enables exception handling and specifies the location of the exception-handling code within a procedure. Here's how the **On Error GoTo** statement works:

```
On Error { GoTo [ line | 0 | -1 ] | Resume Next }
```

Here are the parts of this statement:

- **GoTo** *line*—Enables the exception-handling code that starts at the line specified in the required *line* argument. The *line* argument is any line label or line number. If an exception occurs, program execution goes to the given location. (Note that the specified line must be in the same procedure as the **On Error** statement.)

- **GoTo 0**—Disables the enabled exception handler in the current procedure and resets it to **Nothing**.

- **GoTo -1**—Same as **GoTo 0**.

- **Resume Next**—Specifies that when an exception occurs, execution skips over the statement that caused the problem and goes to the statement immediately following. Execution continues from that point.

> **NOTE:** If a trappable exception occurs in a procedure, you can handle that exception in an exception handler. But what if you call another procedure, and an exception occurs before control returns from that procedure? If the called procedure has an exception handler, the code in that exception handler will be executed. However, if the called procedure does not have an exception handler, control will return to the exception handler in the calling procedure. In this way, control moves back up the calling chain to the closest exception handler.

Here's an example showing how to use the **On Error GoTo** statement that uses a division by zero to create an overflow exception. In this case, I'm directing execution to the label "Handler", which you create by placing this label on a line of its own, followed by a colon—note that I also place an **Exit Sub** statement before the exception handler so that the exception-handling code isn't executed inadvertently during normal program execution:

```
Module Module1
    Sub Main()
        Dim int1 = 0, int2 = 1, int3 As Integer
        On Error Goto Handler
        int3 = int2 / int1
        Exit Sub
Handler:
        .
        .
        .
    End Sub
End Module
```

I can add exception-handling code in the exception handler like this:

```
Module Module1
    Sub Main()
        Dim int1 = 0, int2 = 1, int3 As Integer
        On Error Goto Handler
        int3 = int2 / int1
        Exit Sub
Handler:
        System.Console.WriteLine("Overflow error!")
    End Sub
End Module
```

Now, when this console application runs, you'll see "Overflow error!". You can also handle specific exceptions in different ways, depending on which exception occurred, by checking the **Err** object's **Number** property, which holds the exception's number. Here, I'm handling only arithmetic overflow exceptions, which are exception number 6:

```
Module Module1
    Sub Main()
        Dim int1 = 0, int2 = 1, int3 As Integer
        On Error Goto Handler
        int3 = int2 / int1
        Exit Sub
Handler:
        If (Err.Number = 6) Then
            System.Console.WriteLine("Overflow error!")
        End If
    End Sub
End Module
```

The **Err** object also has a new **GetException** method that returns an
exception object. For more on these objects, see the Immediate Solutions section "Using Structured Exception Handling" later in this chapter. Using the **TypeOf** and **Is** keywords in an **If** statement, you can
handle exception objects such as **OverflowException** like this:

```
Module Module1
    Sub Main()
        Dim int1 = 0, int2 = 1, int3 As Integer
        On Error Goto Handler
        int3 = int2 / int1
        Exit Sub
Handler:
        If (TypeOf Err.GetException() Is OverflowException) Then
            System.Console.WriteLine("Overflow error!")
        End If
    End Sub
End Module
```

Now that structured exception handling has been added to Visual
Basic, the real attraction of unstructured exception handling is the
Resume statement (see the next section).

*TIP: System errors during calls to Windows dynamic link libraries (DLLs) do not throw
exceptions, which means that they can't be trapped with Visual Basic exception trapping.
When calling DLL functions, you should check each return value for success or failure and, in
case of failure, check the value in the **Err** object's **LastDLLError** property.*

Using **Resume Next** and **Resume** *Line*

One of the most useful aspects of unstructured exception handling is the **Resume** statement, which lets you resume program execution even after an exception has occurred. You can use **Resume** to resume execution with the statement that caused the exception, **Resume Next** to resume execution with the statement after the one that caused the exception, and **Resume** *line*, where *line* is a line number or label that specifies where to resume execution. Here's an example using **Resume Next**, which lets you skip over the line that caused the problem:

```
Module Module1
    Sub Main()
        Dim int1 = 0, int2 = 1, int3 As Integer
        On Error Goto Handler
        int3 = int2 / int1
        System.Console.WriteLine("Program completed...")
        Exit Sub
Handler:
        If (TypeOf Err.GetException() Is OverflowException) Then
            System.Console.WriteLine("Overflow error!")
            Resume Next
        End If
    End Sub
End Module
```

Here's what you see when you run this console application:

```
Overflow error!
Program completed...
```

Here's an example using the **Resume** *line* format:

```
Module Module1
    Sub Main()
        Dim int1 = 0, int2 = 1, int3 As Integer
        On Error Goto Handler
        int3 = int2 / int1
Nextline:
        System.Console.WriteLine("Program completed...")
        Exit Sub
Handler:
        If (TypeOf Err.GetException() Is OverflowException) Then
            System.Console.WriteLine("Overflow error!")
            Resume Nextline
```

```
         End If
      End Sub
End Module
```

You can also use an **On Error Resume Next** or **On Error Resume** *line* statement to make Visual Basic continue program execution after an exception has occurred. This form is sometimes preferable to the **On Error GoTo** form if you don't want to write an explicit exception handler:

```
Module Module1
   Sub Main()
      Dim int1 = 0, int2 = 1, int3 As Integer
      On Error Resume Next
      int3 = int2 / int1
      .
      .
      .
```

Using **On Error GoTo 0**

To turn off unstructured exception handling, you can use the **On Error GoTo 0** or **On Error GoTo -1** statement. Here's an example:

```
Module Module1
   Sub Main()
      Dim int1 = 0, int2 = 1, int3 As Integer
      On Error Goto Handler
      int3 = int2 / int1
      On Error Goto 0   'Turn error handling off
      System.Console.WriteLine("Program completed...")
Handler:
      If (TypeOf Err.GetException() Is OverflowException) Then
         System.Console.WriteLine("Overflow error!")
         Resume Next
      End If
   End Sub
End Module
```

Getting an Exception's Number and Description

To find out more information about what type of exceptions occurred, you can use the **Err** object's **Number** and **Description** properties, like this:

```
Module Module1
    Sub Main()
        Dim int1 = 0, int2 = 1, int3 As Integer
        On Error Goto Handler
        int3 = int2 / int1
        System.Console.WriteLine("Program completed...")
Handler:
        System.Console.WriteLine( _
            "Error number {0} occurred: {1}", _
            Err.Number, Err.Description)
    End Sub
End Module
```

Here's what you see when you run this console application:

```
Error number 6 occurred: Exception of type
    System.OverflowException was thrown.
```

TIP: You can determine the object that caused the exception by using the Visual Basic **Err** object's **Source** property. This property holds the name of the object or application that caused the exception. For example, if you connect to Microsoft Excel and it generates an exception, Excel sets **Err.Number** to its error code for that exception, and it sets **Err.Source** to "Excel.Application".

Using Structured Exception Handling

Microsoft has added structured exception handling to Visual Basic, and, as you might expect, it's now considered the recommended method of exception handling. In fact, it is appropriate to call the **On Error GoTo** method of exception handling unstructured because using this statement only sets the internal exception handler in Visual Basic; it certainly doesn't add any structure to your code, and if your code extends over procedures and blocks, it can be hard to figure out what exception handler is working when.

Structured exception handling is based on a particular statement, the **Try . . . Catch . . . Finally** statement, which is divided into a **Try** block, optional **Catch** blocks, and an optional **Finally** block. The **Try** block contains code where exceptions can occur, and the **Catch** block contains code to handle the exceptions that occur. If an exception occurs in the **Try** block, the code *throws* the exception—actually an object based on the Visual Basic **Exception** class—so that it can be caught and handled by the appropriate **Catch** statement. After the rest of the statement finishes, execution is always passed to the **Finally** block, if one exists. Here's what the **Try . . . Catch . . . Finally** statement looks like in general:

```
Try
    [ tryStatements ]
    [Catch [ exception1 [ As type1 ] ] [ When expression1 ]
        catchStatements1
        [Exit Try] ]
    [Catch [ exception2 [ As type2 ] ] [When expression2 ]
        catchStatements2
        [ Exit Try ] ]
        .
        .
        .
    [Catch [ exceptionn [ As typen ] ] [ When expressionn ]
        catchStatementsn ]
        [ Exit Try ] ]
    [ Finally
        [ finallyStatements ]
End Try
```

Here are the parts of this statement:

- **Try**—Begins the **Try** block for structured exception handling.

- *tryStatements*—Sensitive statements where you expect exceptions.

- **Catch**—If an exception happens in the **Try** block, the exception is thrown, and each **Catch** statement is examined in order to determine whether it will handle the exception.

- *exception*—A variable name that you give the exception. The value of *exception* is the value of the thrown exception.

- *type*—Specifies the type of the exception you're catching in a **Catch** statement.

- **When**—A **Catch** clause with a **When** clause will catch exceptions only when *expression* evaluates to **True**.

- **expression**—An expression used to select exceptions to handle. It must be convertible to a **Boolean** value. **expression** is often used to filter exceptions by number.

- **catchStatements**—Statements to handle exceptions occurring in the **Try** block.

- **Exit Try**—Statement that breaks out of the **Try . . . Catch . . . Finally** structure. Execution is transferred to the code immediately following the **End Try** statement. Note that **Exit Try** is not allowed in **Finally** blocks.

- **Finally**—A block that is always executed when execution leaves any part of the **Try** statement.

NOTE: *If a Try statement does not contain any Catch blocks, it must contain a Finally block.*

- **finallyStatements**—Statements that are executed after all other exception processing has occurred.

TIP: *Bear in mind that if exceptions occur that the code does not specifically handle, Visual Basic will default to its normal exception message.*

If you supply the optional **Finally** statement, the corresponding statement block is always the last code to be executed just before control leaves **Try . . . Catch . . . Finally**. This is true even if an unhandled exception occurs or if you execute an **Exit Try** statement. Note that you can have any number of **Catch** statements (however, you must have at least one **Catch** statement or a **Finally** statement).

Here's an example; in this case, the exception-prone code executes a division by zero, which generates an arithmetic overflow exception. Note that I place the sensitive code in the **Try** block and the exception-handling code in the **Catch** block:

```
Module Module1
    Sub Main()
        Dim int1 = 0, int2 = 1, int3 As Integer
        Try
            int3 = int2 / int1
            System.Console.WriteLine("The answer is {0}", int3)
        Catch
            System.Console.WriteLine( _
                "Exception: Arithmetic overflow!")
        End Try
    End Sub
End Module
```

Here's what you see when you run this console application:

```
Exception: Arithmetic overflow!
```

You also can get more information about the exception by getting an exception object. I'll do that here by catching any exception based on the **Exception** class—which means all exceptions—and using the exception object's **ToString** method to display information about the exception:

```
Module Module1
    Sub Main()
        Dim int1 = 0, int2 = 1, int3 As Integer
        Try
            int3 = int2 / int1
            System.Console.WriteLine("The answer is {0}", int3)
        Catch e As Exception
            System.Console.WriteLine(e.ToString)
        End Try
    End Sub
End Module
```

Here's what you see when you run this code:

```
System.OverflowException: Exception of type
 System.OverflowException was thrown.

   at Microsoft.VisualBasic
   .Helpers.IntegerType.FromObject(Object Value)
   at ConsoleApp.Module1.Main() in
    C:\vbnet\ConsoleApp\Module1.vb:line 5
```

This kind of information is more useful to the programmer than to the user. For the user, you might display the message in the exception object's message property (that is, use **e.message** instead), which gives you this:

```
Exception of type System.OverflowException was thrown.
```

That's a little better, but it's best to catch individual exceptions yourself and customize the messages you display to your application. Take a look at the next section for the details.

Filtering Exceptions in the **Catch** Block

When you're handling exceptions, you usually want to handle different types of exceptions differently, according to the nature of the exception that occurred. This process is called *filtering*. Filtering exceptions with **Catch** blocks can be done in two ways. First, you can filter on specific classes of exceptions, which means that you have to prepare for the various exceptions you want to handle.

Exceptions are based on the Visual Basic **Exception** class (which, like all other objects in Visual Basic, is based on the **Object** class). In general, when you use Visual Basic statements that are capable of throwing exceptions, the Visual Basic documentation will tell you what possible exceptions each statement may throw. However, that won't help in tracking down exceptions that occur when you're simply using the general syntax of the language, such as when you divide two numbers and an overflow exception occurs. To track down what class such an exception corresponds to, you could take a look at the Visual Basic documentation for the **Exception** class, which lists the classes derived from it:

```
Object
    Exception
        ApplicationException
        CodeDomSerializerException
        InvalidPrinterException
        IOException
        IsolatedStorageException
        PathTooLongException
        CookieException
        ProtocolViolationException
        WebException
        MissingManifestResourceException
        SUDSGeneratorException
        SUDSParserException
        SystemException
        UriFormatException
        SoapException
```

Each derived class itself has many derived classes, and if you keep searching (each class in the previous code is a hyperlink in the documentation, so you just keep clicking), you'll eventually find the **OverflowException** class, which is based on the **ArithmeticException** class, which is based on the **SystemException** class, which is based on the **Exception** class:

```
Object
    Exception
        SystemException
            ArithmeticException
                OverflowException
```

An easier way to do this, if you can generate the exception you're anticipating, is to use the **Exception** class's **getType** method (such as **e.getType**) to get the type of the exception as a string. Here's an example where I'm providing code to explicitly handle overflow exceptions:

```
Module Module1
    Sub Main()
        Dim int1 = 0, int2 = 1, int3 As Integer
        Try
            int3 = int2 / int1
            System.Console.WriteLine("The answer is {0}", int3)
        Catch e As OverflowException
            System.Console.WriteLine( _
                "Exception: Arithmetic overflow!")
        End Try
    End Sub
End Module
```

The second exception-filtering option lets you use the **Catch** statement to filter on any conditional expression, using the **When** keyword. This option is often used to filter by exception number, which you can check with the **Err** object's **Number** property. Here's an example that filters overflow exceptions by number (which is exception number 6 in Visual Basic .NET):

```
Module Module1
    Sub Main()
        Dim int1 = 0, int2 = 1, int3 As Integer
        Try
            int3 = int2 / int1
            System.Console.WriteLine("The answer is {0}", int3)
        Catch When Err.Number = 6
            System.Console.WriteLine( _
                "Exception: Arithmetic overflow!")
        End Try
    End Sub
End Module
```

Using Multiple **Catch** Statements

You can use multiple **Catch** statements when you filter exceptions. Here's an example that specifically handles overflow, invalid-argument, and argument-out-of-range exceptions:

```
Module Module1
    Sub Main()
        Dim int1 = 0, int2 = 1, int3 As Integer
        Try
            int3 = int2 / int1
            System.Console.WriteLine("The answer is {0}", int3)
        Catch e As System.OverflowException
            System.Console.WriteLine( _
                "Exception: Arithmetic overflow!")
        Catch e As System.ArgumentException
            System.Console.WriteLine( _
                "Exception: Invalid argument value!")
        Catch e As System.ArgumentOutOfRangeException
            System.Console.WriteLine( _
                "Exception: Argument out of range!")
        End Try
    End Sub
End Module
```

If you want to add a general exception handler to catch any exceptions not filtered, you can add a **Catch** block for the **Exception** class at the end of the other **Catch** blocks:

```
Module Module1
    Sub Main()
        Dim int1 = 0, int2 = 1, int3 As Integer
        Try
            int3 = int2 / int1
            System.Console.WriteLine("The answer is {0}", int3)
        Catch e As System.ArgumentOutOfRangeException
            System.Console.WriteLine( _
                "Exception: Argument out of range!")
        Catch e As System.ArgumentException
            System.Console.WriteLine( _
                "Exception: Invalid argument value!")
        Catch e As Exception
            System.Console.WriteLine("Exception occurred!")
        End Try
    End Sub
End Module
```

Related solutions:	Found on page:
Creating **Sub** Procedures	108
Creating Functions	111

Using **Finally**

The code in the **Finally** block, if one exists, is always executed in a
Try . . . Catch . . . Finally statement, even if no exception occurred
and even if you execute an **Exit Try** statement. This allows you to
deallocate resources; here's an example with a **Finally** block:

```
Module Module1
    Sub Main()
        Dim int1 = 0, int2 = 1, int3 As Integer
        Try
            int3 = int2 / int1
            System.Console.WriteLine("The answer is {0}", int3)
        Catch e As System.OverflowException
            System.Console.WriteLine( _
                "Exception: Arithmetic overflow!")
        Catch e As System.ArgumentException
            System.Console.WriteLine( _
                "Exception: Invalid argument value!")
        Catch e As System.ArgumentOutOfRangeException
            System.Console.WriteLine( _
                "Exception: Argument out of range!")
        Finally
            System.Console.WriteLine( _
                "Execution of sensitive code " & _
                "is complete")
        End Try
    End Sub
End Module
```

Here's what you see when you execute this console application:

```
Exception: Arithmetic overflow!
Execution of sensitive code is complete
```

6. The Visual Basic
Language: Exception
Handling

Throwing an Exception

You can throw an exception using the **Throw** statement, and you can also rethrow a caught exception using the **Throw** statement. Here's an example where I'm explicitly throwing an overflow exception:

```
Module Module1
    Sub Main()
        Try
            Throw New OverflowException()
        Catch e As Exception
            System.Console.WriteLine(e.Message)
        End Try
    End Sub
End Module
```

TIP: *It's even possible to mix structured and unstructured exception handling to some extent. If you're using unstructured exception handling, you can get an exception object with the **Err** object's **GetException** method and throw that exception in a **Try** block.*

Chapter 7

Windows Forms

In Brief

In this chapter, we start to get visual. As you know, the two types of forms in Visual Basic .NET are Windows forms and Web forms. This chapter is all about working with Windows forms.

There's a great deal to learn about Windows forms in Visual Basic, and you'll take a look at it all here. You'll see how to customize forms; how to work with multiple forms; how to use the **MsgBox** function to create message boxes; how to create, hide, and show forms in code; how to add controls at runtime; and much more. I'll begin the chapter with an overview of Visual Basic Windows forms.

All About Windows Forms

Forms are what you work with in form designers; they represent the windows that will appear in your application. However, it's become common to refer to both the windows under design and the windows in your running application as forms in Visual Basic applications.

The whole power of Visual Basic has been that you can develop forms visually, adding controls and other items from the toolbox. In VB .NET, the support for Windows forms is in the **System.Windows.Forms** namespace, and the form class is **System.Windows.Forms.Form**. The **Form** class itself is based on the **Control** class, which means that forms share a lot of the properties and methods that controls do. Here's what the class hierarchy looks like for the **Form** class; every level is derived from the one above it (note that all classes are derived from the **Object** class):

```
Object
    MarshalByRefObject
        Component
            Control
                ScrollableControl
                    ContainerControl
                        Form
```

You can see a form in a form designer in the Visual Basic Integrated Development Environment (IDE) in Figure 7.1, which shows several aspects of forms. At the top of the form is the *title bar*, which displays the form's title; here that's just Form1. At the right in the title bar is

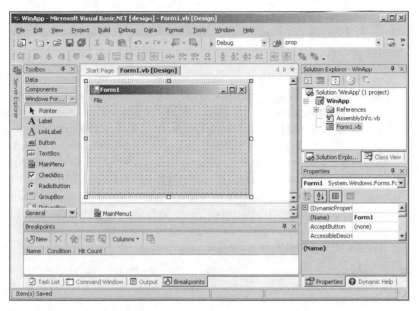

Figure 7.1   A form under design.

the *control box*, including the minimizing/maximizing buttons and the close button. These are controls the user takes for granted in most windows, although we'll see that they are inappropriate in others, such as dialog boxes.

Under the title bar comes the *menu bar*, if one exists. In Figure 7.1, the form has one menu—the File menu. Under the menu bar, forms can have *toolbars*, as you see in the IDE itself.

The main area of a form—the area where everything takes place—is called the *client area*. In general, Visual Basic code works with controls in the client area and leaves the rest of the form to Visual Basic. (In fact, the client area is itself a window.)

Finally, the whole form is surrounded by a *border*. Several types of borders can be used, as you'll see when working with dialog boxes and using the fixed, nonresizable borders appropriate to them.

The important class for Windows forms is the **Form** class in the **System.Windows.Forms** namespace. Each form in this namespace is an instance (that is, an object) of that class. As mentioned in Chapter 3, objects are instances of classes, much as an integer variable is an instance of the **Integer** type. (You can think of a class as a type that you create objects from.) As you also know, classes can have *members—fields* (data items), *methods* (built-in procedures), and *properties* (data items accessed through an interface on the basis of methods).

Now that we're actually starting to work with classes such as the **Form** class, it's important to understand the two kinds of class members. First, some members are inherent to the *class* itself (accessed through the class), such as **Form.ActiveForm**, or just **ActiveForm**. For these members—called static, shared, or class members—you don't need an object. Second, some members, called instance or object members, are built into *objects*, such as **MyForm1.BackColor**. With this type, **MyForm1** is an instance of the **Form** class, where you do need an object. In other words, the difference is that to use class members, you don't need an object of that class to work with, and with object members, you do. To sum it up:

- *Static/shared members* are *class members*, accessed directly using the class like this: ***classname.membername***. No object is needed.

- *Instance members* are *object members*, accessed by using an instance of a class (an object) like this: ***objectname.membername***.

I prefer the terms "class members" and "object members" because that makes clear what kinds of members they are, but the VB .NET documentation often uses the terms "Static (Shared) members" and "Instance members."

NOTE: *For more information on this topic, see the section "Class vs. Object Members" in the In Brief section of Chapter 10, where you'll see how to create both class and object members from scratch.*

With all that under our belts, I can talk about the members of the **Form** class. The **Form** class has only one class property, **ActiveForm**, which holds the currently active form for the entire application. If you want to determine what window has the focus (that is, is the target of keystrokes), use the **ActiveForm** property. However, the **Form** class does have many object properties, such as **Left**, **Right**, **Top**, and **Bottom**, which give the coordinates of the various edges of the form, and **Visible**, which indicates whether the form is visible. Some of these object properties are public, some private to the object, and some protected (that is, accessible only to objects of the **Form** class or objects of classes derived from **Form**).

Windows forms also support *events*, which we've discussed as far back as Chapter 1. Events let you know that something's happened with a form; for example, when you click a form, a **Click** event occurs, and when the form is closed, a **Closed** event occurs.

Creating Windows Applications

We've already created Windows applications in Chapter 1. Doing so is easy—you just open the New Project dialog box with the New Project button in the Start page or with the New|Project menu item in the File menu. Then you select the Visual Basic Projects folder in the Project Types box at the right in this dialog box, select the Windows Application icon in the Templates box, give a new Name (I'll call this project WinHello) and Location to the application in the boxes of the same names, and click OK. This creates a Windows project and solution as you see in Figure 7.1; these are the files that are created and what they mean:

- *WindowsApp.vbproj*—A Visual Basic project

- *AssemblyInfo.vb*—General information about an assembly, including version information

- *Form1.vb*—A form's code file

- *Form1.resx .NET*—An XML-based resource template

- *WindowsApp.vbproj.user*—The file that stores project user options

- *WindowsApp.sln*—The solution file, storing the solution's configuration

- *WindowsApp.suo*—The file that stores solution user options

- *bin*—Directory for binary executables

- *obj*—Directory for debugging binaries

All these files are created for us automatically by Visual Basic. As you can see in Figure 7.1, however, not much is happening in this program yet. It's time to add some *controls*.

Adding Controls to Forms

In Windows, users interact with your program using controls: scrollbars, buttons, text boxes, menus, and so on—all the user interface elements Windows users are accustomed to. In VB .NET, you use the toolbox, introduced in Chapter 2, to add controls to a form.

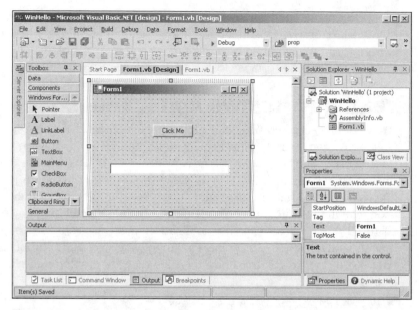

Figure 7.2   Adding controls to a form.

To make this more concrete, add a button and a text box to the new Windows application you just created, as you see in Figure 7.2. Visual Basic gives these controls new names automatically—**Button1** and **TextBox1**.

In this example, the application should display text in the text box when the user clicks on the button, so change the **Text** property of the button to **"Click Me"**, as you see in Figure 7.2, using the Properties window. Then delete the text in the text box so that it appears empty. This creates the user interface of our application.

Handling Events

Although you've added two controls to your program, a button and a text box, they don't actually do anything when the program runs. We want to display a message when the user clicks on the button, so double-click the button now to open the form's code designer to this **Sub** procedure:

```
Private Sub Button1_Click(ByVal sender As System.Object, _
    ByVal e As System.EventArgs) Handles Button1.Click

End Sub
```

This is the event handler for the button's **Click** event, and it's called when the button is clicked. This **Sub** procedure is passed the object that caused the event (the button object itself) and an **EventArgs** object that has more information about the event. Note also the **Handles Button1.Click** part at the end, which indicates that this **Sub** procedure handles the **Click** event of **Button1**. In VB6, event handlers such as this could have different numbers of arguments, depending on the event, but in VB .NET, event handlers are written to take two—and only two—arguments. To place text in **TextBox1** when the button is clicked, we need only add this code:

```
Private Sub Button1_Click(ByVal sender As System.Object, _
    ByVal e As System.EventArgs) Handles Button1.Click
    TextBox1.Text = "Welcome to Visual Basic"
End Sub
```

Now you can run the application, as you see in Figure 7.3. When you click the button, the message appears in the text box, as you also see in that figure.

In this way, you can add code to an object's default event handler. To add code to a different event handler, select the object in the left-hand drop-down list box in a code designer and select the event you want to add code to in the right-hand drop-down list box. Visual Basic will add an event handler for that event.

That gives you the introduction you need; now it's time to start handling detailed issues in the Immediate Solutions.

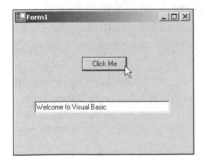

Figure 7.3   Running a Windows application.

Immediate Solutions

Setting Title Bar Text

Setting the text in the title bar of a form couldn't be easier. At design time, you just change the form's **Text** (formerly **Caption**) property. You also can set the **Text** property at runtime in code like this:

```
Private Sub Button1_Click(ByVal sender As System.Object, _
    ByVal e As System.EventArgs) Handles Button1.Click
        Text = "Welcome to my Application"
End Sub
```

NOTE: *Technically, you should use Me.Text in this case, but the current form is the default in this code, so you don't have to specify the Me keyword.*

Adding and Removing Min/Max Buttons

Forms usually come with minimizing and maximizing buttons as well as a close box at the upper right. However, that's not appropriate in all cases, as we'll see when we design dialog boxes later in this chapter. (See the section "Creating Dialog Boxes.") To remove these buttons, you can set the form's **ControlBox** property to **False**. You can also remove the minimizing and maximizing buttons independently with the **MaximizeBox** and **MinimizeBox** properties.

TIP: *If you're thinking of designing a dialog box, take a look at the dialog box material later in this chapter—besides removing the control box, you should also set the dialog box's border correctly, add OK and Cancel buttons, and take care of a few more considerations.*

You also can set what buttons are in a form by setting its border type. For example, if you set the border style to a fixed type, the minimizing and maximizing buttons will disappear.

Setting a Form's Border

You set a form's border style with its **FormBorderStyle** property. Here are the possible values for that property:

- **Fixed3D**—A fixed, three-dimensional border
- **FixedDialog**—A thick, fixed dialog box–style border
- **FixedSingle**—A fixed, single-line border
- **FixedToolWindow**—A tool window border that is not resizable
- **None**—No border
- **Sizable**—A resizable border
- **SizableToolWindow**—A resizable tool window border

Setting a Form's Initial Position

You can use a form's **StartPosition** property to specify its initial position on the screen. You assign this property values from the **FormStartPosition** enumeration. Here are the possible values:

- **CenterParent**—The form is centered within the bounds of its parent form.
- **CenterScreen**—The form is centered on the current display and has the dimensions specified in the form's size.
- **Manual**—The **Location** and **Size** properties of the form will determine its starting position on the screen.
- **WindowsDefaultBounds**—The form is positioned at the Windows default location and has the bounds determined by Windows default.
- **WindowsDefaultLocation**—The form is positioned at the Windows default location and has the dimensions specified in the form's size.

Here's how you can set a form's **StartPosition** property from code:

```
Form1.StartPosition = FormStartPosition.CenterScreen
```

7. Windows Forms

Moving and Sizing Forms and Controls in Code

In Visual Basic 6 and earlier, you could use the **Move** method to move forms and controls (and optionally set their dimensions) and the **Height** and **Width** methods to set their dimensions. In VB .NET, you use the **SetBounds** method to move forms and controls (and optionally set their dimensions) and the **Size** and **Location** properties to set their dimensions.

You set the **Size** property to a new **Size** object and the **Location** property to a new **Point** object. The dimensions you set in the **Size** and **Point** objects are measured in pixels, as are all measurements in Visual Basic; you create these objects by passing x and y dimensions to their class's constructors, like this:

```
Size(x_dimension, y_dimension)
Point(x_location, y_location)
```

TIP: In the Visual Basic screen coordinate system, the upper left of the screen is the origin, (0, 0). Positive x values increase downward and positive y values increase to the right.

Here's an example. Suppose you wanted to change the size and location of both a form and a button on the form when the user clicks a button. You can do that like this (the origin of coordinates for the form is the upper left of the screen, and the origin for the button contained in the form is the upper left of the form's client area):

```
Private Sub Button1_Click(ByVal sender As System.Object, _
    ByVal e As System.EventArgs) Handles Button1.Click
        Size = New Size(100, 100)
        Location = New Point(0, 0)
        Button1.Size = New Size(100, 50)
        Button1.Location = New Point(0, 0)
End Sub
```

You can also use the **SetBounds** method to do the same thing:

```
Overloads Public Sub SetBounds(ByVal x As Integer, _
    ByVal y As Integer, _
    ByVal width As Integer, ByVal height As Integer)
```

Here are the arguments you pass to **SetBounds**:

- *x*—The new **Left** property value of the control
- *y*—The new **Right** property value of the control
- *width*—The new **Width** property value of the control
- *height*—The new **Height** property value of the control

As you see with the **Overloads** keyword in the previous code, **SetBounds** is *overloaded*, which means that more than one form of this method exists. Here is the other form (Visual Basic will know which form you want to use depending on how many arguments you pass):

```
Overloads Public Sub SetBounds( ByVal x As Integer, _
   ByVal y As Integer, _
   ByVal width As Integer, ByVal height As Integer, _
   ByVal specified As BoundsSpecified)
```

This form has a new argument, *specified*, which is a combination of values from the **BoundsSpecified** enumeration. Here are the possible values of *specified*:

- **All**—Specifies that both **Location** and **Size** property values of the control are indicated
- **Height**—Specifies that the height of the control is indicated
- **Location**—Specifies that both x and y coordinates of the control are indicated
- **None**—Specifies that no bounds are indicated
- **Size**—Specifies that both **Width** and **Height** property values of the control are indicated
- **Width**—Specifies that the width of the control is indicated
- **X**—Specifies that the left edge of the control is indicated
- **Y**—Specifies that the top edge of the control is indicated

For example, to set the bounds in terms of the **X** item, use **BoundsSpecified.X**.

To use **SetBounds** to do the same thing as in the code at the beginning of this section, you can do this:

```
Private Sub Button1_Click(ByVal sender As System.Object, _
    ByVal e As System.EventArgs) Handles Button1.Click
        SetBounds(0, 0, 100, 100)
        Button1.SetBounds(0, 0, 100, 50)
End Sub
```

TIP: *One way of creating simple animation is to use a picture box control to display an image and use the **SetBounds** method to move it around a form.*

Showing and Hiding Controls and Forms

Showing and hiding controls and forms is easy: just use the control's or form's **Visible** property. Setting this property to **True** displays the control or form; setting it to **False** hides it. Here's an example that makes a button disappear (probably much to the user's surprise) when the user clicks on it:

```
Private Sub Button1_Click(ByVal sender _
    As System.Object, ByVal e As System.EventArgs) _
    Handles Button1.Click
        Button1.Visible = False
End Sub
```

You can also use the **Show** and **Hide** methods of controls and forms to show and hide them. For example, when the user clicks on **Button1**, we can hide **Form2** and show **Form3** this way:

```
Private Sub Button1_Click(ByVal sender _
    As System.Object, ByVal e As System.EventArgs) _
    Handles Button1.Click
        Form2.Hide()
        Form3.Show()
End Sub
```

Using the **MsgBox** Function

You can use the **MessageBox** class built into the .NET framework to display messages and accept input from the user. Here's how the **MsgBox** function works:

```
Public Function MsgBox(Prompt As Object _
    [, Buttons As MsgBoxStyle = MsgBoxStyle.OKOnly _
    [, Title As Object = Nothing]]) As MsgBoxResultArguments
```

Here are the arguments you pass to this function:

- *Prompt*—A string expression displayed as the message in the dialog box. The maximum length is about 1,024 characters (depending on the width of the characters used).

- *Buttons*—The sum of values specifying the number and type of buttons to display, the icon style to use, the identity of the default button, and the modality of the message box. If you omit *Buttons*, the default value is zero. The possible constants for the *Buttons* argument are in Table 7.1.

- *Title*—String expression displayed in the title bar of the dialog box. Note that if you omit *Title*, the application name is placed in the title bar.

Table 7.1   MsgBox constants.

Constant	Value	Description
OKOnly	0	Shows OK button only.
OKCancel	1	Shows OK and Cancel buttons.
AbortRetryIgnore	2	Shows Abort, Retry, and Ignore buttons.
YesNoCancel	3	Shows Yes, No, and Cancel buttons.
YesNo	4	Shows Yes and No buttons.
RetryCancel	5	Shows Retry and Cancel buttons.
Critical	16	Shows Critical Message icon.
Question	32	Shows Warning Query icon.
Exclamation	48	Shows Warning Message icon.
Information	64	Shows Information Message icon.
DefaultButton1	0	First button is default.
DefaultButton2	256	Second button is default.
DefaultButton3	512	Third button is default.
ApplicationModal	0	Application modal, which means that the user must respond to the message box before continuing work in the current application.
SystemModal	4096	System modal, which means that all applications are unavailable until the user dismisses the message box.
MsgBoxSetForeground	65536	Specifies the message box window as the foreground window.
MsgBoxRight	524288	Text will be right aligned.
MsgBoxRtlReading	1048576	Specifies that text should appear as right to left on RTL systems, such as Hebrew and Arabic.

7. Windows Forms

TIP: *If you want the message box prompt to be more than one line of text, you can force separate lines of text by using a carriage return character **(Chr(13))**, a linefeed character **(Chr(10))**, or a carriage return/linefeed together **(Chr(13) & Chr(10))** between each line.*

Note also that this function returns a value from the **MsgBoxResult** enumeration. Here are the possible **MsgBoxResult** values, indicating which button in the message box the user clicked on:

- **OK**
- **Cancel**
- **Abort**
- **Retry**
- **Ignore**
- **Yes**
- **No**

For example, here's how we use **MsgBox** in an example I'll call MsgBoxer. In this case, I'm adding OK and Cancel buttons to the message box, adding an information icon, and making the message box *modal* (which means that you have to dismiss it before doing anything else). I also check to see whether the user clicked on the OK button, in which case I display the message "You clicked OK" in a text box:

```
Private Sub Button1_Click(ByVal sender As System.Object, _
    ByVal e As System.EventArgs) Handles Button1.Click
    Dim Result As Integer
    Result = MsgBox( _
        "This is a message box!", MsgBoxStyle.OKCancel + _
        MsgBoxStyle.Information + _
        MsgBoxStyle.SystemModal, "Message Box")
    If (Result = MsgBoxResult.OK) Then
        TextBox1.Text = "You clicked OK"
    End If
End Sub
```

You can see the results of this code in Figure 7.4.

Figure 7.4   A message box created with the **MsgBox** function.

Working with Multiple Forms

You've designed your program, and it's a beauty: an introductory form to welcome the user, a data entry form to get data from the user, a summary form to display the data analysis results, and a logon form to connect to the Internet—it's all there.

Suddenly, it occurs to you: Aren't Visual Basic Windows projects organized into modules, classes, and forms? How does the code in one form reach the code in another—that is, how can the code in the analysis module read what the user has entered in the data entry form? It's time to take a look at working with multiple forms.

To see how to create multiple-form applications and how to communicate between forms, create a new Windows application. I'll call this example MultiWindow; when I create this application, it has only one Windows form, **Form1**. To add another, select the Project|Add Windows Form item to open the Add New Item dialog box you see in Figure 7.5; select the Windows Form icon in the Templates box and click Open. This adds a new form, **Form2**, to the project, as you see in the IDE in Figure 7.6.

Here I'll add a text box, **TextBox1**, to **Form2**, as you see in Figure 7.6. When the user clicks a button in **Form1**, the program will read the text in that text box and display it in a text box in **Form1**. In **Form1**, I start by creating a new object of **Form2** and calling it **OtherWindow**:

```
Dim OtherWindow As New Form2()
```

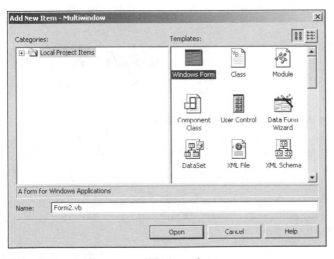

Figure 7.5   Adding a new Windows form.

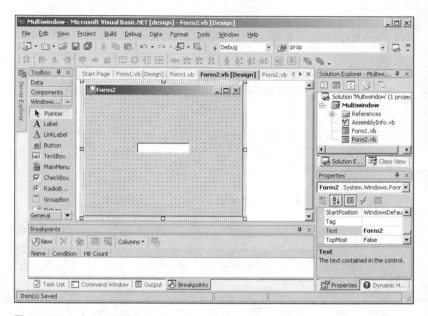

Figure 7.6   A new Windows form.

Place this declaration anywhere in the code for **Form1**, outside any procedure, like this:

```
Public Class Form1
    Inherits System.Windows.Forms.Form
    Dim OtherWindow As New Form2()
        .
        .
        .
```

TIP: *You can also select the (Declarations) item in the right-hand drop-down list box in the code designer to move to this area of your code automatically.*

To display this new form as soon as the program starts and **Form1** is displayed, double-click **Form1** to bring up its **Load** event handler, which is called when **Form1** is about to be displayed. You can show the second form with its **Show** method:

```
Private Sub Form1_Load(ByVal sender As System.Object, _
    ByVal e As System.EventArgs) Handles MyBase.Load
    OtherWindow.Show()
End Sub
```

Now add a button, **Button1**, to **Form1**; give it the text "Read text"; and also add a text box to **Form1**. When the user clicks on this button, I want to read the text in the text box in **OtherWindow** and display it in the text box in **Form1**. To do that, I can access the text box in the **OtherWindow** object as **OtherWindow.TextBox1** and the **Text** property of that text box as **OtherWindow.TextBox1.Text**. To display this text in the text box in **Form1**, I can use this code (note that I also hide the second window with the **OtherWindow** object's **Hide** method):

```
Private Sub Button1_Click(ByVal sender As System.Object, _
    ByVal e As System.EventArgs) Handles Button1.Click
    TextBox1.Text = OtherWindow.TextBox1.Text
    OtherWindow.Hide()
End Sub
```

Now when the user types something into the text box in the second window—as you see in Figure 7.7—and clicks on Read Text, the second window disappears, and the text from its text box appears in the text box in **Form1**, as you see in Figure 7.8. This example is a success.

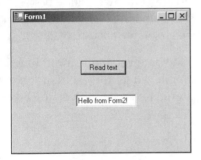

Figure 7.7   A multiwindow application.

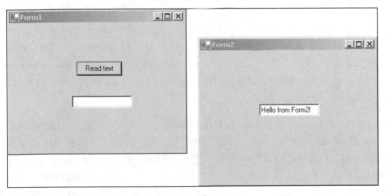

Figure 7.8   Accessing data between forms.

Setting the Startup Form

Now the program is complete, and you've saved writing the best for last: the opening form in which you greet the user. Unfortunately, that greeting form is **Form249**, and when you actually test the program, Visual Basic pops **Form1**, the Import File dialog box, onto the screen first. How can you make the program start with **Form249**?

Just right-click your project in the Solutions Explorer, select Properties, and select the Common Properties folder and the General item in the box at the left. Next, select **Form249** from the Startup Object drop-down list on the right, click OK, and you're done. That's it—now the program will display the form you've selected first when the program runs.

Creating Dialog Boxes

Sometimes nothing will do but to create your own dialog boxes. Visual Basic supports message boxes and input boxes, but they're very basic—in real applications, you'll need to create custom dialog boxes.

To see how this works, create a new Windows application now; I'll call this example Dialog. In this example, I'll let the user enter some text in a dialog box and read the entered text when the dialog box is closed.

Creating a Dialog Box

To create the dialog box, add a new Windows form, **Form2**, to the project and add two buttons with the captions "OK" and "Cancel" to this form, as well as a text box. Set the **Text** property of this form to **"Enter your text"** to set the text in the title bar and add a *label* control above the text box with the prompt "Enter your text:", as you see in Figure 7.9. Label controls simply display text like this prompt. To create this label, drag a **Label** control from the toolbox to **Form2** and set its **Text** property.

In addition, set the **FormBorderStyle** property of **Form2** to **FixedDialog**, giving it a dialog box border, and set the **ControlBox** property to **False** to remove the control box (the minimize, maximize, and close buttons at the upper right). Also, set the **ShowInTaskbar** property of **Form2** to **False**—this means that when this dialog box appears, it will not display an icon in the Windows task bar, which dialog boxes shouldn't.

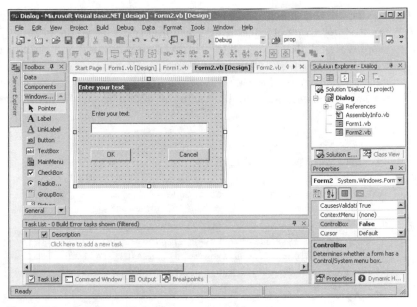

Figure 7.9   Creating a dialog box.

Finally, set the **DialogResult** property of the OK button to **OK** and the same property of the Cancel button to **Cancel**. This property returns a value of the **DialogResult** enumeration when the dialog box is closed so that you can determine which button the user has clicked on. Here are the possible settings for this property:

- **OK**
- **Cancel**
- **Abort**
- **Retry**
- **Ignore**
- **Yes**
- **No**
- **None**

Displaying Data from Dialog Boxes

You'll need some way of displaying your new dialog box from **Form1**, the form that appears when the application starts, so add a button, **Button1**, to **Form1** now, giving it the text "Enter your text". Also, you'll need a way of displaying the text that is read from the dialog, so add a text box, **TextBox1**, to **Form1** now.

To display the dialog box when the user clicks on Enter Your Text, create a new object of the **Form2** dialog box class, **DialogBox**. To display this dialog box, use the **ShowDialog** method, not the **Show** method, because **ShowDialog** will return a **DialogResult** value indicating what button the user clicked on. If the user clicked on OK, the text from the text box will display in the dialog box in the main form:

```
Public Class Form1
    Inherits System.Windows.Forms.Form
    Dim DialogBox As New Form2()

'Windows Form Designer generated code

    Private Sub Button1_Click(ByVal sender As System.Object, _
        ByVal e As System.EventArgs) Handles Button1.Click
        If DialogBox.ShowDialog = DialogResult.OK Then
            TextBox1.Text = DialogBox.TextBox1.Text
        End If
    End Sub
End Class
```

Creating Accept and Cancel Buttons

The last step is to add some code to the dialog box, **Form2**, to close the dialog box when the user clicks on a button. Also, set the dialog box's **AcceptButton** and **CancelButton** properties to indicate which button is the accept button and which is the cancel button; this allows the user to press Enter to select the accept (OK) button and Esc to select the Cancel button:

```
Public Class Form2
    Inherits System.Windows.Forms.Form

'Windows Form Designer generated code

    Private Sub Form2_Load(ByVal sender As System.Object, _
        ByVal e As System.EventArgs) Handles MyBase.Load
        Me.AcceptButton = Button1
        Me.CancelButton = Button2
    End Sub

    Private Sub Button1_Click(ByVal sender As System.Object, _
        ByVal e As System.EventArgs) Handles Button1.Click
        Me.Close()
    End Sub
```

```
    Private Sub Button2_Click(ByVal sender As System.Object, _
        ByVal e As System.EventArgs) Handles Button2.Click
        Me.Close()
    End Sub
End Class
```

And that completes the code—now run the application, as shown in Figure 7.10. The dialog box appears when you click the button in **Form1**, and you can enter text in it. When you click OK, the dialog box disappears, and the text you entered appears in the text box in **Form1**, as you see in Figure 7.11. Everything works as planned.

TIP: *One good rule for constructing dialog boxes is to always add a Cancel button so that if the user has opened the dialog box by mistake, it can be closed without consequences.*

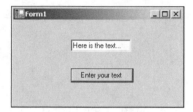

Figure 7.10   Displaying a newly created dialog box.

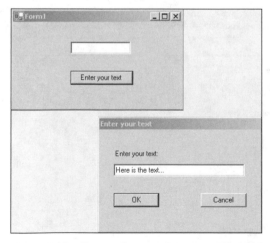

Figure 7.11   Recovering text from a created dialog box.

7. Windows Forms

Adding and Removing Controls at Runtime

You can add or remove controls to your application at runtime—you need only use the **Add** or **Remove** methods of the form's **Controls** collection. You'll see collections later in the book; they let you operate on a number of objects at once, as with the **Add** and **Remove** methods.

Here's an example I'll call AddControls that adds a new text box at runtime—all you have to do is create a new text box in code, give it a size and location, set its text, and use the **Add** method when the user clicks on a button:

```
Private Sub Button1_Click(ByVal sender As System.Object, _
    ByVal e As System.EventArgs) Handles Button1.Click
    Dim NewTextBox As New TextBox()
    NewTextBox.Size = New Size(100, 20)
    NewTextBox.Location = New Point(100, 100)
    NewTextBox.Text = "Hello from Visual Basic"
    Me.Controls.Add(NewTextBox)
End Sub
```

You can see the results in Figure 7.12; when the user clicks on a button, a new text box appears in the form.

Related solution:	Found on page:
Adding Buttons at Runtime	173

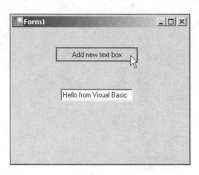

Figure 7.12   Adding controls at runtime.

Chapter 8

Windows Forms: Core Controls

In Brief

In this chapter, we'll take a look at some of the core Windows forms controls in Visual Basic .NET. Controls are those visual elements that the user interacts with by typing into or clicking on, such as text boxes or buttons. I don't have the space in this book to cover them all—take a look at the *Visual Basic .NET Black Book* for that—and it wouldn't be appropriate in this book anyway, which is about the core Visual Basic language. However, by looking at the core set of controls, you'll find it easy to work with other controls in most cases.

Here, we'll take a look at text boxes, labels, buttons, checkboxes, and radio buttons. In the next chapter, we'll take a look at another core control: menus. Like all Windows controls, these controls are based on the **Control** class. The many controls derived from this class inherit a lot of functionality from it, so we'll look first at their common base class, the **Control** class. This will give us a good foundation for this chapter and those to come.

The Control Class

The **Control** class is in the **System.Windows.Forms** namespace. It serves as a base class for the Windows controls you'll see, such as text boxes. For example, here's the class hierarchy for text boxes, where the **MarshalByRefObject** class is derived from the **Object** class, the **Component** class is derived from **MarshalByRefObject**—all the way through the **Control** class and up to the **TextBox** class:

```
Object
    MarshalByRefObject
        Component
            Control
                TextBoxBase
                    TextBox
```

Because Windows controls are based on the **Control** class, they inherit many properties, methods, and events from that class, and you can find those properties, methods, and events in the *Visual Basic .NET Black Book* or the Visual Basic documentation.

NOTE: *Keep in mind that the **Form** class is also derived from **Control**, so it also shares these properties, methods, and events.*

Text Boxes

Every Windows user is familiar with text boxes: They're exactly what their name implies—boxlike controls in which you can enter text. Text boxes can be multiline, have scrollbars, be read-only, and have many other attributes. The **TextBox** class is derived from the **TextBoxBase** class, which is based on **Control**.

Windows forms text boxes are used to get input from the user or to display text. The **TextBox** control is used generally for editable text, although it can also be made read-only. Text boxes can display multiple lines, wrap text to the size of the control, and add basic formatting, such as quotation marks and masking characters for passwords.

The text displayed by the control is contained in the **Text** property. By default, you can enter up to 2,048 characters in a text box. If you set the **MultiLine** property to **True** to make the control accept multiple lines of text, you can enter up to 32KB of text. The **Text** property can be set at design time with the Properties window, at runtime in code, or by user input at runtime. The current contents of a text box can be retrieved at runtime by reading the **Text** property. You've seen how to do this already, as in this example, which inserts text into a text box:

```
Private Sub Button1_Click(ByVal sender As System.Object, _
    ByVal e As System.EventArgs) Handles Button1.Click
    TextBox1.Text = "Hello from Visual Basic"
End Sub
```

You can set or read text from text boxes at runtime, and the user can enter and edit text in text boxes as well. You can limit the amount of text entered into a **TextBox** control by setting the **MaxLength** property to a specific number of characters. **TextBox** controls also can be used to accept passwords if you use the **PasswordChar** property to mask characters.

You also can restrict text from being entered in a **TextBox** control by creating an event handler for the **KeyDown** event, letting you validate each character entered in the control. And you can restrict any data entry in a **TextBox** control by setting the **ReadOnly** property to **True**.

Labels

You use labels to identify parts of your application. Usually, labels are used to display text that cannot be edited by the user. Your code can change the text displayed by a label. Labels are based directly on the **Control** class.

The caption for a label is stored in the **Text** property. Because you can change that caption in code, labels can act somewhat like noneditable text boxes, displaying text and messages to the user. The **TextAlign** (formerly **Alignment**) property allows you to set the alignment of the text within the label.

Here's another interesting aspect of labels—they cannot receive the focus (that is, become the selected target of keystrokes), but you can set up mnemonic characters for them with the **UseMnemonic** property; just specify a mnemonic character in the caption by preceding it with an "&" character. In that case, when the user presses Alt and the mnemonic character, the focus goes to the control after the label (that is, the control that the label is labeling), which lets you support keyboard navigation for the many controls that don't support mnemonic characters. You also can support images in labels with the **Image** property or with the **Image** and **ImageList** properties together.

Buttons

There is no more popular control in Visual Basic than buttons, with the possible exception of text boxes. Buttons are the plain controls that you simply click and release, the buttons you see everywhere in Visual Basic applications are usually just rounded, rectangular, gray buttons with a caption, as you see in an example I'll call Buttons, which is shown in Figure 8.1.

Buttons provide the most popular way of creating and handling an event in code—every Visual Basic programmer is familiar with the button **Click** event. Buttons can be clicked on with the mouse or activated with the Enter key if the button has the focus.

Buttons are also very popular in dialog boxes. As you've seen in Chapter 7, you can set the **AcceptButton** or **CancelButton** property of a

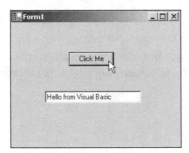

Figure 8.1   A button at work.

form to let users click on a button by pressing the Enter or Esc key—
even if the button doesn't have focus. And when you display a form
using the **ShowDialog** method, you can use the **DialogResult** property of a button to specify the return value of **ShowDialog**.

You can also change the button's appearance, giving it an image or align-
ing text and images in it as you like. You can even make it look flat for
a "Web" look, setting the **FlatStyle** property to **FlatStyle.Flat**. Or you
can set the **FlatStyle** property to **FlatStyle.Popup**, which means that
it looks flat until the mouse pointer passes over it, when the button
pops up to give it the standard Windows button appearance.

Checkboxes

Checkboxes are also familiar controls. You click on a checkbox to
select it and click on it again to deselect it. When you select a checkbox,
a check appears in it, indicating that the box is indeed selected. You
use a checkbox to let the user choose non-exclusive options, such as
toppings on a pizza (cheese, anchovies, pepperoni, and so on) or fill-
ings in a sandwich (ham, cheese, lettuce, and the like). The checkbox
control can display an image, text, or both. You can see some
checkboxes at work in Figure 8.2 in an example I'll call CheckBoxes.

You can use the **Appearance** property to specify whether the
checkbox appears as a typical checkbox or as a button. The **FlatStyle**
property determines the style and appearance of the control. If the
FlatStyle property is set to **FlatStyle.System**, the user's operating
system sets the appearance of the control.

In addition, the **ThreeState** property determines whether the control supports two or three states. For standard checkboxes, you use
the **Checked** property to get or set the value of a checkbox control,

Figure 8.2   Checkboxes at work.

but for three-state checkboxes, which support an "indeterminate" state, you use the **CheckState** property. The indeterminate state is sort of a middle state between checked and unchecked. For example, if you use a checkbox to specify that selected text in a text control of some type should be in italics but have selected text that is partly normal and partly italic text, the checkbox can show the indeterminate state—in which a checkbox appears on a gray background—to show that neither the checked nor the unchecked state fully applies.

Radio Buttons

Radio buttons, also called option buttons, are similar to checkboxes— the user can select and deselect them—except for two things: They are round where checkboxes are square, and you usually use radio buttons together in groups.

In fact, that's the functional difference between checkboxes and radio buttons—checkboxes can work independently, but radio buttons are intended to work in groups. When you select one radio button in a group, the others are automatically deselected. For example, although you might use checkboxes to select trimmings on a sandwich (of which more than one can exist), you would use radio buttons to let the user select one of a set of exclusive options, such as the current day of the week. You can see radio buttons at work in Figure 8.3 in an example I'll call RadioButtons.

When the user selects one radio button in a group, the others clear automatically. All radio buttons in a given container, such as a form, make up a group. To create multiple groups on one form, you place each additional group in its own container, such as a group box or panel control.

Figure 8.3   Radio buttons at work.

Like checkboxes, you use the **Checked** property to get or set the state of a radio button. Radio buttons can display text, an image, or both. In addition, a radio button's appearance may be altered to appear as a toggle-style button, as we'll see later in the chapter, or as a standard radio button by setting the **Appearance** property.

And that's enough overview—it's time to start creating these controls, text boxes, rich text boxes, labels, and link labels in your Windows applications.

Immediate Solutions

Creating Text Boxes

Creating a text box is easy enough—you just double-click on the text box item in the toolbox or drag a text box from the toolbox to a Windows form. That's all it takes. But what if you want to start customizing your text box? See the next section.

Creating Multiline, Word-Wrap Text Boxes

You've got a text box all set up for user feedback, and it can hold about 60 characters of text. Surely, that's enough, you think. But when you start reading the users' comments, you find that they're all favorable but truncated (for example, "I loved your program! In fact, let me say that I never s"). Maybe it's worthwhile to allow the user to enter more text.

You can do that by setting the text box's **MultiLine** property to **True**, converting a text box into a multiline text box, complete with word wrap. The result appears in Figure 8.4. Now your program's users can type in line after line of text.

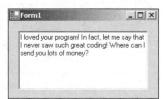

Figure 8.4   Creating a multiline text box.

Accessing Text in a Text Box

Java, C++, Visual Basic—a programmer has to switch between many languages these days. So how do you set the text in a text box again? Is there a **SetText** method? No, you use the **Text** property, like this:

```
Private Sub Button1_Click_1(ByVal sender As System.Object, _
    ByVal e As System.EventArgs) Handles Button1.Click
    TextBox1.Text = "Hello from Visual Basic"
End Sub
```

When the user clicks the command button **Button1**, the text "Hello from Visual Basic" appears in the text box. And you can recover text from a text box in the same way:

```
Private Sub Button1_Click_1(ByVal sender As System.Object, _
    ByVal e As System.EventArgs) Handles Button1.Click
    Dim strText As String
    strText = TextBox1.Text
End Sub
```

Selecting and Replacing Text in a Text Box

To work with part of the text in a text box, you select the text you want using three properties:

- **SelectionLength**—Returns or sets the number of characters selected

- **SelectionStart**—Returns or sets the starting point of text selected; indicates the position of the insertion point if no text is selected

- **SelectedText**—Returns or sets the string containing the currently selected text; consists of a zero-length string ("") if no characters are selected

---

TIP: *While on the topic of text selection, I might note the **HideSelection** property, which, when **True**, turns off text selection highlighting when your program loses the focus.*

For example, here's how to select all the text in a textbox and replace it with "Hello from Visual Basic". Note the use of the **Len** function to get the length of the text currently in the text box:

```
Private Sub Button1_Click(ByVal sender As System.Object, _
    ByVal e As System.EventArgs) Handles Button1.Click
    TextBox1.SelectionStart = 0
    TextBox1.SelectionLength = Len(TextBox1.Text)
    TextBox1.SelectedText = "Hello from Visual Basic"
End Sub
```

That's how it works when you want to select some text—you specify the beginning of the selected text in **SelectionStart** and the end in **SelectionLength** and refer to the text with the **SelectedText** property. Note that text selected under program control this way does *not* appear highlighted in the text box; when the user selects text, the text will appear highlighted, and these properties will be set automatically.

Creating a Password Control

It's time to heighten security—users of your new SuperSpecialDataBase program are worried about the low security of your program, so you can add a little security with password controls. Visual Basic can help.

To convert a standard text box into a password box, you just assign some character (usually an asterisk, "*") to the text box's **PasswordChar** property. After that, your program can read the text in the text box, but only the password character will appear on the screen each time the user types a character, as shown in Figure 8.5.

TIP: You may be concerned that someone can copy the text in a password control and paste it into a word processor to read it, but, in fact, clipboard handling from the text box is disabled if you're using a password character.

Figure 8.5   Creating a password control.

Using Labels Instead of Text Boxes

Using labels instead of text boxes has several advantages in a Visual Basic program. Labels display read-only text (although you *can* make text boxes read-only by setting their **ReadOnly** property to **True**), and they give the appearance of text directly on the form; this can look much better than a text box on occasion. For example, you might want to display the result of a calculation in a label instead of a text box so that the user can't edit that result.

In fact, you can make text boxes and labels resemble each other. To make a text box look like a label, in the Properties window set the text box's **BackColor** property to **Control**, its **ReadOnly** property to **True**, and its **BorderStyle** property to **None**. To make a label look like a text box, set its **BackColor** property to **Window** and its **BorderStyle** property to **Fixed3D**.

Handling Button Clicks

I've covered this topic before, as far back as Chapter 1, but for completeness, I'll include it again here; you respond to button clicks with the button's **Click** event. To add a click event handler, just double-click on the button at design time, adding a **Sub** procedure such as this one to your code:

```
Private Sub Button1_Click(ByVal sender As System.Object,
    ByVal e As System.EventArgs) Handles Button1.Click

End Sub
```

Place the code you want to execute when the button is clicked on in this **Sub** procedure; this code is from the Buttons example:

```
Private Sub Button1_Click(ByVal sender As System.Object, _
    ByVal e As System.EventArgs) Handles Button1.Click
    TextBox1.Text = "Hello from Visual Basic"
End Sub
```

Here the **sender** argument is the button object itself that caused the event, and the **e** argument is a simple **EventArgs** object that doesn't contain any additional useful information, such as where the button was clicked.

All types of buttons have a **Click** event—they wouldn't be much use otherwise—as well as a double-click event, **DoubleClick** (formerly **DblClick** in VB6 and earlier). Note that if you double-click on a checkbox, you select and then deselect it (or deselect and then select it), so you're back to where you started. If you double-click on a radio button, however, you select it no matter what its original state and cause a **DoubleClick** event.

Showing and Hiding Buttons

In the last section, you saw that you can disable buttons using the **Enabled** property. However, it's an inefficient use of space (and frustrating to the user) to display a lot of disabled buttons. If you have to disable several buttons, you should hide them.

To make a button disappear, just set its **Visible** property to **False**. To make it reappear, set the **Visible** property to **True**. You can set this property at either design time or runtime. Here's how to make a button disappear when you click on it (and probably startle the user):

```
Private Sub Button1_Click(ByVal sender As System.Object, _
    ByVal e As System.EventArgs) Handles Button1.Click
    Button1.Visible = False
End Sub
```

You can also use the **Control** class's **Show** and **Hide** methods to show and hide buttons.

TIP: *If your program shows and hides buttons, you can rearrange the visible buttons to hide any gaps using the buttons'* ***SetBounds*** *method.*

Resizing and Moving Buttons from Code

Your new April Fool's program has an Exit button, but it moves around and resizes itself, making it a moving target for the user to try to hit. Your coworkers think it's hilarious, and they love it. Your boss hates it and asks to see you to discuss time management—immediately.

In Visual Basic 6 and earlier, you could use the **Move** method to move forms and controls (and optionally set their dimensions) and the **Height** and **Width** methods to set their dimensions. In VB .NET, you use the **SetBounds** method to move forms and controls (and optionally set their dimensions) and the **Size** and **Location** properties to set their dimensions.

You set the **Size** property to a new **Size** object and the **Location** property to a new **Point** object. The dimensions you set in the **Size** and **Point** objects are measured in pixels, as are all measurements in

Visual Basic, and you create these objects by passing x and y dimensions to their class's constructors like this:

```
Size(x_dimension, y_dimension)
Point(x_location, y_location)
```

TIP: *In the Visual Basic screen coordinate system, the upper left of the screen is the origin, (0, 0). Positive x values increase downward and positive y values increase to the right.*

Here's an example. Say that you wanted to change the size and location of a button in a form when the user clicks on that button. You can do that like this (the origin of coordinates for the form is the upper left of the screen, and the origin for the button contained in the form is the upper left of the form's client area):

```
Private Sub Button1_Click(ByVal sender As System.Object, _
    ByVal e As System.EventArgs) Handles Button1.Click
        Button1.Size = New Size(100, 50)
        Button1.Location = New Point(0, 0)
End Sub
```

You can also use the **SetBounds** method to do the same thing; this method is overloaded and has several forms—here's a popular one:

```
Overloads Public Sub SetBounds(ByVal x As Integer, _
    ByVal y As Integer, _
    ByVal width As Integer, ByVal height As Integer)
```

Here are the arguments you pass to **SetBounds**:

- *x*—The new **Left** property value of the control
- *y*—The new **Right** property value of the control
- *width*—The new **Width** property value of the control
- *height*—The new **Height** property value of the control

Adding Buttons at Runtime

Your new program lets the user add options to customize things, and you want to display a new button for each option. Is there a way to add buttons to a Visual Basic program at runtime?

Yes, there is. You can do that by declaring new buttons and adding them to the form's **Controls** collection with the **Add** method. You can also give each new button its own event handler with the **AddHandler** method, using the **AddressOf** operator to find the address of the appropriate event handler, like this:

```
Public Class Form1
        Inherits System.Windows.Forms.Form
        Dim WithEvents Button1 As Button
        Dim WithEvents Button2 As Button
        Dim WithEvents Button3 As Button
        Friend WithEvents Button4 As Button
        Friend WithEvents TextBox1 As TextBox

        'Windows Form Designer generated code "

        Private Sub Button4_Click(ByVal sender As System.Object, _
            ByVal e As System.EventArgs) Handles Button4.Click
            Button1 = New Button()
            Button2 = New Button()
            Button3 = New Button()

            Button1.Size = New Size(80, 30)
            Button1.Location = New Point(115, 20)
            Button1.Text = "Button 1"

            Button2.Size = New Size(80, 30)
            Button2.Location = New Point(115, 60)
            Button2.Text = "Button 2"

            Button3.Size = New Size(80, 30)
            Button3.Location = New Point(115, 100)
            Button3.Text = "Button 3"

            Controls.Add(Button1)
            Controls.Add(Button2)
            Controls.Add(Button3)

            AddHandler Button1.Click, AddressOf Button1_Click
            AddHandler Button2.Click, AddressOf Button2_Click
            AddHandler Button3.Click, AddressOf Button3_Click
        End Sub

        Private Sub Button1_Click(ByVal sender As System.Object, _
            ByVal e As System.EventArgs)
            TextBox1.Text = "You clicked button 1"
        End Sub
```

```
Private Sub Button2_Click(ByVal sender As System.Object, _
    ByVal e As System.EventArgs)
    TextBox1.Text = "You clicked button 2"
End Sub


Private Sub Button3_Click(ByVal sender As System.Object, _
    ByVal e As System.EventArgs)
    TextBox1.Text = "You clicked button 3"
End Sub

End Class
```

That's all it takes.

Creating Checkboxes

You've already seen how to create checkboxes in the In Brief section
of this chapter. You can handle checkbox **CheckChanged** events,
which happen when the **Checked** property changes. Here's some code
from the CheckBoxes example:

```
Private Sub CheckBox1_CheckedChanged(ByVal _
    sender As System.Object, _
    ByVal e As System.EventArgs) Handles _
    CheckBox1.CheckedChanged
    TextBox1.Text = "You clicked check box 1"
End Sub
```

You can see the results of this code in Figure 8.2, earlier in the chapter.

Getting a Checkbox's State

You've added all the checkboxes you need to your new program,
WinBigSuperCasino, and you've connected those checkboxes to **Click**
event handlers. But now there's a problem: When the users set the
current amount of money they want to bet, you need to check whether
they've exceeded the limit they've set for themselves. But they set
their limit by clicking on other checkboxes—how can you determine
which one they've checked?

You can see whether a checkbox is checked by examining its **Checked** property. This property can be set to either **True** or **False**. Here's an example. In this case, I'll change a button's caption if a checkbox, **Check1**, is checked, but not otherwise:

```
Private Sub Button1_Click(ByVal sender As System.Object, _
    ByVal e As System.EventArgs) Handles Button1.Click
    If CheckBox1.Checked Then
        Button1.Text = "The check mark is checked"
    End If
End Sub
```

Setting a Checkbox's State

Your new program, SuperSandwichesToGoRightNow, is just about ready, but there's one hitch. You use checkboxes to indicate what items are in a sandwich (cheese, lettuce, tomato, and more) to let the users custom-build their sandwiches, but you also have a number of specialty sandwiches with preset ingredients. When the user selects one of those already built sandwiches, how do you set the ingredients checkboxes to show what's in them?

You can set a checkbox's state by setting its **Checked** property to **True** or **False**, as in this code:

```
Private Sub Button1_Click(ByVal sender As System.Object, _
    ByVal e As System.EventArgs) Handles Button1.Click
    CheckBox1.Checked = True
End Sub
```

TIP: *How can you make a checkbox appear checked when your program first starts? Just set its **Checked** property to **True** at design time.*

Creating Three-State Checkboxes

In VB6 and earlier, you could set any checkbox to one of three states—now you need to set the checkbox's **ThreeState** property to **True** to indicate that you want it to support three states.

By default, checkboxes are two-state controls; you use the **Checked** property to get or set the value of a two-state checkbox. You use the **CheckState** property to get or set the value of the three-state checkbox. The three states are as follows:

- **Checked**—A check appears in the checkbox.

- **Unchecked**—No check appears in the checkbox.

- **Indeterminate**—A check appears in the checkbox on a gray background.

These three states are discussed in the In Depth section of this chapter. You can see a checkbox in the indeterminate state in Figure 8.6.

TIP: *If the **ThreeState** property is set to **True**, the **Checked** property will return **True** for either a checked or an indeterminate state.*

If you've set the checkbox's **ThreeState** property to **True**, you can set its **CheckState** property to **CheckState.Indeterminate** at design time or runtime to set the checkbox to the indeterminate state:

```
Private Sub CheckBox1_CheckedChanged(ByVal _
    sender As System.Object, _
    ByVal e As System.EventArgs) Handles _
    CheckBox1.CheckedChanged _
    TextBox1.Text = "You clicked check box 1"
    CheckBox1.CheckState = CheckState.Indeterminate
End Sub
```

Figure 8.6   A checkbox in the indeterminate state.

Creating Radio Buttons

You've already seen how to create radio buttons in the In Depth section of this chapter. You can handle radio button **CheckChanged** events, which happen when the **Checked** property changes; here's some code from the RadioButtons example:

```
Private Sub RadioButton1_CheckedChanged(ByVal _
    sender As System.Object, _
    ByVal e As System.EventArgs) Handles _
    RadioButton1.CheckedChanged _
    TextBox1.Text = "You clicked radio button 1"
End Sub
```

You saw the results of this code in Figure 8.3, earlier in the chapter.

Getting a Radio Button's State

You can check whether a radio button is selected with the **Checked** property (formerly the **Value** property in VB6 and earlier). A radio button's **Checked** property has only two settings: **True** if the button is selected and **False** if not.

Here's an example showing how to determine whether a radio button is selected. In this case, I display a message in a message box that indicates whether a radio button, **RadioButton1**, is selected:

```
Private Sub Button1_Click(ByVal sender As System.Object, _
    ByVal e As System.EventArgs) Handles Button1.Click
    If RadioButton1.Checked Then
        MsgBox ("The Radio Button is selected.")
    Else
        MsgBox ("The Radio Button is not selected.")
    End If
End Sub
```

That's all there is to it.

Setting a Radio Button's State

Besides examining a radio button's state, you can also set it using the **Checked** property. The **Checked** property can take two values: **True** or **False**. Here's an example. In this case, I just set a radio button, **RadioButton1**, to its selected state by setting its **Checked** property to **True**:

```
Private Sub Button1_Click(ByVal sender As System.Object, _
    ByVal e As System.EventArgs) Handles Button1.Click
    RadioButton1.Checked = True
End Sub
```

That's all it takes.

Windows Forms: Menus

In Brief

In the previous chapter, you looked at some of the core Windows controls in Visual Basic .NET; in this chapter, you'll see another important core control, but one that doesn't work like the others: menus. If you're familiar with Visual Basic 6, you'll find many differences from it in VB .NET. For example, now menus have their own control instead of a separate menu editor. (Giving menus their own control is more in line with the Visual Basic philosophy, so that's an improvement.)

Every Windows user is familiar with menus; you wouldn't get far in Windows without them. Menus are those controls that allow the user to make selections and also hide away those selections when they're not needed, saving space in Windows applications, which is always at a premium. (Imagine replacing all the menu items in a real-world Windows application with buttons in the main window.)

In Visual Basic, the **MainMenu** control represents the container for the menu structure of a form; you can assign a control of this type to a form's **Menu** property at runtime. Menus are made up of **MenuItem** objects that represent the individual parts of a menu—menu items can be a parent menu or a menu item in a menu. You can see the menu application you'll develop in this chapter, which I'll call Menus, in Figure 9.1. Here, I've opened the File menu in the menu bar and opened a submenu two levels deep.

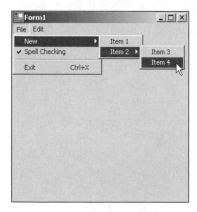

Figure 9.1   The Menus application.

All kinds of options are available here—you can add submenus that will pop up when the user clicks on an arrow in a menu item, display checkmarks, create menu separators (horizontal bars used in menus to group menu items), assign shortcut keys (such as Ctrl+H) to menu items, and even draw the appearance of menu items yourself. These actions are supported by **MenuItem** objects, not **MainMenu** objects.

TIP: Don't forget that if you're going to release your programs for public consumption you need to adhere to a number of menu conventions in Windows. For example, if a menu item opens a dialog box, you should add an ellipsis (...) after its name (such as Print...). Many shortcuts are already standard, such as Ctrl+S for Save, Ctrl+X for Cut, Ctrl+V for Paste/ View, Ctrl+C for Copy, and so on. The File menu should be the first menu, and an Exit item should be at the bottom of that menu. Menus in the menu bar that don't open a menu but instead perform some action immediately (sometimes called bang menus) should have an exclamation point (!) after their names (such as Connect!).

Menu Items

Menus such as File or Edit and the items in those menus are supported with the **MenuItem** class. This class supports the controls in your menu system, and it's their **Click** event that you add code to in order to make that menu system active.

This class provides properties that enable you to configure the appearance and functionality of a menu item. To display a checkmark next to a menu item, use the **Checked** property. You can use this feature to identify a menu item that is selected in a list of mutually exclusive menu items. You can use the **Shortcut** property to define a keyboard combination (such as Ctrl+X) that can be pressed to select the menu item and set the **ShowShortcut** property to **True** to display that key combination in the menu item's caption. In addition, **MenuItem** objects themselves can have other **MenuItem** objects attached to them to display submenus.

To set the caption of a menu or menu item, you use the **Text** property. Setting the **Text** property to a hyphen (-) converts the menu item into a menu separator, one of those horizontal bars that help group menu items together. (You can even have separators in menu bars, in which case they're vertical.) Prefacing a character in a menu item's caption with an ampersand (&) underlines that character and makes it into an access key, which means that the user can select that item by pressing Alt and that character. For example, giving a menu item the caption "E&xit" makes X the access key for this menu item.

You can enable and disable menu items with the **Enabled** property and show or hide them with the **Visible** property.

NOTE: *For a **MenuItem** to be displayed, you have to add it to a **MainMenu** (or **ContextMenu**) object.*

MenuItem objects in a Multiple Document Interface (MDI) application—where one window contains others—work in a special way. When an MDI child window appears, its menu is merged with the MDI parent window (so no menu system appears in the child). You can specify how menu items should be added to the MDI parent window with the **MergeOrder** and **MergeType** properties. You can also use the **MergeMenu** method to specify how this merging occurs.

TIP: *MenuItem objects cannot be used in multiple places at the same time, such as in a **MainMenu** object and a **ContextMenu** object. However, you can use the **CloneMenu** method to create a copy of a **MenuItem** object for use in another location.*

The most common menu item event that you handle is **Click**, which means that the user has clicked a menu item and your code should respond to it. However, other events exist here as well—the **Popup** event lets you perform tasks before a menu is displayed because it happens just before a menu item is displayed. And the **Select** event happens when a menu item is selected (that is, highlighted). This enables you to perform tasks such as displaying help for menu items when the user places the mouse cursor over those items.

Context Menus

Another popular type of menus is *context menus*. You use **ContextMenu** controls to give users access to frequently used menu commands and bring them up by right-clicking another control. You can see a context menu at work in an example I'll call ContextMenus in Figure 9.2. Usually, you use context menus to display control-specific options, such as Cut, Copy, and Paste, in text boxes.

You associate context menus with other controls by setting the control's **ContextMenu** property to the **ContextMenu** control. The central property of the **ContextMenu** control is the **MenuItems** property; you can add menu items to a context menu at design time or in code by creating **MenuItem** objects and adding them to the **MenuItems** collection of the context menu.

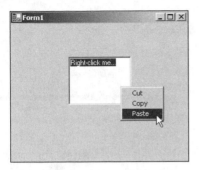

Figure 9.2   A context menu.

NOTE: *You can reuse* **MenuItem** *objects from a main menu in a context menu if you use the* **CloneMenu** *method of the* **MenuItem** *class.*

As with main menus, context menu items can be disabled, hidden, or deleted. You also can show and hide context menus yourself with the **ContextMenu** control's **Show** and **Hide** methods. You can handle the menu item's **Click**, **Select**, and **Popup** events, as you can in main menus. In fact, the only major difference here is that context menus are not divided into separate menus, such as File, Edit, Window, and so on.

TIP: *A context menu can be associated with a number of other controls, but as you'd expect, each control can have only one context menu.*

Immediate Solutions

Creating Menus

So how do you create menus in Visual Basic? The simplest way to do so is at design time because you need only add a **MainMenu** control from the toolbox to a Windows form. When you do so, the **MainMenu** control appears in the component tray under the form designer, as you see in Figure 9.3. (In fact, it would be more proper to call this a **MainMenu** component because it doesn't inherit the **Control** class and it appears in the component tray. Nonetheless, Visual Basic calls this a **MainMenu** control.)

Note the Type Here box in Figure 9.3. To create a new menu, you just double-click that text to open a text box that you can use to enter the caption for menus and menu items. When you're creating a new menu item, Type Here boxes appear in all the other places you can enter text. To create a new menu in the menu bar, add a submenu to the current menu item, as you see in Figure 9.4, where I'm editing the menu system in the Menus example. Using this control is intuitive

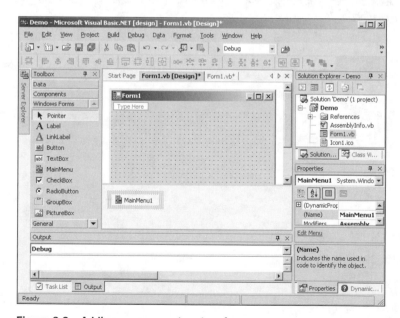

Figure 9.3   Adding a menu system to a form.

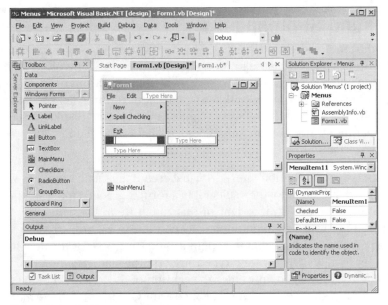

Figure 9.4   Adding menu items to a form.

and easy—all you have to do is to enter text in the Type Here boxes and double-click the resulting menus and menu items to add code to their **Click** events in the corresponding code designer. To drag menu items around, repositioning them after you've given them a caption, just use the mouse.

How do you make the menu items you've added to a menu system active? For each menu and menu item you add at design time, Visual Basic creates a **MenuItem** object, and you can handle its **Click** event. For example, the last menu item in the File menu is the Exit item in the Menus project. It turns out that this item is **MenuItem4** in this example, so when I double-click it in the form designer, its **Click** event opens in the code designer, and I can use the **End** statement to end the program:

```
Private Sub MenuItem4_Click(ByVal sender As System.Object, _
    ByVal e As System.EventArgs) Handles MenuItem4.Click
    End
End Sub
```

Now when the user clicks the Exit menu item at runtime, the program will terminate.

Creating Submenus

In the previous section, you got your start with menus, creating simple menu items. You also can create submenus, which involves giving menu items to menu items. When a menu item has a submenu, a right-pointing arrow appears in that menu item at runtime, as you saw in Figure 9.1. Clicking that arrow opens the submenu, displaying additional menu items. And submenus can have submenus, which can have other submenus, and so on.

It's easy to create submenus—you just create the menu item you want to add a submenu to, then select it in a form designer. Doing so opens a Type Here box to the right of that menu item; you can enter the captions for the submenu items, as you see in Figure 9.5. Selecting the first item in the submenu opens a Type Here box for the next item under it as well as another Type Here box for a new submenu to the right of it. You need only enter the caption of the submenu items you want, then double-click them to open their **Click** event in the matching code designer.

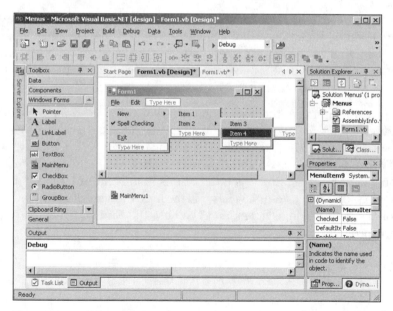

Figure 9.5   Adding submenu items to a form.

For example, you can add code to display a message box when a menu item is selected, like this:

```
Private Sub MenuItem6_Click(ByVal sender As System.Object, _
    ByVal e As System.EventArgs) Handles MenuItem6.Click
    MsgBox("You clicked my favorite item!")
End Sub
```

To see this in action, take a look at Figure 9.1, which shows how the submenus work in the Menus example.

Adding Checkmarks to Menu Items

You can also add a checkmark to a menu item, which you usually use to indicate that a specific option has been selected—you can see an example in front of the Spell Checking menu item in Figure 9.1. To add a checkmark to a menu item at design time, just click to the left of its caption. A checkbox is there, and if you click on it, you'll toggle a checkmark on and off; you can see the checkmark in Figure 9.5.

You can use the **Checked** property of a **MenuItem** object to toggle the checkmark; **True** means the checkmark is displayed, **False** means it's hidden. In the Menus example, the checkmark in front of the Spell Checking item toggles on and off when you select that item because I flip the logical sense of the **Checked** property with the **Not** operator that we saw in Chapter 4:

```
Private Sub MenuItem7_Click(ByVal sender As System.Object, _
    ByVal e As System.EventArgs) Handles MenuItem7.Click
    MenuItem7.Checked = Not MenuItem7.Checked
End Sub
```

Related solution:	Found on page:
Using Visual Basic Operators	82

Creating Menu Access Keys

Access keys make it possible to select menu items from the keyboard using the Alt key. For example, if you make the "F" in the File menu's caption an access key and the "x" in the Exit menu item an access key, the user can select the Exit item by pressing Alt+F to open the File menu, then Alt+X to select the Exit item.

To give an item an access key, you precede the access key in its caption with an ampersand (&). In this example, that means using the captions "&File" and "E&xit". Access keys are underlined in menu captions, as you see in Figure 9.5, as visual cues to the user.

Note that you still have to open a menu item's menu to be able to use its access key. If you want to assign a key to a menu item that can be used without first opening that item's menu, use a shortcut instead; see the next section.

Creating Menu Shortcuts

You can create shortcuts for menu items, which are key combinations that, when pressed, will select that item, firing its **Click** event. You set a shortcut with the **Shortcut** property. To display the shortcut next to the menu item's caption at runtime, you set the **ShowShortcut** property to **True** (it's **True** by default).

For instance, in the Menus example, I've given the Exit item in the File menu a shortcut of Ctrl+X, as you can see next to its caption in Figure 9.1. When the user presses Ctrl+X, this item is activated. To assign a shortcut key combination to a menu item at design time, just select a shortcut key combination from the list that appears when you select the **Shortcut** property of any menu item in the Properties window. At runtime, you can use members of the **Shortcut** enumeration to do the same thing, as in this code:

```
menuItem1.Shortcut = Shortcut.CtrlX
```

Remember that shortcuts will select their corresponding menu item even if no menu is open at the time. If you want to make sure that the user must first open the item's menu, use access keys instead; see the previous section.

Changing a Menu Item's Caption at Runtime

To change a menu item's caption at runtime, you need only set its **Text** property. Here's an example:

```
Private Sub MenuItem1_Popup(ByVal sender As Object, _
    ByVal e As System.EventArgs) Handles MenuItem6.Popup
    MenuItem1.Text = "I've been clicked!"
End Sub
```

Creating Menu Separators

If you take a look at Figure 9.1, you'll see a horizontal line in the File menu above the Exit item. That line is a menu separator, and you can use it to separate the items in a menu into functional groupings.

To create a menu separator, as in the Menus example, you can assign a single hyphen (-) to a menu item's **Text** property (just type a hyphen in the Type Here box when you're creating the menu item). That's all it takes—Visual Basic will make the menu item into a menu separator for you automatically.

Using the **Popup** Event

The **MenuItem Popup** event occurs when a menu item is about to be displayed, and you can execute code to configure the item in this event's handler. For example, you might have an item that lets the user connect to the Internet, and you might want to set the caption to "Connect" if the user is presently disconnected and to "Disconnect" if connected. Here's an example that uses this event to display a message box before the corresponding menu item is displayed:

```
Private Sub MenuItem6_Popup(ByVal sender As Object, _
    ByVal e As System.EventArgs) Handles MenuItem6.Popup
    MsgBox("I'm about to open my submenu!")
End Sub
```

Showing and Hiding Menu Items

To show and hide menu items, you can use their **Visible** property
(they don't have **Show** or **Hide** methods). Here's an example from
the Menus code; when you select the item with the caption "Item 4"
from the submenu system, the program will hide the menu item with
the caption "Item 1":

```
Private Sub MenuItem8_Click(ByVal sender As System.Object, _
    ByVal e As System.EventArgs) Handles MenuItem8.Click
    MsgBox("Hiding item 1...")
    MenuItem5.Visible = False
End Sub
```

Disabling Menu Items

To disable, or "gray out," a menu item so that it can't be selected, you
set its **Enabled** property to **False**. Here's an example:

```
Private Sub MenuItem8_Click(ByVal sender As System.Object, _
    ByVal e As System.EventArgs) Handles MenuItem8.Click
    MsgBox("Disabling item 1...")
    MenuItem5.Enabled = False
End Sub
```

Drawing Menu Items Yourself

Well, your new menu system looks good, but it's just not right. Wouldn't
it be much nicer if you could draw people's faces instead of just text?

You can, if that's what you want. To show how this works, take a look
at a new example I'll call DrawMenuItem, in which I'm drawing an
ellipse in a menu item, as you see in Figure 9.6.

Here's how you do it. First, you set the menu item's **OwnerDraw** property to **True**. Next, you add code to the menu item's **MeasureItem**
event to let Visual Basic know how big you want to make this item
when displayed. To pass this information back to Visual Basic, you're
passed an object of the **MeasureItemEventArgs**, and you set this
object's **ItemHeight** and **ItemWidth** properties in pixels, like this:

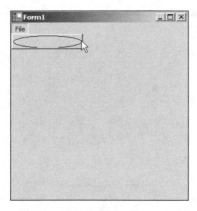

Figure 9.6   Drawing a menu item.

```
Private Sub MenuItem2_MeasureItem(ByVal sender As Object, _
    ByVal e As System.Windows.Forms.MeasureItemEventArgs) _
    Handles MenuItem2.MeasureItem
    e.ItemHeight = 20
    e.ItemWidth = 100
End Sub
```

Next, you draw the item with a **Graphics** object passed to you in the menu item's **DrawItem** event. In this case, I'll do that by creating a black pen object to draw with and by drawing an ellipse with it. Note in particular that the boundaries that you're supposed to draw inside are passed to you as a **Bounds** object (you can use the **Height** and **Width** properties of this object to get more information):

```
Private Sub MenuItem2_DrawItem(ByVal sender As Object, _
    ByVal e As System.Windows.Forms.DrawItemEventArgs) _
    Handles MenuItem2.DrawItem
    Dim pen As New Pen(Color.Black)
    e.Graphics.DrawEllipse(pen, e.Bounds)
End Sub
```

And, of course, you can handle other events as before for this menu item, such as the **Click** event:

```
Private Sub MenuItem2_Click(ByVal sender As System.Object, _
    ByVal e As System.EventArgs) _
    Handles MenuItem2.Click
    MsgBox("You clicked item 1")
End Sub
```

Creating Menus in Code

So far in this chapter, you've designed and built menu systems at design time, but you can create menu systems at runtime as well—just create a **MainMenu** object, add the **MenuItem** objects you want to it, and assign the **MainMenu** object to a form's **Menu** property. Here's an example, which I'll call CreateMenus, that does exactly that. You can see the menu system that this example creates when you click its Create Menu button, shown in Figure 9.7.

Here's the code this example uses to create the menu system you see in Figure 9.7. Note that you need only create **MenuItem** objects and use the **MenuItems** collection's **Add** method to add them to menus or other menu items:

```
Dim mainMenu1 As New MainMenu()

Dim WithEvents menuItem1 As New MenuItem()
Dim WithEvents menuItem2 As New MenuItem()
Dim WithEvents menuItem3 As New MenuItem()
Dim WithEvents menuItem4 As New MenuItem()

Private Sub Button1_Click(ByVal sender As System.Object, _
    ByVal e As System.EventArgs) Handles Button1.Click
    menuItem1.Text = "File"
    menuItem2.Text = "New"
    menuItem3.Text = "Text File..."
    menuItem3.Checked = True
    menuItem3.Shortcut = Shortcut.CtrlT
    menuItem4.Text = "Image..."
    menuItem4.Shortcut = Shortcut.CtrlI
    menuItem2.MenuItems.Add(menuItem3)
    menuItem2.MenuItems.Add(menuItem4)
    AddHandler menuItem3.Click, AddressOf MenuItem3_Click
    menuItem1.MenuItems.Add(menuItem2)
    mainMenu1.MenuItems.Add(menuItem1)
    Menu = mainMenu1
End Sub

Private Sub MenuItem3_Click(ByVal sender As System.Object, _
    ByVal e As System.EventArgs) Handles menuItem2.Click
    MsgBox("You clicked me!")
End Sub
```

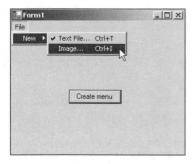

Figure 9.7   Creating menus from code.

Creating Context Menus

Creating context menus is much like creating standard menus—you
need only add a **ContextMenu** control to a Windows form, as you
see in Figure 9.8. The caption for this context menu is simply "Context Menu", but everything else is the same as creating any standard
menu (see the section "Creating Menus" earlier in this chapter)—just
give the items in the menu the captions you want, as you also see in
Figure 9.8.

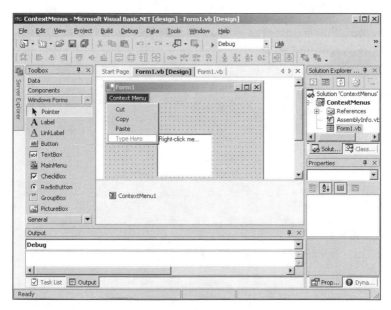

Figure 9.8   Creating a context menu.

Now you can connect code to the context menu items as you can with any **Click** events:

```
Private Sub MenuItem3_Click(ByVal sender As System.Object, _
    ByVal e As System.EventArgs) Handles MenuItem3.Click
    MsgBox("You clicked the Paste item")
End Sub

Private Sub MenuItem2_Click(ByVal sender As System.Object, _
    ByVal e As System.EventArgs) Handles MenuItem2.Click
    MsgBox("You clicked the Copy item")
End Sub

Private Sub MenuItem1_Click(ByVal sender As System.Object, _
    ByVal e As System.EventArgs) Handles MenuItem1.Click
    MsgBox("You clicked the Cut item")
End Sub
```

Finally, assign the context menu control, such as **ContextMenu1**, to the **ContextMenu** property of the control you want to connect it to. In the ContextMenus example, I've connected this context menu to a multiline text box; when the user right-clicks on this text box, the context menu appears, as you see in Figure 9.2, and you can select the items in that menu.

TIP: You also can make context menus appear whenever you want to from your code—just set their **Visible** property to **True**.

Object-Oriented Programming

In Brief

Just about everything you do in Visual Basic .NET involves objects in some way—even simple variables are based on the Visual Basic **Object** class. And all your code has to appear in a class of some sort, even if you're using a module or structure; these are also types of classes now. For these reasons, it's important to understand object-oriented programming (OOP) in Visual Basic—now more than ever before. This and the following chapter are dedicated to OOP.

I haven't looked at OOP in detail until now because you didn't really need to understand a great deal of the programming aspect of it. Visual Basic comes with thousands of built-in classes, ready to use, so you didn't have to plumb the depths too much. You knew that Windows forms are classes, based on the **System.Windows.Forms.Form** class, and that the code was part of that class:

```
Public Class Form1
    Inherits System.Windows.Forms.Form

    Private Sub Form1_Load(ByVal sender As System.Object, _
    ByVal e As System.EventArgs) Handles MyBase.Load
        .
        .
        .
    End Sub

End Class
```

But that's just a start. To go farther, you're going to have to create your own classes and objects.

Classes and Objects

You've already become familiar with the idea behind classes and objects, as discussed in Chapter 3. The idea is that classes are a type, and objects are examples, or *instances*, of that type. The relationship between classes and objects is much like the relationship between cookie cutters and cookies—you use the cookie cutter to create new cookies. Just think of the numeric data types such as **Integer**, which is a type, and a specific integer variable, **myInteger233**, which is an instance of that type. In fact, the **Integer** type is a class in Visual Basic, and variables of that type are in fact objects.

It's easy to create classes and objects in Visual Basic. To create a class, you only need to use the **Class** statement, which, like other compound statements in Visual Basic, needs to end with **End Class**:

```
Public Class DataClass
        .
        .
        .
End Class
```

This creates a new class named **DataClass**. You can create an object of this class, **data**, like this—note that you must use the **New** keyword to create a new instance of a class:

```
Dim data As New DataClass()
```

You can also do it like this:

```
Dim data As DataClass = New DataClass()
```

That's all there is to it, but not much is happening here. It's when you start giving classes their own methods, fields, properties, and events that things become more useful.

Fields, Properties, Methods, and Events

Fields, properties, methods, and events are called the *members* of a class. Inside the class, members are declared as either **Public**, **Private**, **Protected**, **Friend**, or **Protected Friend**:

- **Public**—Gives variables public access, which means that no restrictions are placed on their accessibility.

- **Private**—Gives variables private access, which means that they are accessible only from within their class, including any nested procedures.

- **Protected**—Gives variables protected access, which means that they are accessible only from within their own class or from a class derived from that class. Note that you can use **Protected** only at the class level (which means that you can't use it inside a procedure) because you use it to declare members of a class.

- **Friend**—Gives variables friend access, which means that they are accessible from within the program that contains their declaration as well as from anywhere else in the same assembly.

- **Protected Friend**—Gives variables both protected and friend access, which means that they can be used by code in the same assembly as well as by code in derived classes.

The *fields* of a class, also called the class's *data members,* are much like built-in variables (although they may also be constants). For example, I can declare a field named **value** to the **DataClass** class you just saw by declaring a variable with that name:

```
Public Class DataClass
    Public value As Integer
End Class
```

Now I can refer to that field in an object of this class using the familiar *object.field* syntax of Visual Basic:

```
Dim data As New DataClass()
data.value = 5
```

You can also make fields hold constant values with **Const**:

```
Public Class Class1
    Public Const Field1 As Integer = 0
        .
        .
        .
End Class
```

Using fields like this can give you direct access to the data stored inside an object, and that's unusual in OOP because you usually want to check the data being stored in your objects to make sure it's legal first. (For example, you might want to make sure that the number of computers stored in your warehouse is not assigned negative numbers.) An easy way of guarding access to the data in your objects is to use *properties.* You're familiar with properties of objects, such as these:

```
TextBox1.Size = New Size(150, 20)
TextBox1.Location = New Point(80, 20)
TextBox1.Text = "Hello from Visual Basic"
```

Properties are retrieved and set like fields but are handled with the **Property Get** and **Property Set** procedures, which provide more control on how values are set or returned. You first saw how to create properties in Chapter 5. You'll see more on properties in the next chapter, such as creating write-only and read-only properties.

Methods represent the object's built-in procedures. For example, a class named **Animal** may have methods named **Sleeping** and **Eating**. You define methods by adding procedures, either **Sub** routines or functions, to your class; for example, here's how I might implement the **Sleeping** and **Eating** methods:

```
Public Class Animal
    Public Sub Eating()
        MsgBox("Eating...")
    End Sub

    Public Sub Sleeping()
        MsgBox("Sleeping...")
    End Sub
End Class
```

Now I can create a new object of the **Animal** class and call the **Eating** method in the familiar way:

```
Dim pet As New Animal()
pet.Eating()
```

And, as we all know, *events* allow objects to perform actions whenever a specific occurrence takes place. For example, when you click a button, a **Click** event occurs, and you can handle that event in an event handler, as you've already done so many times. As an example, I'll create a custom event, **ThreeClick**, in the next chapter, which will be triggered when you click a button three times. You'll be able to set up an event handler for that event that looks like this:

```
Private Sub tracker_ThreeClick(ByVal Message As String) _
    Handles tracker.ThreeClick
    TextBox1.Text = Message
End Sub
```

Class vs. Object Members

Here's another important distinction to understand when dealing with members in OOP: class members versus object members. Members that apply to a class and are invoked with the class name are called *shared*, *static*, or *class* members; the members that apply to objects created from the class are called *instance* or *object* members. For example, if **TextBox1** is an object, its **Text** property is an instance or object member because you use it with the object's name: **TextBox1.Text = "Hello from Visual Basic"**.

On the other hand, you can make members shared or class members, which you use with the class name, if you use the **Shared** keyword. Using this keyword makes a member into a class member, which you can use with just the class name—no object needed. (It also makes all objects share that member, as you'll see in this chapter.) Here's an example; in this case, I'll add a class method named **Add** to a class named **Mathematics**—this method takes just two integers and adds them, returning their sum:

```
Public Class Mathematics
    Shared Function Add(ByVal x As Integer, _
        ByVal y As Integer) As Integer
        Return x + y
    End Function
End Class
```

Now I can use this new class method using the name of the class, **Mathematics**, without needing an object of that class:

```
Private Sub Button1_Click(ByVal sender As System.Object, _
    ByVal e As System.EventArgs) Handles Button1.Click
    TextBox3.Text = Mathematics.Add(TextBox1.Text, _
        TextBox2.Text)
End Sub
```

As you'll see in this chapter, using the **Shared** keyword also means that the shared method or data member is shared across all instances of its class. For example, if a class has a shared data member named **Count**, every object of that class uses the same memory location for **Count**.

Abstraction, Encapsulation, Inheritance, and Polymorphism

Fields, properties, methods, and events are only one part of OOP. Generally, a language such as Visual Basic is object oriented if it supports the following:

- *Abstraction*—The ability to create an abstract representation of a concept in code (as an object named **employee** is an abstraction of a real employee).

- *Encapsulation*—The separation between implementation and interface. In other words, when you encapsulate an object, you make its code and data *internal* and no longer accessible to the outside except through a well-defined interface. This is also called *data hiding*.

- *Polymorphism*—Creating procedures that can operate on objects of different types. For example, if both **person** and **employee** objects have a **last_name** property, a polymorphic procedure can use both objects' **last_name** property. Visual Basic handles polymorphism with both late binding and multiple interfaces, both of which I'll cover later in this book.

- *Inheritance*—The ability to derive new classes from other classes. The idea here is that if you were to create, for example, a class for a specific Visual Basic form and then derive a new type of form from that class, the derived class would *inherit* all the class functionality of the base, even before you start adding code or customizing the new form.

In fact, inheritance is such an important topic that the next chapter is dedicated to it. Using inheritance, you can derive a new class, the *derived class*, from a *base class*. The derived class inherits all the members of the base class, unless you specifically *override* them. What does that mean? Take a look at the next section.

Overloading, Overriding, and Shadowing

Overloading, overriding, and shadowing are important concepts in Visual Basic OOP. All three of these techniques allow you to create multiple members with the same name. Here's how they work, in overview:

- *Overloaded*—Members provide different versions of a property or method that have the same name but that accept a different number of parameters (or parameters of different types).

- *Overridden*—Properties and methods replace an inherited property or method. When you override a member from a base class, you replace it. Overridden members must accept the same data type and number of arguments.

- *Shadowed*—Members create a local version of a member that has broader scope. You can also shadow a type with any other type. For example, you can declare a property that shadows an inherited method with the same name.

Structures and Modules

Classes are so popular in OOP that other programming constructs—in particular, structures and modules—are now based on them. Structures were originally a halfway solution between variables and true objects that allowed you to create your own data types, much like adding fields to a class. As with classes, however, structures can now support methods. Modules in Visual Basic are designed primarily to hold code, but now they can also support members, just like classes.

Although structures support many of the same features as classes, including the ability to support fields, methods, events, and properties, it's important to realize that the following features of classes are not supported by structures:

- Structures cannot explicitly inherit from any other type.

- Structures cannot inherit from other structures.

- You cannot define a nonshared constructor that doesn't take any arguments for a structure. You can, however, define a nonshared constructor that does take arguments. The reason for this is that every structure has a built-in public constructor without arguments that initializes all the structure's data members to their default values. That means that **Dim employee As EmployeeStruct** is the same as **Dim employee As EmployeeStruct = New EmployeeStruct( )**.

- You cannot override the **Finalize** method in a structure.

- The declarations of data members in a structure cannot include initializers or the **New** keyword, or set initial sizes for arrays.

- If you declare data members with **Dim**, their default access in structures is public, not private, as in classes and modules.

- Structure members cannot be declared as **Protected**.

- Structures are *value types* rather than *reference types*. This means, for example, that assigning a structure instance to another structure, or passing a structure instance to a **ByVal** argument, causes the entire structure to be copied.

TIP: You have to perform equality testing with structures, testing member by member for equality.

In addition, modules are a reference type similar to classes, but with some important distinctions:

- The members of a module are implicitly shared.

- Modules can never be instantiatcd.

- Modules do not support inheritance.

- Modules cannot implement interfaces.

- A module can be declared only inside a namespace.

- Modules cannot be nested in other types.

- You can have multiple modules in a project, but note that members with the same name in two or more modules must be qualified with the name of their module when used outside that module.

Now it's time to start digging into the specific details in the Immediate Solutions.

Immediate Solutions

Creating Classes

So how do you actually create a class? You use the **Class** statement:

```
[ <attrlist> ] [ Public | Private | Protected |
  Friend | Protected Friend ]
[ Shadows ] [ MustInherit | NotInheritable ] Class name
  [ Implements interfacename ]
    [ statements ]
End Class
```

Here are the various parts of this statement:

- *attrlist*—Optional. This is the list of attributes for this class. You separate multiple attributes with commas.

- **Public**—Optional. Classes declared **Public** have public access; no restrictions are placed on the use of public classes.

- **Private**—Optional. Classes declared **Private** have private access, so the class is accessible only within its declaration context.

- **Protected**—Optional. Classes declared **Protected** have protected access, which means that they are accessible only from within their own class or from a derived class.

- **Friend**—Optional. Classes declared **Friend** have friend access, which means that they are accessible only within the program that contains their declaration.

- **Protected Friend**—Optional. Classes declared **Protected Friend** have both protected and friend accessibility.

- **Shadows**—Optional. Indicates that this class shadows a programming element in a base class.

- **MustInherit**—Optional. Indicates that the class contains methods that must be implemented by a deriving class.

- **NotInheritable**—Optional. Indicates that the class is a class from which no further inheritance is allowed.

- *name*—Required. The name of the class.

- *interfacename*—Optional. The name of the interface implemented by this class.

- *statements*—Optional. The statements that make up the variables, properties, events, and methods of the class.

Each attribute in the ***attrlist*** part has the following syntax:

```
<attrname [({ attrargs | attrinit })]> Attrlist
```

Here are the parts of the ***attrlist*** part:

- ***attrname***—Required. The name of the attribute.

- ***attrargs***—Optional. The list of arguments for this attribute. You separate multiple arguments with commas.

- ***attrinit***—Optional. The list of field or property initializers. You separate multiple initializers with commas.

You place the members of the class inside the class itself. You can also nest class declarations. You've already seen a number of examples; here's how to set up a class named **DataClass**:

```
Public Class DataClass
    Private value As Integer

    Public Sub New(ByVal newValue As Integer)
        value = newValue
    End Sub

    Public Function GetData() As Integer
        Return value
    End Function
End Class
```

Creating Objects

You can create objects of a class using the **Dim** statement; this statement is used at the module, class, structure, procedure, or block level:

```
[ <attrlist> ] [{ Public | Protected
| Friend | Protected Friend |
Private | Static }] [ Shared ]
[ Shadows ] [ ReadOnly ] Dim
[ WithEvents ] name[ (boundlist) ]
[ As [ New ] type ] [ = initexpr ]
```

Here are the parts of this statement:

- ***attrlist***—A list of attributes that apply to the variables you're declaring in this statement. You separate multiple attributes with commas.

- **Public**—Gives variables public access, which means that no restrictions are placed on their accessibility. You can use **Public** only at the module, namespace, or file level (which means that you can't use it inside a procedure). Note that if you specify **Public**, you can omit the **Dim** keyword if you want to.

- **Protected**—Gives variables protected access, which means that they are accessible only from within their own class or from a class derived from that class. You can use **Protected** only at the class level (which means that you can't use it inside a procedure) because you use it to declare members of a class. Note that if you specify **Protected**, you can omit the **Dim** keyword if you want to.

- **Friend**—Gives variables friend access, which means that they are accessible from within the program that contains their declaration as well as from anywhere else in the same assembly. You can use **Friend** only at the module, namespace, or file level (which means that you can't use it inside a procedure). Note that if you specify **Friend**, you can omit the **Dim** keyword if you want to.

- **Protected Friend**—Gives variables both protected and friend access, which means that they can be used by code in the same assembly as well as by code in derived classes.

- **Private**—Gives variables private access, which means that they are accessible only from within their declaration context (usually a class), including any nested procedures. You can use **Private** only at the module, namespace, or file level (which means that you can't use it inside a procedure). Note that if you specify **Private**, you can omit the **Dim** keyword if you want to.

- **Static**—Makes variables static, which means that they'll retain their values, even after the procedure in which they're declared ends. You can declare static variables inside a procedure or a block within a procedure but not at the class or module level. Note that if you specify **Static**, you can omit the **Dim** keyword if you want to, but you cannot use either **Shadows** or **Shared**.

- **Shared**—Declares a shared variable, which means that it is not associated with a specific instance of a class or structure but can be shared across many instances. You access a shared variable by referring to it either with its class or structure name or with the variable name of an instance of the class or structure. You can use **Shared** only at the module, namespace, or file level (but not at the procedure level). Note that if you specify **Shared**, you can omit the **Dim** keyword if you want to.

- **Shadows**—Makes this variable a shadow of an identically named programming element in a base class. A shadowed element is unavailable in the derived class that shadows it. You can use **Shadows** only at the module, namespace, or file level (but not inside a procedure). This means that you can declare shadowing variables in a source file or inside a module, class, or structure but not inside a procedure. Note that if you specify **Shadows**, you can omit the **Dim** keyword if you want to.

- **ReadOnly**—Means that this variable can only be read and not written. This can be useful for creating constant members of reference types, such as an object variable with preset data members. You can use **ReadOnly** only at the module, namespace, or file level (but not inside procedures). Note that if you specify **Shadows**, you can omit the **ReadOnly** keyword if you want to.

- **WithEvents**—Specifies that this variable is used to respond to events caused by the instance that was assigned to the variable. Note that you cannot specify both **WithEvents** and **New** in the same variable declaration.

- *name*—The name of the variable. You separate multiple variables with commas. If you specify multiple variables, each variable is declared of the data type given in the first **As** clause encountered after its *name* part.

- *boundlist*—Used to declare arrays; gives the upper bounds of the dimensions of an array variable. Multiple upper bounds are separated with commas. An array can have up to 60 dimensions.

- **New**—Means that you want to create a new object immediately. If you use **New** when declaring an object variable, a new instance of the object is created. Note that you cannot use both **WithEvents** and **New** in the same declaration.

- *type*—The data type of the variable. Can be **Boolean**, **Byte**, **Char**, **Date**, **Decimal**, **Double**, **Integer**, **Long**, **Object**, **Short**, **Single**, or **String** or the name of an enumeration, structure, class, or interface. To specify the type, you use a separate **As** clause for each variable, or you can declare a number of variables of the same type by using common **As** clauses. If you do not specify *type*, the variable takes the data type of *initexpr*. Note that if you don't specify either *type* or *initexpr*, the data type is set to **Object**.

- *initexpr*—An initialization expression that is evaluated and the result assigned to the variable when it is created. Note that if you declare more than one variable with the same **As** clause, you cannot supply *initexpr* for those variables.

Each attribute in the *attrlist* list must use this syntax:

```
<attrname [({ attrargs | attrinit })]>
```

Here are the parts of the *attrlist* list:

- *attrname*—The name of the attribute.
- *attrargs*—The list of arguments for this attribute. You separate multiple arguments with commas.
- *attrinit*—The list of field or property initializers for this attribute. You separate multiple arguments with commas.

When you create a new object from a class, you use the **New** keyword. You can do that in either of these ways:

```
Dim employee As New EmployeeClass()
Dim employee As EmployeeClass = New EmployeeClass()
```

If you omit the **New** keyword, you're just declaring a new object, and it's not yet created:

```
Dim employee As EmployeeClass
```

Before using the object, you must explicitly create it with **New**:

```
employee = New EmployeeClass()
```

As discussed in the In Brief section of this chapter, classes often use constructors that let you configure objects with data. You write constructors by giving a method the name **New**, and you'll see more on constructors in the next chapter.

Creating Structures

Traditionally, structures were used to let you create your own complex data types. For example, if you wanted to store both an employee's ID value (an integer) and an employee's name (a string) in one variable, you could create a new structure named, say, **Employee**, like this:

```
Public Structure Employee
    Public Name As String
    Public ID As Integer
End Structure
```

This creates a new data type. Now you can declare a variable of this new type and access the data fields in it, like this:

```
Dim employee As Employee
employee.Name = "Cary Grant"
employee.ID = 101
```

Now, however, structures are much like classes and can support events, methods, and properties as well as fields. To create a structure, you use the **Structure** statement at the module or the class level:

```
[ <attrlist> ] [{ Public | Protected | Friend |
Protected Friend | Private }] Structure name
    [ variabledeclarations ]
    [ proceduredeclarations ]
End Structure
```

You can see the parts of this statement in the section "Creating Objects" earlier in this chapter, with these additions:

- *name*—Required. The name of the structure.

- *variabledeclarations*—Optional. One or more **Dim**, **Friend**, **Private**, or **Public** statements declaring variables that are the data members of the structure. Note that these declarations follow the same rules as they do outside a structure.

- *proceduredeclarations*—Optional. One or more declarations of **Function**, **Property**, or **Sub** procedures that are the method members of the structure. Note that these declarations follow the same rules as they do outside a structure.

Each attribute in the *attrlist* part has the following syntax:

```
<attrname [({ attrargs | attrinit })]> Attrlist
```

Here are the parts of *attrlist*:

- *attrname*—Required. The name of the attribute.

- *attrargs*—Optional. The list of positional arguments for this attribute. You separate multiple arguments with commas.

- *attrinit*—Optional. The list of field or property initializers for this attribute. You separate multiple initializers with commas.

Note that you must declare every data member of a structure. This means that every statement in the *variabledeclarations* part must contain **Dim**, **Friend**, **Private**, or **Public**. If **Option Strict** is **On**, you must also include the **As** clause in every statement. Members declared with **Dim** default to public access, and members declared without the **As** clause default to the **Object** data type.

TIP: *You cannot initialize the value of any data member of a structure as part of its declaration. You must either initialize a data member by means of a parameterized constructor on the structure or assign a value to the member after you've created an instance of the structure.*

You can assign one structure variable to another of the same type, and all the members will be copied as well. However, to compare structures at this time in Visual Basic, you must compare each member individually, although that may change in the future.

As mentioned, structures support many of the same features as classes. However, as discussed in the In Brief section of this chapter, a number of features of classes are not supported in structures—see the In Brief section for more information.

Chapter 11

Object-Oriented Programming: Constructors, Methods, Properties, and Events

If you need an immediate solution to:	See page:
Creating Constructors	219
Using **Is** to Compare Objects	220
Creating Data Members	221
Creating Class (Shared) Data Members	221
Creating Methods	223
Creating Class (Shared) Methods	224
Creating Properties	226
Creating Class (Shared) Properties	227
Creating Events	228
Creating Class (Shared) Events	231
Overloading Methods and Properties	231
Getting Rid of Objects When You're Done with Them	233
Triggering Garbage Collection	234
Creating Class Libraries	234
Creating Namespaces	236
Using the **Finalize** Method (Creating Destructors)	237

In Brief

In this chapter, we're going to continue with object-oriented programming (OOP), taking a look at creating constructors, destructors, methods, properties, and more. As you know, you create objects with the **New** keyword, as you've seen, like this:

```
Dim data As New DataClass()
```

When you create an object, you might want to customize that object with data. For example, when you create an object of a class named **Employee**, you might want to store the employee's name, phone number, ID number, and so on in that object. To do that, you can use *constructors*, which I first discussed in Chapter 3. You pass data to a constructor by enclosing it in parentheses following the class name when you're creating an object. The parentheses in the previous code are empty because I was not passing anything to a constructor there. (Technically, each class comes with a default constructor built in that takes no arguments.) However, you might want to store a value, such the integer 5, in an object of a class named **DataClass**, like this:

```
Dim data As New DataClass(5)
```

How do you create a constructor? You add a **Sub** procedure named **New** to a class—that's all it takes. For example, here's how that might look for the **DataClass** class; in this case, I'm storing the value passed to **New** in a private data member named **value** and adding a method named **GetData** to return that stored value as needed:

```
Public Class DataClass
    Private value As Integer

    Public Sub New(ByVal newValue As Integer)
        value = newValue
    End Sub

    Public Function GetData() As Integer
        Return value
    End Function
End Class
```

Now I can store the value 5 inside an object of the **DataClass** class simply by passing 5 to the constructor, and I can retrieve that value with the **GetData** method:

```
Dim data As New DataClass(5)
MsgBox(data.GetData())
```

The life cycle of objects ends when they leave scope or are set to **Nothing** and are released by the .NET framework. Visual Basic controls the release of system resources using procedures called *destructors*. In Visual Basic, objects have constructors far more often than they have destructors because you typically use destructors only to clean up after an object (deallocating resources, for example, or informing other objects that the current object will no longer be available). The **Finalize** destructor is the one you normally use; **Finalize** is called automatically by the system when an object is destroyed (which means that you should not explicitly call **Finalize** yourself). The .NET framework automatically runs the **Finalize** destructor and destroys objects when the system determines that such objects are no longer needed.

---

*TIP: The **Sub New** and **Sub Finalize** procedures in Visual Basic .NET replace the **Class_Initialize** and **Class_Terminate** methods used in earlier versions of Visual Basic to initialize and destroy objects.*

Unlike the **Class_Terminate** procedure of VB6 and earlier, you're not supposed to be able to determine exactly when the .NET framework will execute the **Finalize** method. You can be sure only that the system will call **Sub Finalize** some time after the last reference to an object is released. The delay between when an object leaves scope and when it is actually destroyed occurs because the .NET framework uses a system called *reference-tracing garbage collection*, which releases unused resources every now and then. Garbage collection is automatic, and it ensures that unused resources (usually memory) are always released without any extra work on your part.

To get rid of an object, then, you assign it the value **Nothing**. The next time garbage is collected, the object will be removed from memory.

TIP: In the Visual Basic documentation, you'll read a great deal about how you can't trigger garbage collection yourself, but the fact is that you can. See the section "Triggering Garbage Collection" in the Immediate Solutions in this chapter.

An OOP Example

Examples always help. Here's an example, which I'll name ComboBoxesData, that stores objects in a combo box, and each object holds its name and index in the combo box. When the user selects an item in the combo box, the code recovers the data from the object corresponding to the selected item and displays that data.

To make this work, I create a class named

DataItem, which uses a **New** constructor to store each item's name and index value as internal, private data:

```
Public Class DataItem
    Private Data As Single
    Private Name As String

    Public Sub New(ByVal NameArgument As String, _
        ByVal Value As Single)
        Name = NameArgument
        Data = Value
    End Sub
        .
        .
        .
End Class
```

In addition, I'll add two methods to this class—**ToString**, which returns the name of the item (and which actually overrides the **ToString** method built into the **Object** class, which is the ultimate base class of every class), and **GetData**, which returns the index value of the item:

```
Public Class DataItem
    Private Data As Single
    Private Name As String

    Public Sub New(ByVal NameArgument As String, _
        ByVal Value As Single)
        Name = NameArgument
        Data = Value
    End Sub

    Overrides Function ToString() As String
        Return CStr(Name)
    End Function
```

```
    Public Function GetData() As Single
        Return Data
    End Function
End Class
```

Now I can create 20 objects of this class and place them into a combo box with the combo box's **AddRange** method this way when the program's form first loads:

```
Public Class Form1
    Inherits System.Windows.Forms.Form

    'Windows Form Designer generated code

    Private Sub Form1_Load(ByVal sender As System.Object, _
        ByVal e As System.EventArgs) Handles MyBase.Load
        Dim Objects(20) As DataItem
        ComboBox1.BeginUpdate()
        Dim intLoopIndex As Integer
        For intLoopIndex = 0 To 20
            Objects(intLoopIndex) = _
                New DataItem("Item " & intLoopIndex, _
                CSng(intLoopIndex))
        Next
        ComboBox1.Items.AddRange(Objects)
        ComboBox1.EndUpdate()
    End Sub
End Sub
```

Then, when the user changes the selection in the combo box, I can recover the selected item with the combo box's **SelectedItem** property and use the **GetData** method I have given that item to recover the item's internal data:

```
Public Class Form1
    Inherits System.Windows.Forms.Form

    'Windows Form Designer generated code

    Private Sub Form1_Load(ByVal sender As System.Object, _
        ByVal e As System.EventArgs) Handles MyBase.Load
        Dim Objects(20) As DataItem
        ComboBox1.BeginUpdate()
        Dim intLoopIndex As Integer
        For intLoopIndex = 0 To 20
            Objects(intLoopIndex) = _
                New DataItem("Item " & intLoopIndex, _
```

```
                    CSng(intLoopIndex))
            Next
            ComboBox1.Items.AddRange(Objects)
            ComboBox1.EndUpdate()
        End Sub

        Private Sub ComboBox1_SelectedIndexChanged(ByVal sender As _
            System.Object, ByVal e As System.EventArgs) Handles _
            ComboBox1.SelectedIndexChanged
            MsgBox("The data for the item you selected is: " & _
                CType(ComboBox1.SelectedItem, DataItem).GetData())
        End Sub
    End Class
```

Now you can understand all that's going on in this code. You can see this example, ComboBoxData, at work in Figure 11.1.

Now it's time to start looking into some of the more detailed aspects of what I've been discussing, and I'll do that in the Immediate Solutions section of this chapter.

Figure 11.1   The ComboBoxData example.

Immediate Solutions

Creating Constructors

As discussed in the In Brief section of this chapter, as well as in Chapter 3, constructors are special methods that let you configure the objects you create from a class. You've already dealt with constructors throughout this book, as in this code, where I'm passing data to the constructors for the **Size** and **Point** classes:

```
Private Sub Button1_Click(ByVal sender As System.Object, _
    ByVal e As System.EventArgs) Handles Button1.Click
    Dim TextBox1 As New TextBox()
    TextBox1.Size = New Size(150, 20)
    TextBox1.Location = New Point(80, 20)
    TextBox1.Text = "Hello from Visual Basic"
    Me.Controls.Add(TextBox1)
End Sub
```

So how do you create a constructor? You add a **Sub** procedure named **New** to a class—that's all it takes. For example, here's how that might look for a class named **DataClass**; in this case, I'm storing the value passed to **New** in a private data member named **value**:

```
Public Class DataClass
    Private value As Integer

    Public Sub New(ByVal newValue As Integer)
        value = newValue
    End Sub

    Public Function GetData() As Integer
        Return value
    End Function
End Class
```

Now I can store the value 5 inside an object of the **DataClass** class simply by passing 5 to the constructor:

```
Dim data As New DataClass(5)
MsgBox(data.GetData())
```

Note that all classes have a default constructor that doesn't take any
arguments; this constructor exists so that you can create objects without providing an explicit **New Sub** procedure and doesn't do anything special. (However, if you derive a new class from a base class
and add a constructor to the derived class, Visual Basic will complain
if you don't call the base class's constructor from the derived class's
constructor and if an explicit base class constructor that takes no
arguments is not present.)

TIP: More on constructors is coming up in the next chapter, when we start deriving classes
from base classes.

Using **Is** to Compare Objects

Here's something that's important to know: If you want to know
whether two objects are really the same object, you should use the **Is**
keyword instead of the standard comparison operators. If the two
objects you're checking are the same object, **Is** returns **True**. Here's
an example, where I'm checking which button of several has been
clicked; the clicked button is passed in the **sender** argument:

```
Private Sub Button_Click(ByVal sender As System.Object, _
    ByVal e As System.EventArgs)
    If sender Is Button1 Then
        TextBox1.Text = "You clicked button 1"
    End If
    If sender Is Button2 Then
        TextBox1.Text = "You clicked button 2"
    End If
    If sender Is Button3 Then
        TextBox1.Text = "You clicked button 3"
    End If
End Sub
```

Creating Data Members

As discussed in the In Brief section of the previous chapter, the fields of a class, also called the class's data members, are much like built-in variables. For example, in the In Brief section of this chapter, I declared a field named **value** in a class named **DataClass**:

```
Public Class DataClass
    Public value As Integer
End Class
```

Now I can refer to that field in an object of this class using the familiar *object.field* syntax of Visual Basic:

```
Dim data As New DataClass()
data.value = 5
```

You can also make fields hold constant values with **Const**:

```
Public Class Class1
    Public Const Field1 As Integer = 0
    .
    .
    .
End Class
```

These data members are object data members—you use them with a specific object. However, you can also create class data members; see the next section for the details.

Related solution:	Found on page:
Declaring Variables	62

Creating Class (Shared) Data Members

You can use the **Shared** keyword to create class data members. You can use a class data member with the name of the class alone, no object needed. For example, say that you have a class named **Mathematics** and declare a shared variable named **Pi**:

```
Public Class Mathematics
    Public Shared Pi As Double = 3.1415926535
End Class
```

Now you can use **Pi** as a class variable with the **Mathematics** class directly, no object needed:

```
integer5 = Mathematics.Pi
```

Pi is more naturally handled as a constant; you can use **Const** instead of **Shared** to create a shared constant that works the same way (except that you can't assign values to it because it's a constant):

```
Public Class Mathematics
    Public Const Pi As Double = 3.1415926535
End Class
```

Variables that you declare with the **Shared** keyword are called shared because they're shared over all instances of the class. For example, take a look at this example I'll name Shared—in this case, I'm adding a shared data member named **Data** to the **Mathematics** class, and each instance of this class will now see the same value stored in **Data**. To show this, I'll add a method named **Increment** to the **Mathematics** class, which increments the value in **Data** by 1 and returns the new value:

```
Public Class Mathematics
    Shared Data As Integer = 0

    Public Function Increment() As Integer
        Data += 1
        Return Data
    End Function
End Class
```

Next, I create two different objects of the **Mathematics** class, **Object1** and **Object2**. Both of these objects will share the same internal **Data** member, which you can see by clicking the buttons in this program—one button uses the **Increment** method of **Object1**, and the other button uses the **Increment** method of **Object2**. No matter how much you alternate between the buttons, you'll see that the value in **Data** (which appears in a text box) increments steadily because both objects are working on the same value. Here's what the code looks like:

```
Dim Object1, Object2 As New Mathematics()

Private Sub Button2_Click(ByVal sender As System.Object, _
    ByVal e As System.EventArgs) Handles Button2.Click
    TextBox4.Text = "Count = " & Object1.Increment
End Sub

Private Sub Button3_Click(ByVal sender As System.Object, _
    ByVal e As System.EventArgs) Handles Button3.Click
    TextBox4.Text = "Count = " & Object2.Increment
End Sub
```

You can see this program at work in Figure 11.2—the two buttons that use **Object1** and **Object2** are at the bottom, and the text box that reports the new value stored in the **Data** member is beneath them. No matter which button you click, the displayed value increments steadily, demonstrating that, indeed, both objects are sharing the same value in **Data**.

Related solution:	Found on page:
Declaring Variables	62

Creating Methods

As discussed in the In Brief section of this chapter, methods represent the object's built-in procedures. For example, a class named **Animal** may have methods named **Sleeping** and **Eating**. You define methods by adding procedures, either **Sub** procedures or functions, to your class; for example, here's how I might implement the **Sleeping** and **Eating** methods:

```
Public Class Animal
    Public Sub Eating()
        MsgBox("Eating...")
    End Sub

    Public Sub Sleeping()
        MsgBox("Sleeping...")
    End Sub
End Class
```

Now I can create a new object of the **Animal** class and call the **Eating** method in the familiar way:

```
Dim pet As New Animal()
pet.Eating()
```

In general, you can add whatever functions or **Sub** procedures you want to your class, including those that accept parameters and those that return values, as you saw earlier in this chapter:

```
Public Class DataClass
    Private value As Integer

        Public Sub New(ByVal newValue As Integer)
            value = newValue
        End Sub

        Public Function GetData() As Integer
            Return value
        End Function
End Class
```

Note that these methods are object methods—you use them with an object. However, you can also create class methods. See the next section for the details.

Related solutions:	Found on page:
Creating **Sub** Procedures	108
Creating Functions	111

Creating Class (Shared) Methods

When you create a class method, you can use it with the class alone, no object needed. For example, in the Shared example, I added a function named **Add** to the **Mathematics** class and made it a class method by using the **Shared** keyword. Now I can use the **Add** method like this: **Mathematics.Add**, that is, with the name of the class alone. Here's how I add two integers in text boxes in the Shared example when the user clicks on the button with the equals sign (=) caption you see in Figure 11.2:

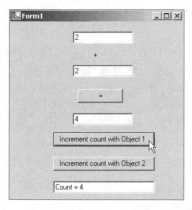

Figure 11.2   Using a shared data member.

```
Private Sub Button1_Click(ByVal sender As System.Object, _
    ByVal e As System.EventArgs) Handles Button1.Click
    TextBox3.Text = _
        Mathematics.Add(TextBox1.Text, TextBox2.Text)
End Sub

Public Class Mathematics
    Shared Function Add(ByVal x As Integer, ByVal y As Integer)
_
        As Integer
        Return x + y
    End Function
End Class
```

You can see the results in Figure 11.2, where the numbers in the two text boxes are added and the sum is displayed when the user clicks the = button. Note that you can only use shared data in a shared method or the values that are passed to you, as I've done here, unless you provide a specific object to work with.

Creating Properties

As discussed in the In Brief section of this chapter, you often don't
want to give code outside an object direct access to the data in the
object. Instead, you can use properties, which use methods to set or
get an internal value. You saw how to do that in Chapter 5; here's an
example from that chapter where I'm adding a property to a module:

```
Module Module2
    Private PropertyValue As String
    Public Property Prop1() As String
        Get
            Return PropertyValue
        End Get
        Set(ByVal Value As String)
            PropertyValue = Value
        End Set
    End Property
End Module
```

See the section "Creating Properties" in Chapter 5 for all the details,
including how to create indexed properties. Note that you can make
properties write-only with the **WriteOnly** keyword (and you must
omit the **Get** method):

```
Module Module2
    Private PropertyValue As String
    Public WriteOnly Property Prop1() As String
        Set(ByVal Value As String)
            PropertyValue = Value
        End Set
    End Property
End Module
```

You can make properties read-only with the
ReadOnly keyword (and you must omit the **Set** method):

```
Module Module2
    Private PropertyValue As String
    Public
ReadOnly Property Prop1() As String
        Get
            Return PropertyValue
        End Get
    End Property
End Module
```

Related solution:	*Found on page:*
Creating Properties	116

Creating Class (Shared) Properties

You can make properties shared with the **Shared** keyword, which means that you can use them with the class name and don't need a specific object to work with. However, in a shared property, you can work only with shared data or data passed to you, or you must provide a specific object to work with. Here's an example where I'm creating and working with a shared property:

```
Public Class Mathematics
    Shared Data As Integer = 0
    Shared Property Property1()
        Get
            Return Data
        End Get
        Set(ByVal Value)
            Data = Value
        End Set
    End Property
End Class

Private Sub Button1_Click(ByVal sender As System.Object, _
ByVal e As System.EventArgs) Handles Button1.Click
    Mathematics.Property1 = 5
End Sub

Private Sub Button2_Click(ByVal sender As System.Object, _
ByVal e As System.EventArgs) Handles Button2.Click
    TextBox1.Text = Mathematics.Property1
End Sub
```

Related solution:	*Found on page:*
Creating Properties	116

Creating Events

You can design and support your own events using OOP in Visual Basic by using the **Event** statement:

```
[ <attrlist> ] [ Public | Private | Protected | Friend |
Protected Friend] [ Shadows ] Event eventname[(arglist)]
[ Implements interfacename.interfaceeventname ]
```

Here are the parts of this statement:

- *attrlist*—Optional. The list of attributes that apply to this event. You separate multiple attributes with commas.

- **Public**—Optional. Events declared **Public** have public access, which means that no restrictions are placed on their use.

- **Private**—Optional. Events declared **Private** have private access, which means that they are accessible only within their declaration context.

- **Protected**—Optional. Events declared **Protected** have protected access, which means that they are accessible only from within their own class or from a derived class.

- **Friend**—Optional. Events declared **Friend** have friend access, which means that they are accessible only within the program that contains the its declaration.

- **Protected Friend**—Optional. Events declared **Protected Friend** have both protected and friend accessibility.

- **Shadows**—Optional. Indicates that this event shadows an identically named programming element in a base class.

- *eventname*—Required. The name of the event.

- *interfacename*—The name of an interface.

- *interfaceeventname*—The name of the event being implemented.

Each attribute in the

attrlist part has the following syntax:

```
<attrname [({ attrargs | attrinit })]> Attrlist
```

Here are the parts of *attrlist*:

- *attrname*—Required. The name of the attribute.

- *attrargs*—Optional. The list of arguments for this attribute. You separate multiple arguments with commas.

- *attrinit*—Optional. The list of field or property initializers for this attribute. You separate multiple initializers with commas.

The *arglist* argument has the following syntax:

```
[ <attrlist> ] [ ByVal | ByRef ] varname[ ( ) ]
[ As type ] Arglist
```

Here are the parts of *arglist*:

- *attrlist*—Optional. The list of attributes for this argument. You separate multiple attributes with commas.

- **ByVal**—Optional. Specifies that the argument is passed by value. (**ByVal** is the default.)

- **ByRef**—Optional. Specifies that the argument is passed by reference.

- *varname*—Required. The name of the variable representing the argument being passed to the procedure.

- *type*—Optional. The data type of the argument passed to the procedure; may be **Byte**, **Boolean**, **Char**, **Short**, **Integer**, **Long**, **Single**, **Double**, **Decimal**, **Date**, **String** (variable length only), **Object**, a user-defined type, or an object type.

Let's see an example; I'll call this one Events. In this case, I'll create a custom event called **ThreeClick** that occurs when you click a button three times. To keep track of how many times the button has been clicked, I'll use an object called **tracker**, of a class I'll call **ClickTrack**:

```
Public Class ClickTrack
    .
    .
    .
End Class
```

To implement the **ThreeClick** event, I use the **Event** statement, indicating that the event handler for this event should be passed one argument, a string holding a message (which will indicate that the event occurred):

```
Public Class ClickTrack
    Public Event ThreeClick(ByVal Message As String)
    .
    .
    .
End Class
```

How can you make this event actually occur? You just use the **RaiseEvent** method. In this case, you must pass **RaiseEvent** a message you want to associate with this event (if you had given **ThreeClick** two arguments, you'd have to pass **RaiseEvent** two arguments, and so on). You can keep track of the number of button clicks with a **Sub** procedure named **Click** and raise the **ThreeClick** event when three clicks have occurred, passing that event's handler the string "You clicked three times":

```
Public Class ClickTrack
    Public Event ThreeClick(ByVal Message As String)
    Public Sub Click()
        Static ClickCount As Integer = 0
        ClickCount += 1
        If ClickCount >= 3 Then
            ClickCount = 0
            RaiseEvent ThreeClick("You clicked three times")
        End If
    End Sub
End Class
```

That's how you make a custom event occur—with **RaiseEvent**. I'll need an object of this new **ClickTrack** class, and I'll call that object **tracker**. Note that I declare it using the**WithEvents** keyword to indicate that this new object can handle events:

```
Dim WithEvents tracker As New ClickTrack()
```

Now that I've created a new event, I can also write an event handler for it—I just need to make sure that I accept the right number of arguments and use a **Handles** clause to indicate what event I'm handling (which is **tracker.ThreeClick** in this case). When the event occurs, I'll display the message I've associated with the event in a text box:

```
Private Sub tracker_ThreeClick(ByVal _
    Message As String) Handles _
    tracker.ThreeClick
    TextBox1.Text = Message
End Sub
```

All that's left is to keep calling the **tracker** object's **Click** method until the **ThreeClick** event occurs, and I can do that with a button this way:

```
Private Sub Button1_Click(ByVal sender As System.Object, _
    ByVal e As System.EventArgs) Handles Button1.Click
    tracker.Click()
End Sub
```

You can see the result in Figure 11.3. Now you're creating and handling custom events.

Creating Class (Shared) Events

Events (see the previous section to see how to create custom events) can also be declared as **Shared**:

```
Public Shared Event ThreeClick(ByVal Message As String)
```

That's good to know because, for example, shared methods can raise only shared events.

Overloading Methods and Properties

In OOP, methods and properties can be *overloaded*, which means that you can define a method or property multiple times with different argument lists. For example, say that you had a method named **Draw** that can draw rectangles and triangles. For rectangles, you might need only four arguments in your argument list—the x and y coordinates of the upper-left and lower-right corners of the rectangle. However, for triangles, you might need six arguments, corresponding to the x and y coordinates of the three vertices of the triangle. To handle this,

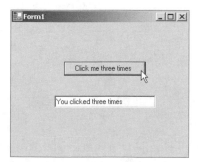

Figure 11.3   Using custom events.

you can overload **Draw** to handle four or six arguments just by defining the method twice with two different argument lists. (Note that to be different, an argument list need not have a different *number* of arguments—arguments are considered different if they're of different data types, too.)

TIP: *Don't confuse overloading with overriding; overriding is something that happens with inheritance, where a base class member is replaced by a different member in the derived class. You'll see more about overriding in Chapter 12.*

Here's an example I'll call Overloading. In this case, I'll create a class named **Notifier** with a method named **Display**, which will display a message box. **Display** will have two versions—you pass the text to display in the message box to the first version and the text and a message box icon to the second. Here, then, is all you do to overload a method—just define it a number of times with different argument lists. Note that I'm adding two buttons to call the two versions of **Display**:

```
Dim notifierObject As New Notifier()

Private Sub Button1_Click(ByVal sender As System.Object, _
    ByVal e As System.EventArgs) Handles Button1.Click
    notifierObject.Display("Hello from Visual Basic!")
End Sub

Private Sub Button2_Click(ByVal sender As System.Object, _
    ByVal e As System.EventArgs) Handles Button2.Click
    notifierObject.Display("Hello from Visual Basic!", _
        MsgBoxStyle.Exclamation)
End Sub

Public Class Notifier
    Public Sub Display(ByVal Message As String)
        MsgBox(Message)
    End Sub

    Public Sub Display(ByVal Message As String, ByVal Icon _
        As MsgBoxStyle)
        MsgBox(Message, Icon)
    End Sub
End Class
```

How does Visual Basic know which overloaded version to use? It need only check the argument list you're passing to the method and find the version of the method that has the same number and types of

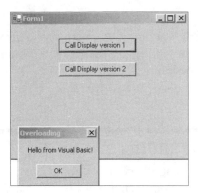

Figure 11.4   Overloading a method.

arguments, in the same order. That's all it takes—you can see the results in Figure 11.4.

You can also use an **Overloads** keyword to indicate that you're overloading a method or property. You don't need to use **Overloads** when you're overloading members of the same class, but it becomes important when you're working with inheritance. See the section "Overloading Base Class Members" in Chapter 12 for the details.

Getting Rid of Objects When You're Done with Them

When you're done with an object and want to get rid of it so that it no longer takes up memory and other resources, what do you do? (This isn't necessarily a problem when you have one such object, but imagine if you have an array of 20,000 of them.) The official way to get rid of objects is to assign them the **Nothing** keyword. That might look like this:

```
Dim notifierObject As New Notifier()
notifierObject.Display("Hello from Visual Basic!")
notifierObject = Nothing
```

This tags the object for garbage collection, which was discussed in the In Brief section of this chapter. When the program gets around to collecting the garbage, this object will be destroyed. Note that you don't have to do this at all unless you explicitly want to get rid of an object; if an object goes out of scope, it is automatically targeted for garbage collection. The Visual Basic documentation goes on a great deal about how you can't determine when garbage collection happens—but you can. See the next section.

Triggering Garbage Collection

In the Visual Basic documentation, you'll read a lot about how you have no control over when garbage collection happens. But it's a little-known fact that you *do* have control over this if you want it. All you have to do is to go behind the scenes to the garbage collector namespace (which is **GC**) and use the **Collect** method:

```
System.GC.Collect()
```

Creating Class Libraries

Now that you're creating classes, we can also take a look at creating class libraries. When you have a large number of classes to handle, you can store them in a class library and compile them into a dynamic link library (DLL) file, which can be used across multiple projects if you wish.

Here's an example named ClassLibraries. In this case, you'll create a class library with two classes, imaginatively called **Class1** and **Class2**. These classes are just for demonstration purposes; both of them will have a method named **Display**, which displays a message box. You pass the text for the message box to the **Class1 Display** method, and the text and a message box icon to the **Class2 Display** method—that's the only difference between these methods. To create a class library, select the NewProject item, and this time select the Class Library icon in the New Project dialog box, use the name ClassLibraries, and click OK.

This creates and opens the following template in a code designer:

```
Public Class Class1

End Class
```

You want to create two classes here, each with a **Display** method, so add this code:

```
Public Class Class1
    Public Sub Display(ByVal Message As String)
        MsgBox(Message)
    End Sub
End Class

Public Class Class2
    Public Sub Display(ByVal Message As String)
        MsgBox(Message, MsgBoxStyle.Exclamation)
    End Sub
End Class
```

To make this class library available to other projects, you compile it into a DLL file using the Build|Build ClassLibraries menu item, which creates, in this case, ClassLibraries.dll.

To use this DLL file, create a new project named Displayer. To do that, use the New|Project menu item and click the Add To Solution radio button in the New Project dialog box. Make this a Windows application named Displayer and click OK. Now make this new project the startup project with the Project|Set As Startup Project menu item. (You can't run a class library project like ClassLibraries, so you need a startup project to test out our code.)

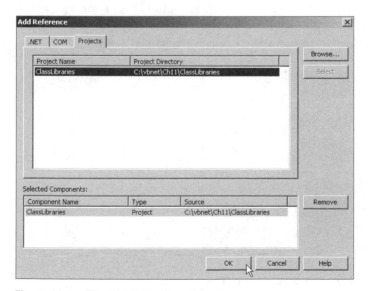

Figure 11.5   The Add Reference dialog box.

To use the classes in ClassLibraries.dll in the Displayer project, select the Project|Add Reference menu item to open the Add Reference dialog box you see in Figure 11.5. Click the Projects tab, double-click the ClassLibraries item to make it appear in the Selected Components box, then click OK.

Now you can use the classes in the ClassLibraries class library; for example, to use **Class1**, you refer to it as **ClassLibraries.Class1**. Here's how I do that in the ClassLibraries example—I create an object of the **ClassLibraries.Class1** class, then use that object's **Display** method like this:

```
Dim cl As New ClassLibraries.Class1()

Private Sub Button1_Click(ByVal sender As System.Object, _
    ByVal e As System.EventArgs) Handles Button1.Click
    cl.Display("Hello from Visual Basic!")
End Sub
```

Now when you click this button, the **Display** method displays a message box as it should, as you see in Figure 11.6.

Creating Namespaces

When you're creating a large number of classes, it can be helpful to divide them up into their own namespaces to help organize things. You already know about namespaces; as the name implies, you use them to create separate spaces so that names can't conflict with other names already declared. To create your own namespace, you can use the **Namespace** statement:

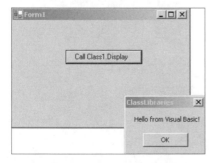

Figure 11.6   Using a class library.

```
Namespace {name | name.name}
    componenttypes
End Namespace
```

Here are the parts of this statement:

- **name**—Required. A unique name that identifies the namespace.

- **componenttypes**—Required. Elements that make up the namespace. These include enumerations, structures, interfaces, classes, delegates, and so on.

Note that namespaces are always public, which means that the declaration of a namespace cannot include any access modifiers. (However, the components inside the namespace may have public or friend access; the default access is friend.)

Here's an example that declares two namespaces, one inside another:

```
Namespace Secret
    'Declares a namespace named Secret.
    Namespace TopSecret
        ' Declares a namespace named TopSecret in Secret.
        Class Documents
            ' Declares the class Secret.TopSecret.Documents.
            .
            .
            .
        End Class
    End Namespace
End Namespace
```

Using the **Finalize** Method (Creating Destructors)

You know how to create constructors, but what about *destructors*, which are run when an object is destroyed? You can place code to clean up after the object, such as saving state information and closing files, in a destructor. In Visual Basic, you can use the **Finalize** method for this purpose. The **Finalize** method is called automatically when the .NET runtime determines that the object is no longer needed.

Here's a quick example I'll call Finalize. In this case, I'm creating an object of a class named **Class1** and adding a **Finalize** method that beeps when the object is destroyed. Here's what the code looks like:

```
Public Class Form1
    Inherits System.Windows.Forms.Form

    'Windows Form Designer generated code

    Dim Object1 As New Class1()
End Class

Public Class Class1
    Protected Overrides Sub Finalize()
        Beep()
    End Sub
End Class
```

TIP: *You have to use the* **Overrides** *keyword with* **Finalize** *because you're actually overriding the* **Finalize** *method built into the* **Object** *class.*

When you run this example, a blank form appears, and an object, **Object1**, of **Class1** is created; when you close the form, **Object1** is destroyed, and the **Beep** method beeps. The usual code you place in **Finalize** is a little more substantial; you can use this method to deallocate resources, disconnect from the Internet, inform other objects that the current object is going to be destroyed, and more.

Chapter 12

Object-Oriented Inheritance

In Brief

This chapter is all about inheritance, which is the process you use to derive one class from another. This is more useful than it may sound because Visual Basic comes with thousands of built-in base classes from which to create derived classes and then customize. There's a great deal to inheritance in Visual Basic .NET, and I don't have the space to cover all of it here; for the full details, see the *Visual Basic .NET Black Book*.

You're already familiar with this process from your work with Windows forms because you derive forms from **System.Windows.Forms.Form** and then customize them with buttons and event handlers like this:

```
Public Class Form1
    Inherits System.Windows.Forms.Form

    'Windows Form Designer generated code

    Private Sub Button1_Click(ByVal sender As System.Object, _
        ByVal e As System.EventArgs) Handles Button1.Click
        .
        .
        .
    End Sub
End Class
```

The **Inherits** statement you see here is used to declare a new class, called the *derived class,* based on an existing class, known as the *base class.* Derived classes inherit and can extend the properties, methods, events, fields, and constants defined in the base class (the exception here is constructors, which are *not* inherited). For example, if you have a class named **Animal** that has a method named **Breathe** and then derive a class named **Dog** from **Animal**, **Dog** will already have the **Breathe** method built in.

By default, any class can serve as a base class unless you explicitly mark it with the **NotInheritable** keyword, as you'll see in this chapter. Let's take a look at an example, which I'll name Inheritance, that puts this into a practical light and will give you a good start on inheritance. In fact, here I'll implement the base class **Animal** and the derived class **Dog** discussed earlier. I start by creating the **Animal** class.

This class will have a method named **Breathing**, which displays the text "Breathing..." in a text box in the program's main Windows form. To get access to that form, I can pass that form to the constructor, **New**, which will store it as **MainForm**:

```
Public Class Animal
    Public MainForm As Form1

    Public Sub New(ByVal form1 As Form1)
        MainForm = form1
    End Sub
    .
    .
    .
End Class
```

Now, in **Breathing**, I can use **MainForm** to display the text "Breathing..." in a text box, **TextBox1**, in the main form:

```
Public Class Animal
    Public MainForm As Form1

    Public Sub New(ByVal form1 As Form1)
        MainForm = form1
    End Sub

    Public Sub Breathing()
        MainForm.TextBox1.Text = "Breathing..."
    End Sub
End Class
```

That's simple enough so far. Now I can derive a new class, **Dog**, from **Animal**—note the **Inherits** statement here:

```
Public Class Dog
    Inherits Animal
    .
    .
    .
End Class
```

However, this raises an issue: How do you pass the form for displaying text to the **Animal** class's constructor so that it can store it in **MainForm**? In other words, when you create an object of the **Dog** class, how can you pass necessary data back to the base class's constructor? You can do that by referring to the base class with the special **MyBase** keyword, which refers to the base class. This means that you can call the base class's constructor as **MyBase.New**. Note that if you do call a base class's constructor, you must do so as the very first line (Visual Basic insists on this) in your derived class's constructor:

```
Public Class Dog
    Inherits Animal

    Public Sub New(ByVal form1 As Form1)
        MyBase.New(form1)
    End Sub
        .
        .
        .
End Class
```

Now the **Dog** class inherits everything the **Animal** class had, such as the **Breathing** method. In addition, it inherits the **MainForm** data member, so I can use that data member when I add a new method to **Dog**, **Barking**:

```
Public Class Dog
    Inherits Animal

    Public Sub New(ByVal form1 As Form1)
        MyBase.New(form1)
    End Sub

    Public Sub Barking()
        MainForm.TextBox1.Text = "Barking..."
    End Sub
End Class
```

In this way, I'm augmenting and customizing the base class in the derived class. For example, now **Dog** supports a **Barking** method in addition to the **Breathing** method. To see the **Dog** class at work, I can create a new **Dog** object, passing its constructor the current form so that it knows what form to display results in and calling its **Breathing** method like this (recall that the **Me** keyword, which you first saw in Chapter 7, refers to the current form):

```
Public Class Form1
    Inherits System.Windows.Forms.Form
```

```
"Windows Form Designer generated code
Dim spot As Dog

Private Sub Button1_Click(ByVal sender As System.Object, _
    ByVal e As System.EventArgs) Handles Button1.Click
    spot = New Dog(Me)
    spot.Breathing()
End Sub
End Class
```

You can see the Inheritance example at work in Figure 12.1. When I click the "Create a dog..." button, the code creates a new **Dog** object, and the **Dog** class's constructor passes the main form back to the **Animal** base class. When you call the **Breathing** method, which is inherited from the base class, the program displays the text "Breathing..." in the main form, as you see in that figure. Now I'm using inheritance.

As I've discussed as far back as Chapter 3, you can control the access that derived classes have to base class members with *access modifiers*.

Access Modifiers

You've been seeing access modifiers throughout the book. You use access modifiers when you declare a class and when you declare the members of the class. Here they are—note that some of them, such as **Protected**, are designed to be used only with inheritance:

- **Public**—Entities declared **Public** have public access. No restrictions are placed on the accessibility of public entities. You can use **Public** only at the module, namespace, or file level.

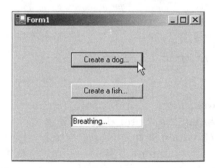

Figure 12.1   The Inheritance example.

- **Protected**—Entities declared **Protected** have protected access. They are accessible only from within their own class or from a derived class. Protected access is not a superset of friend access. You can use **Protected** only at the class level.

- **Friend**—Entities declared **Friend** have friend access. They are accessible from within the program that contains their declaration and from anywhere else in the same assembly. You can use **Friend** only at the module, namespace, or file level.

- **Protected Friend**—Entities declared **Protected Friend** have both protected and friend access. They can be used by code in the same assembly as well as by code in derived classes. The rules for **Protected** and **Friend** apply to **Protected Friend** as well.

- **Private**—Entities declared **Private** have private access. They are accessible only from within their declaration context, including from any nested procedures. You can use **Private** only at the module, namespace, or file level.

Public base class members are available to derived classes and everywhere else, private members are available only in the current class (not in classes derived from that class), protected members are available only in the current class and classes derived from that class, and friend members are available throughout the current assembly. For example, note that I declared the **MainForm** data member in the **Animal** class as **Public**:

```
Public Class Animal
    Public MainForm As Form1

    Public Sub New(ByVal form1 As Form1)
        MainForm = form1
    End Sub
        .
        .
        .
End Class
```

However, this gives **MainForm** more scope than it needs, and it's contrary to the idea of encapsulation and data hiding in object-oriented programming (OOP), which says that objects should be as self-contained as possible (to avoid unintentional naming conflicts or illegal data access). There's no reason all parts of the code should have access to this variable—but classes derived from this class *will* need access to **MainForm**, so I make **MainForm** *protected*, which restricts its scope to the current class (**Animal**) and any classes derived from it (such as **Dog**). This is how **MainForm** is declared in the Inheritance example:

```
Public Class Animal
    Protected MainForm As Form1

    Public Sub New(ByVal form1 As Form1)
        MainForm = form1
    End Sub
    .
    .
    .
End Class
```

Inheritance Modifiers

By default, all classes can serve as base classes in Visual Basic .NET. However, you can use two class-level modifiers, called inheritance modifiers, to modify that behavior:

- **NotInheritable**—Prevents a class from being used as a base class.

- **MustInherit**—Indicates that the class is intended for use as a base class only. Note that objects of **MustInherit** classes cannot be created directly; they can only be created as base class instances of a derived class.

You'll see both of these modifiers in this chapter.

Overloading, Overriding, and Shadowing

Overloading, overriding, and shadowing are also important concepts in Visual Basic OOP. These techniques allow you to create multiple members with the same name. We've already discussed them in the previous chapter; here's how they work in overview:

- *Overloaded* members provide different versions of a property or method that have the same name but that accept a different number of parameters (or parameters of different types).

- *Overridden* properties and methods replace an inherited property or method. When you override a member from a base class, you replace it. Overridden members must accept the same data type and number of arguments.

- *Shadowed* members create a local version of a member that has broader scope. You can also shadow a type with any other type. For example, you can declare a property that shadows an inherited method with the same name.

You saw overloading in the previous chapter, although I'll have a little more to say about it here. In particular, you can use an **Overloads** keyword to indicate that you're overloading a method or property. You don't need to use **Overloads** when you're overloading members of the same class, but it becomes important when you're working with inheritance—see the section "Overloading Base Class Members" later in this chapter.

What's overriding? If an inherited property or method needs to behave differently in the derived class, it can be overridden; that is, you can define a new implementation of the method in the derived class. The following modifiers are used to control how properties and methods are overridden:

- **Overridable**—Allows a property or method in a class to be overridden.

- **Overrides**—Overrides an **Overridable** property or method.

- **NotOverridable**—Prevents a property or method from being overridden. Note that public methods are **NotOverridable** by default.

- **MustOverride**—Requires that a derived class override the property or method. **MustOverride** methods must be declared in **MustInherit** classes.

Let's see an example of overriding at work. In the example I'm calling Inheritance, the base class is **Animal**, and when you call its **Breathing** method, it displays "Breathing...". However, if you were to derive a class named **Fish** from **Animal**, that wouldn't quite be appropriate—you might want this method to display something like "Bubbling..." instead. To do that, you can override the **Animal** class's **Breathing** method in the **Fish** class—you need only mark the **Animal** class's **Breathing** method as **Overridable** and use the **Overrides** keyword when defining the **Breathing** method in the **Fish** class:

```
Public Class Animal
    Protected MainForm As Form1
```

```
Public Sub New(ByVal form1 As Form1)
    MainForm = form1
End Sub

Public Overridable Sub Breathing()
    MainForm.TextBox1.Text = "Breathing..."
End Sub
End Class


Public Class Fish
    Inherits Animal

    Public Sub New(ByVal form1 As Form1)
        MyBase.New(form1)
    End Sub

    Public Overrides Sub Breathing()
        MyBase.MainForm.TextBox1.Text = "Bubbling..."
    End Sub
End Class
```

Now I can declare a **Fish** object named **jaws**, and when I use its overridden **Breathing** method, you'll see "Bubbling...", not "Breathing...":

```
Dim jaws As Fish

Private Sub Button2_Click(ByVal sender As System.Object, _
    ByVal e As System.EventArgs) Handles Button2.Click
    jaws = New Fish(Me)
    jaws.Breathing()
End Sub
```

You can see this code at work in the Inheritance example in Figure 12.2.

Visual Basic Methods Are Virtual

Here's an interesting OOP fact: If you declare an object of the **Animal** class, you can assign any object of a class derived from **Animal**, such as the **Dog** class, to that object:

```
Dim obj As Animal

Private Sub Button2_Click(ByVal sender As System.Object, _
    ByVal e As System.EventArgs) Handles Button2.Click
```

```
obj = New Dog(Me)
          .
          .
          .

End Sub
```

Now you can use all the **Animal** class's members with the **obj** object—but you can't use any members that **Dog** has that **Animal** doesn't (because **obj** is declared as an **Animal** object). For example, the **Dog** class implements its own **Barking** method, and Visual Basic will object if you try to use **obj.Barking**.

So what happens if you use a derived class that has overridden some base class members? For example, the **Fish** class overrides the **Animal** class's **Breathing** method, so if you use this code, will you see "Breathing..." or "Bubbling..."?

```
Dim obj As Animal

Private Sub Button2_Click(ByVal sender As System.Object, _
    ByVal e As System.EventArgs) Handles Button2.Click
    obj = New Fish(Me)
    obj.Breathing()
End Sub
```

Because **obj** is an **Animal** object, you might expect to see "Breathing...", but in fact, you'll see "Bubbling...". That's because all methods are *virtual* in Visual Basic OOP, which means that objects use the latest overridden method. In this case, that means that the **Fish** class's **Breathing** method is used, not the **Animal** base class's **Breathing** method.

Figure 12.2   Overriding a base class method in the Inheritance example.

TIP: *If you are familiar with OOP, It might interest you to know that you can also create pure virtual methods, called abstract methods, with the Visual Basic* **MustInherit** *keyword. Abstract methods can't be used in a base class but must be implemented in a derived class.*

Now it's time to start looking into some of the more detailed aspects of what we've been discussing.

Immediate Solutions

Inheriting from a Base Class

To inherit a base class in a derived class, you use the **Inherits** statement, which makes the derived class inherit the attributes, fields, properties, methods, and events from the base class:

```
Inherits classname
```

Here, *classname* is required, and it's the name of a class being inherited by the class in which the **Inherits** statement is used. You use this statement first thing (before any other statement) in a derived class:

```
Public Class Form1
    Inherits System.Windows.Forms.Form
    .
    .
    .
```

As discussed in the In Brief section of this chapter, you can use access modifiers to indicate how the members of a base class will be inherited and what scope they will have. For more information, see the discussion at the beginning of the In Brief section of this chapter.

Related solution:	Found on page:
Creating Classes	206

Using Public Inheritance

When a member of a class is made public, no restrictions are placed on its scope—it can be used by any part of your program. Public members in a base class become public members of a derived class by default. You make classes and members public with the **Public** keyword (see the section "Access Modifiers" in the In Brief section of this chapter), as I've done many places in the Inheritance example, which is discussed in the In Brief section of this chapter:

```
Public Class Form1
    Inherits System.Windows.Forms.Form

    "Windows Form Designer generated code
    Dim spot As Dog

    Private Sub Button1_Click(ByVal sender As System.Object, _
        ByVal e As System.EventArgs) Handles Button1.Click
        spot = New Dog(Me)
        spot.Breathing()
    End Sub
End Class


Public Class Animal
    Protected MainForm As Form1
    Public Sub New(ByVal form1 As Form1)
        MainForm = form1
    End Sub

    Public Sub Breathing()
        MainForm.TextBox1.Text = "Breathing..."
    End Sub
End Class

Public Class Dog
    Inherits Animal

    Public Sub New(ByVal form1 As Form1)
        MyBase.New(form1)
    End Sub

    Public Sub Barking()
        MainForm.TextBox1.Text = "Barking..."
    End Sub
End Class
```

Using Protected Inheritance

When you declare a member of a base class protected, it's available throughout that class and in any derived classes, but nowhere else. You can see an example of this in the Inheritance example, discussed in the In Brief section of this chapter. In that example, I pass the main Windows form of the program to the **Animal** class's constructor (so that class can display text in the main window), and that form is stored in the **Animal** class's **MainForm** variable. Because derived classes will also need to use **MainForm** but no other classes will, I made that variable protected (this is discussed in the In Brief section of this chapter):

```
Public Class Form1
    Inherits System.Windows.Forms.Form

    "Windows Form Designer generated code
    Dim spot As Dog

    Private Sub Button1_Click(ByVal sender As System.Object, _
        ByVal e As System.EventArgs) Handles Button1.Click
        spot = New Dog(Me)
        spot.Breathing()
    End Sub
End Class

Public Class Animal
    Protected MainForm As Form1
    Public Sub New(ByVal form1 As Form1)
        MainForm = form1
    End Sub

    Public Sub Breathing()
        MainForm.TextBox1.Text = "Breathing..."
    End Sub
End Class

Public Class Dog
    Inherits Animal

    Public Sub New(ByVal form1 As Form1)
        MyBase.New(form1)
    End Sub

    Public Sub Barking()
        MainForm.TextBox1.Text = "Barking..."
    End Sub
End Class
```

Using Private Inheritance

If you make a class member private, it's available only in the present class—not outside that class and not in any class derived from that class. For example, if I made the **MainForm** member of the **Animal** class private in the Inheritance example, as discussed in the previous topic and in the In Brief section of this chapter, that member would not be available in the derived class named **Dog**. That means that this code wouldn't work because I've made **MainForm** private but tried to use it in the derived **Dog** class (note also that the button event handlers are private in the **Form1** class, which means that they can't be used in any class derived from **Form1**):

```
Public Class Form1
    Inherits System.Windows.Forms.Form

    "Windows Form Designer generated code

    Dim spot As Dog
    Dim jaws As Fish

    Private Sub Button1_Click(ByVal sender As System.Object, _
        ByVal e As System.EventArgs) Handles Button1.Click
        spot = New Dog(Me)
        spot.Breathing()
    End Sub

    Private Sub Button2_Click(ByVal sender As System.Object, _
        ByVal e As System.EventArgs) Handles Button2.Click
        jaws = New Fish(Me)
        jaws.Breathing()
    End Sub
End Class

Public Class Animal
    Private MainForm As Form1
    Public Sub New(ByVal form1 As Form1)
        MainForm = form1
    End Sub

    Public Overridable Sub Breathing()
        MainForm.TextBox1.Text = "Breathing..."
    End Sub
End Class
```

```
Public Class Dog
    Inherits Animal

    Public Sub New(ByVal form1 As Form1)
        MyBase.New(form1)
    End Sub

    Public Sub Barking()
        "Will not work now!!!
        MainForm.TextBox1.Text = "Barking..."
    End Sub
End Class

Public Class Fish
    Inherits Animal

    Public Sub New(ByVal form1 As Form1)
        MyBase.New(form1)
    End Sub

    Public Overrides Sub Breathing()
        MainForm.TextBox1.Text = "Bubbling..."
    End Sub
End Class
```

TIP: *If you declare a class **Private**, all the members in it are restricted to that class.*

Using Friend Access

The scope of public members is unlimited, but you can also give members *friend* scope, which restricts them to the current program (that is, the program that contains their declaration) and anywhere else in the same assembly. (Public members, by contrast, are available across assemblies.) You can use the **Friend** keyword in these statements:

- **Class**
- **Const**
- **Declare**
- **Dim**
- **Enum**
- **Event**
- **Function**

- **Interface**
- **Module**
- **Property**
- **Structure**
- **Sub**

You can declare friend access just like any other access modifier; here's an example:

```
Public Class Displayer
    Friend Sub Display(ByVal Text As String)
        MsgBox(Text)
    End Sub
End Class

Dim displayer As New displayer()
Private Sub Button1_Click(ByVal sender As System.Object, _
    ByVal e As System.EventArgs) Handles Button1.Click
    displayer.Display("Hello from Visual Basic!")
End Sub
```

Inheriting Constructors

By default, constructors are *not* inherited in Visual Basic. The idea here is that initializing a derived class's object will be different from initializing an object of the base class, so you're responsible for creating your own constructor in derived classes, if you want to give them one.

TIP: Here's an important point: If you give a derived class a constructor and the base class does not have an explicit constructor that you can call with no arguments, Visual Basic will insist that you call the base class's constructor first thing in the derived class.

You saw an example of using constructors and inheritance in the Inheritance example, as discussed in the In Brief section of this chapter. In that case, I'm deriving the **Dog** class from the **Animal** class. The **Animal** class has a constructor that accepts a form—the main form for the program—and stores it in a protected member named **MainForm**. To pass that form from the **Dog** class's constructor back to the **Animal** class's constructor, I called the **Animal** class's constructor as **MyBase.New** (see the In Brief section of this chapter for more in-depth information):

```
Public Class Form1
    Inherits System.Windows.Forms.Form

    "Windows Form Designer generated code

    Dim spot As Dog

    Private Sub Button1_Click(ByVal sender As System.Object, _
        ByVal e As System.EventArgs) Handles Button1.Click
        spot = New Dog(Me)
        spot.Breathing()
    End Sub
End Class

Public Class Animal
    Protected MainForm As Form1

    Public Sub New(ByVal form1 As Form1)
        MainForm = form1
    End Sub

    Public Sub Breathing()
        MainForm.TextBox1.Text = "Breathing..."
    End Sub
End Class

Public Class Dog
    Inherits Animal

    Public Sub New(ByVal form1 As Form1)
        MyBase.New(form1)
    End Sub

    Public Sub Barking()
        MyBase.MainForm.TextBox1.Text = "Barking..."
    End Sub
End Class
```

Note that if you do call a base class's constructor from a derived class's constructor, that call must be the first line in the derived class's constructor.

Chapter 13

Web Forms

In Brief

In this chapter, we begin our work with Web applications. One of the most important features of Visual Basic .NET is the ability to create distributed applications centered around the Web, so prepare to be amazed. In this chapter, I'll take a look at creating Web applications with Web forms. This represents quite a change from Windows forms and a remarkable amount of programming power.

Working with Web Forms

Web forms are based on ASP.NET (ASP stands for Active Server Pages). Visual Basic will handle the details of working with ASP.NET for you, so in the end it feels much like you're working with a standard Windows Visual Basic project. But the difference is that you're creating a Web page or pages that can be accessed by any browser on the Internet. These Web pages are given the extension .aspx, so, for example, if your program is called CalculateRates, you might end up simply directing users to a Web page called CalculateRates.aspx, which they can open in their browsers.

To create Web applications, you'll need a computer with the Microsoft Internet Information Services (IIS) version 5 or later installed (either locally or on a remote server).

NOTE: *If you want to use FrontPage Server Extensions, the server extensions also must be installed on that server.*

IIS must be running on a Windows machine with the .NET framework installed so that your Visual Basic code can run. Note that for development purposes, you can use IIS locally if you install it on the same machine that you develop programs on. (IIS comes preinstalled in some Windows operating systems, such as Windows 2000 Server, and comes on the CDs for it, but it still has to be installed in others, such as Windows 2000 Professional.)

The Web forms you create need not run in Internet Explorer, but if they don't, a number of features will usually be disabled because they need Internet Explorer to work (see the section "Detecting Browser Type and Capabilities" in the Immediate Solutions section of this chapter). In Web forms, the user interface programming is divided into two distinct pieces: the visual component, which is the Web page itself (this can include scripting code, such as JavaScript—or JScript, the Internet Explorer equivalent—to run in the browser), and the Visual Basic code behind that page (which runs on the server). The visual component has the extension .aspx, and the code that runs on the server has the extension .aspx.vb.

Working with Web Form Controls

Developing a Web form–based application is much like developing a Windows form–based application. Visual Basic will manage the files on the server automatically, and you don't have to explicitly upload or download anything. That's very cool because you can make use of all that Visual Basic already offers you, such as drag-and-drop programming, IntelliSense code prompts, what-you-see-is-what-you-get (WYSIWYG) visual interface designing, project management, and so on. You can fill your Web forms with Web controls, just as you can place Windows controls in a Windows form. But because they run in browsers, Web forms and Web controls are more limited than the Windows variety.

Web Server Controls

The two varieties of Web form controls are server controls and client controls. *Web server controls* run not in the browser but back in the server. That means that when an event occurs, the Web page has to be sent back to the Web server to handle the event. For that reason, Microsoft has restricted Web server control events greatly, mostly handling only **Click**-type events. And by default, many events—such as **SelectedIndexChanged** events in list boxes—are not sent back to the server at all but wait until the whole page is sent ("posted" is the Web term) back to the server (which happens when you click a control that is always handled on the server, such as buttons). However, you *can* force Web server control events, such as **SelectedIndexChanged**, to be sent back to the server at the time they occur if you set the control's **AutoPostBack** property to **True** (see the section "Forcing Event Handling" in the Immediate Solutions section of this chapter).

Because Web server controls such as these are handled back at the server, you can connect Visual Basic code to them. Web server controls often support more functionality than standard HTML controls—but note that they still must run in a browser, so they're actually made up from HTML controls, sometimes in combination with other HTML controls. You can find the Web server controls—

many of which you'll recognize from Windows forms—in Table 13.1. When you want to add these controls to a Web form, you select the Web Forms tab in the toolbox.

HTML Server Controls

Visual Basic creates some Web server controls especially for Web forms, but it also supports the standard HTML controls, such as HTML text fields and HTML buttons. You can turn all standard HTML controls into *HTML server controls*, whose events are handled back at the

Table 13.1   Web server controls.

Control	Description
AdRotator	A control that displays ad banners
Button	A button control
Calendar	A control that displays a calendar for choosing dates
CheckBox	A checkbox control
CheckBoxList	A control that supports a group of checkboxes
DataGrid	A control that displays data in a table of columns
DataList	A control that displays data with more formatting options han a Repeater control
DropDownList	A control that allows users to select items from a list or enter text directly
HyperLink	A control that displays a hyperlink
Image	A control that displays an image
ImageButton	A button that displays an image
Label	A label control
LinkButton	A button that looks like a hyperlink but lets you handle Click events like any other button
ListBox	A list box control
Panel	A panel control
RadioButton	A radio button control
RadioButtonList	A control that supports a group of radio buttons
Repeater	A data control that displays information from a data set using HTML elements
Table	A control that creates an HTML table
TableCell	A control that creates a cell in an HTML table
TableRow	A control that creates a row in an HTML table
TextBox	A text box control

server. To do that, you right-click a control and select the Run As Server Control item. When you do, you can handle such HTML server controls in Visual Basic code in your program by connecting event-handling code to them just as you would in Windows forms. You can find the HTML server controls in Table 13.2. When you want to add these controls to a Web form, you use the HTML tab in the toolbox.

HTML Client Controls

HTML controls don't run on the server by default; they only do so if you right-click a control and select the Run As Server Control item. By default, they are handled in the browser, out of the reach of Visual Basic code. An advantage to operating this way is that if you handle events in the Web client (the browser) instead of the Web server, the whole page doesn't have to make the round-trip to the server, which saves a lot of time. Visual Basic refers to controls handled this way as *HTML client controls*. Because they run in the browser (as such controls might in any Web page), you have to program them with a language the browser understands, such as JavaScript. You do that with

Table 13.2   HTML server controls.

Control	Does this
HtmlAnchor	Creates an <a> element for navigation.
HtmlButton	Creates an HTML button using the <button> element.
HtmlForm	Creates an HTML form.
HtmlGenericControl	Creates a basic control for an HTML element.
HtmlImage	Creates an HTML <img> element.
HtmlInputButton	Creates an HTML button using the <input> element.
HtmlInputCheckbox	Creates an HTML checkbox.
HtmlInputFile	Creates an HTML file upload control.
HtmlInputHidden	Creates an HTML hidden control.
HtmlInputImage	Creates an HTML button that displays images.
HtmlInputRadioButton	Creates an HTML radio button.
HtmlInputText	Creates an HTML text field. (You also can use this control to create password fields.)
HtmlSelect	Creates an HTML select control.
HtmlTable	Creates an HTML table.
HtmlTableCell	Creates a cell in an HTML table.
HtmlTableRow	Creates a row in an HTML table.
HtmlTextArea	Creates an HTML text area (two-dimensional text field).

the Visual Basic HTML editor, which allows you to edit the HTML of the Web page directly. You add these controls to a Web form just as you add HTML server controls—with the HTML tab in the toolbox—but you don't select the Run As Server Control menu item here.

Validation Controls

Besides Web server controls, HTML server controls, and HTML client controls, you also can work with *validation controls* in Web forms. A validation control lets you test a user's input—for example, you can make sure that the user has entered text into a text field. You also can perform more complex tests, such as comparing what's been entered against a pattern of characters or numbers to make sure things are in the right format. To make these more specific tests, validation controls support *regular expressions*, which are special expressions used to check text against a pattern to see how well they match that pattern. You can find the validation controls in Table 13.3.

TIP: I'll cover regular expressions in this book, but for the full story, refer to the Perl Black Book, Second Edition, *which examines regular expressions in great detail.*

User Controls

User controls are controls that you create as Web forms pages. You can embed user controls in Web forms, giving you an easy way to create menus, toolbars, and other elements that users are familiar with from Windows forms.

Table 13.3   Validation controls.

Control	Does this
RequiredFieldValidator	Makes sure the user enters data in this field
CompareValidator	Uses comparison operators to compare user-entered data to a constant value
RangeValidator	Makes sure user-entered data is in a range between given lower and upper boundaries
RegularExpressionValidator	Makes sure user-entered data matches a regular-expression pattern
CustomValidator	Makes sure user-entered data passes validation criteria that you set yourself

Saving a Web Application's State

Here's another place where Web form programming differs from Windows form programming—in saving the current *state* of the data in controls. The problem here is that your data is in a Web page, and the code that works on them is back on the server. Visual Basic makes automatic provision to store the data in Web server controls using HTML hidden fields (that is, HTML **<input>** elements with the **type** attribute set to **"hidden"**), so you don't have to worry about the data in each Web server control (such as the text in a text box). But what about the variables in your program code? They're reset to their default value each time the page is sent on a round-trip to the server, so making sure that the data in your variables is stored is up to you. To see how to do this, see the section "Saving Program Data across Server Round-Trips" in the Immediate Solutions section of this chapter.

You can store the data in a page in two places: in the page itself (that is, in the client) and in the server. To see how this works, take a look at the section "Saving Program Data across Server Round-Trips" in the Immediate Solutions in this chapter; I'll also take a look at them in overview here.

Creating a Web Application

Before you create a Web application, you must have IIS running on the target server (which also must have the .NET framework installed) that will host your application. The reason IIS must be running on the target server is that Visual Basic will create the files you need and host them directly on the server when you create the Web application (usually in the IIS directory named wwwroot).

To create a new Web application, select the File|New menu item in Visual Basic, just as you would to create a new Windows application. This time, however, select the ASP.NET Web Application icon, as shown in Figure 13.1. You can enter the name for the new application, as you see in that figure. I'm going to call this first application First, so I change the URL in the Location box from http://STEVE/WebApplication1 to http://STEVE/First.

Instead of specifying a local or network disk location in the Location box, you enter the location you want to use on a Web server. I'm using a local server (that is, a server on my computer) named STEVE in Figure 13.1, so the location is "http://STEVE". That makes the URL for the main Web form in the First application, which is **WebForm1**, **http://STEVE/First/WebForm1.aspx**. That's the URL that gets launched when I (or someone else) want to run the application. For applications on the Internet, that URL might look something like this: **http://www.starpowder.com/First/WebForm1.aspx**. If you're unsure what server you want to use, click the Browse button next to the Location box in Figure 13.1. To create the Web application, click the OK button.

Similarly, to open a Web application that you've already created, use the File|Open Project From Web menu item (not the File|Open menu item). Visual Basic will ask for the URL of the server to use, then open the Open Project dialog box you see in Figure 13.2. You can browse to the .vbproj file you want and click Open to open it.

After you've created the First Web application, you'll see the main Web form, WebForm1.aspx, open in the Visual Basic Integrated Development Environment (IDE), as shown in Figure 13.3. This new project is like a Windows application project in many ways. For example, you can set project options, such as debugging versus release versions, the same way you would with Windows projects.

You'll also see some new files in the Solution Explorer; here's an overview of what they do:

- *AssemblyInfo.vb*—Contains all the information for your assembly, such as versioning and dependencies

- *Global.asax*—Handles application-level ASP requests

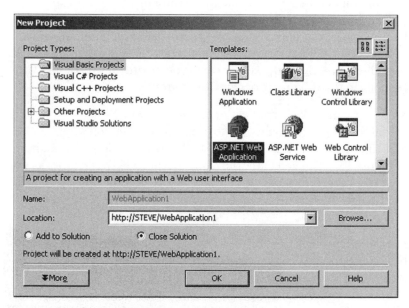

Figure 13.1   Creating a new Web application.

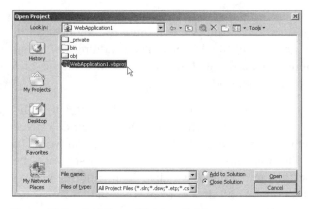

Figure 13.2   Opening a Web application.

- *Styles.css*—Can be used to define default HTML style settings for this Web form
- *Web.config*—Contains application settings for the ASP.NET application
- *Projectname.vsdisco*—An XML file that contains links about an ASP.NET Web application
- *WebForm.aspx*—The Web form itself
- References to these .NET framework namespaces: **System**, **System.Data**, **System.Drawing**, **System.Web**, **System.Web.Services**, and **System.Xml**

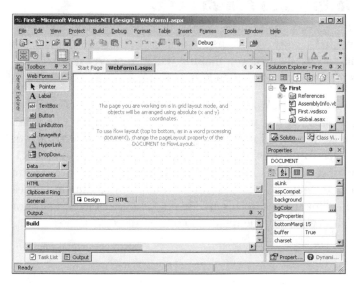

Figure 13.3   Designing a new Web form.

A .vbproj file also exists on the server in the application's folder for the Visual Basic project itself, and you can open the application in Visual Basic using that .vbproj file. When you start adding Visual Basic code to the application, a file with the .aspx.vb extension is created as well, which holds that code.

Note that the text in the Web form in Figure 13.3 indicates that the Web form is in *grid layout mode*, which means that you can place controls where you want them in the Web form, just as you would in a Windows form. The other layout option, which you set with the **pageLayout** property, is *flow layout*, which is the layout that browsers usually use. With flow layout, the controls you add to a Web form "flow," much like the words in a word processor's page, changing position when the page changes size. To anchor your controls, use grid layout. You can set the Web form's properties in the properties window, such as **bgColor**, to set the form's background color, just as you can for Windows controls.

NOTE: *There's a difference between the properties you'll see in the properties window for Web forms versus Windows forms: Web forms support properties that you'll normally find in HTML pages, such as bgColor (for the background color), vLink (for the color of hyperlinks the user has already visited), text (for the foreground color used for text), and so on. Note that these properties start with lowercase letters, unlike Windows forms properties, which start with uppercase letters.*

Adding Controls to a Web Form

You can now add controls to the Web form, just as you can with Windows forms. In this case, you'll use Web server controls, so click the Web Forms tab in the toolbox, making the Web server controls appear in the toolbox, as you see in Figure 13.4.

Just as you would with a Windows form, add two text boxes, **TextBox1** and **TextBox2**, to **WebForm1** and a button with the caption "Click Me". (The small boxed arrow at the upper left in each control indicates a server control, which is run at the server.) Also, add a list box control, **ListBox1**, to **WebForm1** and add six items to it as you would to a Windows form list box; click the ellipsis (...) button in the Items entry in the properties window and enter "Item 0" to "Item 5" in the ListItem Collection Editor dialog box. This gives you the result you see in Figure 13.4.

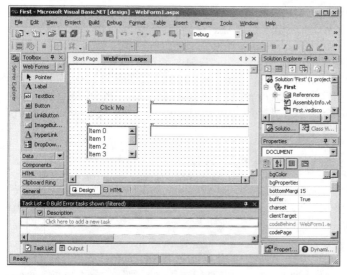

Figure 13.4   Adding Web server controls to a new Web form.

Using HTML Views

The Web form itself, WebForm1.aspx, is where the actual HTML that
browsers will open is stored. You can see that HTML directly if you
click the HTML button at the bottom of the Web form designer (next
to the Design button), as you see in Figure 13.5.

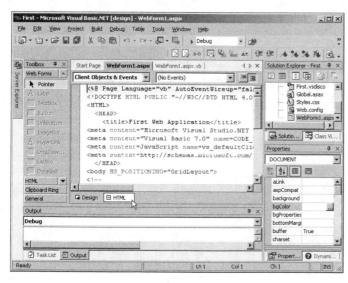

Figure 13.5   The HTML code for WebForm1.aspx.

This is close to the HTML that a Web browser will open, and you can edit this HTML directly. The ASP elements in this document, which begin with **<%@** and **<asp:** will be executed by IIS, which will create standard HTML from them. This HTML is then sent to the browser—that's how ASP works: ASP elements are executed in the server, which creates the HTML corresponding to the various ASP commands. That creates the final HTML that the browser actually sees, without any ASP elements in it.

Handling Events in Code

Double-click the button in **WebForm1** now. Doing so opens the code designer you see in Figure 13.6; the code here is definitely Visual Basic, and it runs on the server.

TIP: *As with Windows forms, you also can select events to add code to in a code designer by selecting the object (such as a control or a Web form) to work with in the left drop-down list box and the event you want to handle in the right drop-down list box.*

The Visual Basic code is stored in a file named WebForm1.aspx.vb. (This is also called the "code-behind" file.) Now that you've double-clicked the button in the Web form, and the corresponding Click event handler opens in the code designer:

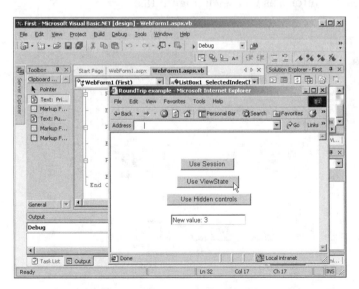

Figure 13.6   The code designer for **WebForm1**.

```
Private Sub Button1_Click(ByVal sender As System.Object, _
    ByVal e As System.EventArgs) Handles Button1.Click
    .
    .
    .
End Sub
```

You can enter code for this button just as you can in Windows forms. For example, to display the message "Welcome to Web programming." in the text box when the button is clicked, you can use this code:

```
Private Sub Button1_Click(ByVal sender As System.Object, _
    ByVal e As System.EventArgs) Handles Button1.Click
    TextBox1.Text = "Welcome to Web programming."
End Sub
```

In the same way, you can add code to display the current selection, when that selection changes, in the list box's **SelectedIndexChanged** event handler:

```
Private Sub ListBox1_SelectedIndexChanged(ByVal sender As _
    System.Object, ByVal e As System.EventArgs) Handles _
    ListBox1.SelectedIndexChanged
    TextBox2.Text = "You selected Item " & sender.SelectedIndex
End Sub
```

Running a Web Application

Now you've written your first Web application, called First. You run it as you would a Windows application. For example, you can use the Debug|Start menu item in the Visual Basic IDE. Doing so starts the application, but this time it'll appear not in a standard window but in your default browser, as you see in Figure 13.7.

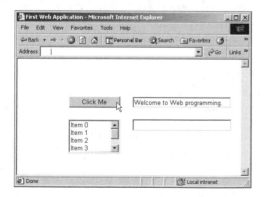

Figure 13.7   Running a Web application.

Of course, you don't need Visual Basic to run a Web application; you can also start the application simply by using a browser and navigating to its startup .aspx form on the server (that's **http://STEVE/Ch13/First/WebForm1.aspx** here; if you were running this page on a Web server named, say, **starpowder.com**, that could be **http://www.starpowder.com/Ch13/First/WebForm1.aspx**). The server will do the rest.

You can see the new Web application at work in Figure 13.7, looking a lot like a Visual Basic Windows application. Now you can click the button, and the message "Welcome to Web programming." appears in the text box, as it should—although note that it takes a round-trip to the server to make that happen. You can see the results in Figure 13.7.

Now try clicking an item in the list box. When you do, nothing happens. Why? I included a list box in this example to show that not all Web server control events are automatically sent back to the server when they occur (to save time by avoiding trips to the server). **Click** events usually are sent back to the server for processing, but not an event such as a list box's **SelectedIndexChanged** event.

Events such as **SelectedIndexChanged** are handled the next time the page is sent back to the server. If you were to change the selection in the list box and then click the "Click Me" button, that would send the form's data back to the server, and when it reappeared, the message "Welcome to Web programming." would appear in the top text box—but the code for the **SelectedIndexChanged** event would also have run, so the bottom text box would indicate which item you selected.

Sometimes you don't want to wait until the form is sent back to the server by other events before handling events, such as **SelectedIndexChanged**. It turns out that you can *force* events, such as **SelectedIndexChanged**, to be handled on the server at the time they occur if you set the control's **AutoPostBack** property to **True**. To see how that works, set the list box's **AutoPostBack** property to **True** and run the application again. When you do and when you change the selection in the list box by clicking a new selection, a message such as "You selected Item 1" appears in the bottom text box, without your having to wait until some other event sends the form back to the server. You can see this in Figure 13.8.

And that's it—pretty cool, huh? To close the application, you close the Web browser or select the Debug|Stop Debugging menu item.

And that's it. Now it's time to start getting into the additional details of all this in the Immediate Solutions section.

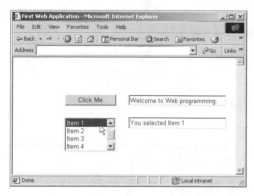

Figure 13.8   Enabling a Web application after **AutoPostBack**.

Immediate Solutions

Initializing a Web Form at Runtime

In Windows forms, you can place code in the **Form_Load** event to initialize the form when it first loads; in Web forms, you use the **Page_Load** event instead:

```
Private Sub Page_Load(ByVal sender As System.Object, _
    ByVal e As System.EventArgs) Handles MyBase.Load
        'Put user code to initialize the page here
    End Sub
```

For an example, see the section "Writing HTML to a Web Form at Runtime" later in this chapter.

Setting Control Layout

You can set the page layout for controls two ways in Web forms using the **pageLayout** property:

- **GridLayout**—This layout is the kind of layout you see in Windows forms. Using grid layout, you can place your controls where you want them, and they'll appear there in your Web page. You can call this kind of positioning *absolute positioning*.

- **FlowLayout**—This layout is the standard layout for controls in HTML pages; the browser can move controls as it wants, letting them "flow." Here, controls follow the same layout as words in a page in a word processor—as the page is resized, the words flow to match. You can call this kind of positioning *relative positioning*.

Forcing Event Handling

As discussed in the In Brief section of this chapter, some events, such as **Click**, cause a Web form to be sent back to the server for event processing, and some, such as **SelectedIndexChanged** in a list box, don't. Sending a Web form back to the server for processing is called "posting it back to the server." Events that aren't automatically posted back to the server are stored and processed when the form is posted back to the server (so, for example, a **SelectedIndexChanged** event would be handled when a **Click** event occurs elsewhere in the page).

To force a control's events to be automatically posted back to the server, and so handled at once, you set the control's

AutoPostBack property to **True**. That's all it takes (this adds the attribute **runat = "server"** to the control's HTML).

Setting Colors in Web Forms and HTML Pages

A number of properties in Web forms can be set to colors (such as **link**, **text**, **bgColor**, and so on). Colors can be specified in HTML pages in two ways: by using a color name (such as **"Red"** or **"Blue"** or **"Magenta"**, which are predefined color names supported by the browser) or by using numbers to denote an RGB color value. In HTML, an RGB color value consists of three two-digit hexadecimal (base 16) numbers (range: 0 to 255, which is to say #00 to #FF in hexadecimal, where # indicates a hexadecimal number) specifying the intensity of the corresponding color in this order: #*RRGGBB*, where *RR* is the red color value, *GG* is the green color value, and *BB* is the blue color value. (See the *HTML Black Book* for more details and examples.) For example, **"#FFFFFF"** is pure white, **"#000000"** is pure black, **"#FF0000"** is pure red, **"#00FF00"** is pure green, **"#0000FF"** is pure blue, **"#FF7F50"** is coral, **"#FF00FF"** is magenta, **"#800000"** is maroon, and so on. Note also that when you select a property that can be set to a color in the properties window, a color picker dialog box opens automatically, allowing you to set colors at design time easily.

Setting Title Bar Text

By default, you'll see the URL of a Web form in the browser's title bar when the Web form is being displayed. If that's not what you want (and it probably won't be), you should give the Web form a title, using the **title** property. For example, I've set this property to "First Web Application" in Figure 13.7.

Related solution:	*Found on page:*
Setting Title Bar Text	146

Setting Hyperlink Colors

You can set the colors used for hyperlinks in a Web form with these Web form properties, taken from HTML:

- **vlink**—The color used for links the user has already visited
- **alink**—The color used for active links—for example, those in the process of being clicked
- **link**—The color used for links before they've been activated or visited

Setting Page Margins

You can set the size of the page margins surrounding the content in a Web form and other HTML pages with these properties (measured in pixels):

- **rightMargin**—Sets the right margin
- **leftMargin**—Sets the left margin
- **topMargin**—Sets the top margin
- **bottomMargin**—Sets the bottom margin

Setting Text Color

You can set the "foreground" color (that is, the default color of text) used in Web forms and HTML pages with the **text** property, mirroring the attribute of the same name in HTML pages.

Creating an Error Page

You can add an error page to jump to when there's an unhandled page exception with the **Page** class's **errorPage** property. Just assign this property the URL of the error page you want to use.

Setting Background Images

As in other Web pages, you can set the background image used in Web forms and HTML pages using the **background** property. You can set this property to the URL of an image at runtime; at design time, you can browse to an image file to assign to this property.

Setting Background Color

In HTML, you set the background color using the **bgColor** attribute, and in Web forms and HTML pages, you can use the property of the same name.

Setting Background Properties

Internet Explorer supports a property for an HTML page's background that other browsers don't: fixed backgrounds. When you make a page's background fixed, it won't scroll when the rest of the page does. This provides a nice effect, rather as though the rest of the page is on a sheet of glass, moving over the background. To make the background fixed in a Web form or HTML page in VB .NET, set its **bgProperties** property to **Fixed**.

Navigating to Another Form

An easy way to let users navigate among the documents in a Web application is to use hyperlinks. To create a hyperlink, you use the Hyperlink tool in the toolbox and set the hyperlink's **navigationURL** property to the URL you want to navigate to. By default, clicking a hyperlink will open a new browser window; to replace the current page with the new page without opening a new window, set the hyperlink's **target** property to "**_self.**"

Redirecting to Another Form

You may want to redirect users from one Web forms page to another if, for example, you are upgrading a page and don't want to display it. To redirect users to another page, you add a line of code to a Web application, for example, in the **Page_Load** event handler:

```
Response.Redirect("http://www.starpowder.com/steve.html")
```

Writing HTML to a Web Form at Runtime

You can write HTML to a Web form at runtime with the **Write** method of the ASP.NET **Response** object. For example, to write the **<h1>** header "Welcome to my page!" in a Web form at runtime (not design time), place this line in the **Page_Load** event handler:

```
Response.Write("<h1>Welcome to my page!</h1>")
```

You can see this at work in an example I'll call WriteHTML in Figure 13.9.

Detecting Browser Type and Capabilities

Web applications can appear in various types of browsers, but the capabilities of your application may be restricted in browsers that VB .NET calls "downlevel." A downlevel browser is one that supports only HTML 3.2. Uplevel browsers, on the other hand, support the following:

Figure 13.9   Writing HTML at runtime.

- ECMAScript (the formal name for JavaScript) version 1.2
- HTML version 4
- Microsoft Document Object Model (MSDOM)
- Cascading style sheets (CSS)

To determine the type and capabilities of the target browser, you can use the properties of the **Request.Browser** object in the **Page_Load** event. You can find these properties in Table 13.4; these properties hold either text or a Boolean value (for example, **Request.Browser.Frames** returns a value of **True** if the browser supports frames, whereas **Request.Browser.Browser** will hold the text "IE" if the browser is Internet Explorer).

Saving Program Data across Server Round-Trips

As discussed in the In Brief section of this chapter, all the data in a Web form isn't necessarily preserved between round-trips to the server. By default, Visual Basic stores the data in Web server controls and HTML server controls in an HTML hidden field in the Web page (that is, HTML **<input>** elements with the **type** attribute set to **"hidden"**), so that data is preserved between round-trips to the server. However, what about the variables in your code? That data isn't stored automatically, so after the page goes to the server and comes back, the values in your variables will be reset to their default values (usually 0).

Table 13.4   Request.Browser properties.

To find this	Use this
Browser type (example: IE6)	Request.Browser.Type
Browser name (example: IE)	Request.Browser.Browser
Version (example: 6.0b)	Request.Browser.Version
Major version (example: 6)	Request.Browser.MajorVersion
Minor version (example: 0)	Request.Browser.MinorVersion
Platform (example: WinNT)	Request.Browser.Platform
Is it a beta version?	Request.Browser.Beta
Is it an AOL browser?	Request.Browser.AOL
Is it Win16?	Request.Browser.Win16
Is it Win32?	Request.Browser.Win32
Supports frames?	Request.Browser.Frames
Supports tables?	Request.Browser.Tables
Supports cookies?	Request.Browser.Cookies
Supports VBScript?	Request.Browser.VBScript
Supports JavaScript?	Request.Browser.JavaScript
Supports Java applets?	Request.Browser.JavaApplets
Supports ActiveX controls?	Request.Browser.ActiveXControls

However, you can make sure the data in your variables is stored over server round-trips, and you can do so in several ways. For example, say that you have a variable named **value1** that you increment every time the user clicks a button, displaying the new value. If you didn't save the value in **value1** between server round-trips, it would be set to 0 after every such trip, and if you incremented it and displayed the resulting value, the user would always see a value of 1, no matter how many times he or she clicked the button. How do you fix this problem?

I'll take a look at a couple of ways of saving the value in **value1** during server round-trips in an example I'll call RoundTrips, which you see in Figure 13.10. When you click any of the three buttons in that example, the code increments one of three counters, whose value is preserved between trips to the server; you'll see "New value: 1", then "New value: 2", then "New value: 3", and so on as you keep clicking a button.

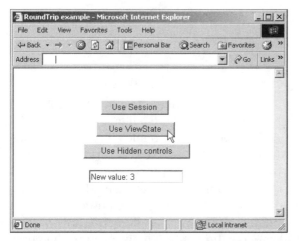

Figure 13.10   Saving program data across server round-trips.

The first technique I'll take a look at, illustrated by the first button in this example, is a server-side technique where you store data on the server using the ASP.NET **Session** object. Each time someone works with your Web application, a new session is created and given a long, randomly generated ID value. You can store and retrieve values using the **Session** object in Visual Basic code; here's how that looks when the user clicks the first button (caption: "Use Session"):

```
Private Sub Button1_Click(ByVal sender As System.Object, _
    ByVal e As System.EventArgs) Handles Button1.Click
    Dim value1 As Integer = Session("value1")
    value1 += 1
    TextBox1.Text = "New value: " & value1
    Session("value1") = value1
End Sub
```

Besides saving values on the server, you also can save them in the Web page itself. By default, Visual Basic stores data in an HTML hidden control in a Web page. The data in that control corresponds to a **StateBag** object, and you can reach that object yourself using a control's **ViewState** property. Because Web forms are based on the **Control** class, you can use the Web form's **ViewState** property to store and retrieve your data across server round-trips. Here's how that works when the user clicks the second button in the RoundTrips example (caption: "Use ViewState"):

```
Private Sub Button2_Click(ByVal sender As System.Object, _
    ByVal e As System.EventArgs) Handles Button2.Click
```

```
      Dim value1 As Integer = Me.ViewState("value1")
      value1 += 1
      TextBox1.Text = "New value: " & value1
      Me.ViewState("value1") = value1
End Sub
```

You also can create your own HTML hidden field in a Web form and use that to store data in. You can add a hidden field to a Web form by clicking the HTML tab in the toolbox and double-clicking the Hidden tool. You need to make this field into a server control so that its data will be preserved across server round-trips, so right-click it and select the Run As Server Control item. Finally, give it an ID value, using the **(id)** property in the Properties window, of **Hidden1**. Now you can access the data in this hidden control as **Hidden1.Value**, so here's how I use this control with the third button in the example (caption: "Use Hidden controls"):

```
Private Sub Button3_Click(ByVal sender As System.Object, _
    ByVal e As System.EventArgs) Handles Button3.Click
    Hidden1.Value += 1
    TextBox1.Text = "New value: " & Hidden1.Value
    End Sub
```

Index

I

ICO file, 37
Icons, specifying, 37
(**id**) property, 280
IDE, 23–46
  Class View window, 37–38
  code designers, 29–32
  Command window, 43–44
  component trays, 40–41
  customizing, 25
  docking windows, 23–24
  Dynamic Help window, 39–40
  forms in, 140–141
  graphical designers, 28–29
  IntelliSense feature, 32–34
  macros, 44
  menu system, 26
  New Project dialog box, 28
  Object Explorer, 34
  Output window, 42
  Properties window, 38–39. *See also*
    Properties window.
  Server Explorer, 41–42
  Solution Explorer, 36–37
  Start Page, 25
  Task List, 42–43
  toolbars, 27
  toolbox, 34–36
If statements, 52
  evaluating code with, 86–87
  evaluating data with, 86–87
  testing values with, 80
If Then...End If statements, 53
If...Else statements, decision making
  with, 86
Ignore setting, 157
IIS, 28, 258
  on target server, 263
IL (Internal Language), 15–16
IL modules, in assemblies, 19
Image control, 260
Image property, 164
ImageButton control, 260
ImageList property, 164
Import statement, 57–58
Imports statement, 57, 104
Increment method, 222–223
Indeterminate state, 177
Index properties, 119
Index values, of properties, 119
Indexes
  array, 71–72

choices based on, returning, 89–90
Information hiding, 45
Inheritance, 203
  from base class, 250
  of constructors, 255–256
  overriding, 232
  private, 253–254
  process of, 240–243
  protected, 252
  public, 250–251
Inheritance modifiers, 245
Inherits statement, 240, 250
initexpr keyword, 60, 64
  in **Dim** statement, 210
  in
    Structure statement, 210
Initialization value, specifying, 65
Inline compilation, 69
Input boxes, 156
Instance members, 56, 142, 201
Instances, 198
  shared members, sharing across, 202
intCountValue variable, 114
Integer data type, 52–53, 66–67
Integer data type class, 198
Integrated Development Environment. *See*
  IDE.
IntelliSense, 32–34
  arguments of, displaying, 33–34
  definition of, 32
  list members of, 33–34
  parameter info of, 33–34
  syntax tips, 33
  turning on and off, 34
Interface statement, **Friend** keyword
  in, 255
interfaceeventname keyword, in **Event**
  statement, 228
interfacemember keyword, 117
interfacename keyword
  in
    Class statement, 207
  in
    Event statement, 228
Internal values, setting or getting, 226
Internet, disconnecting from, 238
Internet Explorer
  background properties support, 275
  Web forms, running in, 258
intValue variable, 89
Invalid-argument exceptions, 136
Invoke method, 116
Is keyword, 83, 85, 87
  comparing objects with, 220

exception handling with, 127
IsArray( ) function, 70
IsDate( ) function, 70
IsDBNull( ) function, 70
IsError( ) function, 70
IsMissing function, 113
IsNothing function, 113
IsNumeric( ) function, 70
IsReference( ) function, 70
ItemHeight property, 192
ItemWidth property, 192

J

.js extension, 20

K

Keyboard combinations, 190
 defining, 183
 displaying, 183
KeyDown event, 163
Keywords, 48–52
 obsolete, 51
 square brackets for, 51

L

Label controls, 260
 creating, 156
Labels, 163–164, 170–171
 advantages of, 170–171
 creating, 122
 images in, supporting, 164–165
 text boxes resembling, 171
Layout modes, 9–10
Left function, 73
leftMargin property, 274
Len function, 73
Like operator, 83, 85
Line-continuation character, 46
Linefeed character, 152
link property, 274
LinkButton control, 260
LinkLabel control, 65
ListBox control, 260
ListItem Collection Editor dialog box, 266–267
Literal values, 52
Location property, 172
 of forms, 148–150

Logical/bitwise operators, 83–85
 order of precedence of, 85
Long data type, 52–53, 66–67
Loop index, 91–92
Loops
 For, 91–92
 controlling, 94
 Do, 90–91
 For Each...Next, 92–93
 nesting of, 45
 With statement and, 94
 While, 93–94

M

Macros, 44
Magic numbers
 avoiding, 45
 definition of, 45
Main Sub procedure, 100
MainForm data member, 241
MainMenu control, 186
Manifests, 19
Manual value, 147
MarshalByRefObject class, 162
MaximizeBox property, 146
MaxLength property, 163
MDI (Multiple Document Interface), 184
Me keyword, 146, 242
MeasureItem event, 192
MeasureItemEventArgs object, 192
Members, 199–201. *See also* Object members.
 class members, 142, 199–202
 overloaded, 203
 overloading, 245
 overriding, 203, 246
 shadowing, 203, 246
Menu access keys, 189–190
Menu bars, in Windows forms, 141
Menu items, 182–184
 active, 187
 checkmarks in, adding, 189
 disabling, 184, 192
 displaying, 184
 displaying checkmarks in, 189
 drawing, 192
 enabling, 184
 hiding checkmarks in, 189
 list of, 184
 showing, 192
Menu items captions, changing, 191
Menu property, 182

public scope, 106
Screen coordinate system, 148, 173
Select Case statement, 87–88
Select event, 184
SelectedIndexChanged event handler, 269
SelectedIndexChanged events, 259
  server processing of, 270
SelectionLength property, 169–170
SelectionStart property, 169–170
SelectionText property, 169–170
sender arguments, 171
Sensitive data, protecting, 45
Server controls, 259–260
  AutoPostBack property, 259
  code, connecting with, 259–260
  HTML server controls, 260–261
  list of, 260
  setting, 260–261
Server Explorer, 24, 41–42
Server extensions, FrontPage, 258
Servers
  Microsoft IIS 5.0 on, 9
  posting Web forms to, 273
  saving data between round-trips to,
    263, 277–280
Session object, 279
Set As Startup Object menu item, 37
Set As Startup Project menu item, 235
Set block, 117
Set procedure, 116–117
Set Startup Project menu item, 37
SetBounds method, 172–173
  arguments of, 173
  of forms, 148–150
  overloading, 149
  rearranging, 172
Setup And Deployment Projects folder, 28
Shadowing, 203, 245–247
Shadows keyword, 60, 64
  in
  Class statement, 206
  in
  Dim statement, 209
  in
  Event statement, 228
  in
  Structure statement, 209
  in
  Sub statement, 109
Shared data, 225
Shared data members, creating, 221–223
Shared events, creating, 231
Shared keyword, 63–64, 109
  creating class data members with,
    221–223

creating class events with, 231
creating class methods with, 224
creating class properties with, 227
  in
  Dim statement, 208–209
  for members, 202
  in
  Structure statement, 208–209
Shared members, 55, 142, 201
  sharing across instances, 202
Shared methods, creating, 224–225
Shared properties, creating, 227
Short data type, 52–53, 66–67
Short-circuiting, 84
Shortcut property, 183, 190
Show method, 150, 172
ShowDialog method, 158, 165
ShowInTaskbar property, 156
ShowShortcut property, 183
  displaying, 190
  setting, 190
Single data type, 52–53, 66–67
Sizable value, 147
SizableTool Window value, 147
Size objects, 148, 172–173
Size property, 172
  of forms, 148–150
Sizing handles, 4–5
Solution Explorer, 19
  AssemblyInfo.vb file, 37
  Class View window, 37–38
  Form1.vb file, 37
  hierarchy of, 36–37
  References folder, 37
Solutions, 19–20
  adding projects to current, 20
  building, 22
  debug mode, 21
  modes, setting, 21–22
  projects in, 20
  properties of, setting, 36
Sort order, 87
SPC function, 76
specified argument, 149
Square brackets ([]), 51
Standard arrays, 71–72
  declarations of, 71–72
Start Page, 25
  replacing, 26
Start Page tab, 24
StartPosition property, 147
Startup form, setting, 156
Startup projects, creating, 235
StateBag object, 279–280

VB.NET Core Language (Little) Black Book Quick Reference

The Property Statement

```
[ <attrlist> ] [ Default ] [ Public | Private | Protected | Friend |
Protected Friend ] [ ReadOnly | WriteOnly ] [Overloads | Overrides ]
[Overridable | NotOverridable] | MustOverride | Shadows | Shared]
Property varname([ parameter list ]) [ As typename ] [ Implements
interfacemember ]

    [ <attrlist> ] Get
        [ block ]
    End Get
    [ <attrlist> ] Set(ByVal Value As typename )
        [ block ]
    End Set
End Property
```

Redimensioning Arrays

```
ReDim [Preserve]
varname(subscripts) [As type] [, varname(subscripts) [As type]] . .
.
```

The Arithmetic Operators

- **^ Operator**: exponentiation
- *** Operator**: multiplication
- **/ Operator**: division
- **\ Operator**: integer division
- **Mod Operator**: modulus
- **+ Operator**: addition
- **- Operator**: subtraction

The Comparison Operators

Operator	True if	False if	Null if
<	expression1 < expression2	expression1 >= expression2	expression1 or expression2 = Null
<=	expression1 <= expression2	expression1 > expression2	expression1 or expression2 = Null
>	expression1 >expression2	expression1 <= expression2	expression1 or expression2 = Null
>=	expression1 >= expression2	expression1 < expression2	expression1 or expression2 = Null
=	expression1 =expression2	expression1 <> expression2	expression1 or expression2 = Null
<>	expression1 <> expression2	expression1 = expression2	expression1 or expression2 = Null

The Logical Operators

- **And Operator**: And operations
- **Eqv Operator**: compares two logical values
- **Imp Operator**: performs a logical implication on two values
- **Not Operator**: flips its operand's logical value
- **Or Operator**: Or operations
- **Xor Operator**: exclusive Or operations

Operator Precedence

Arithmetic	Comparison	Logical
Exponentiation (^)	Equality (=)	Not
Negation (−)	Inequality (<>)	And
Multiplication and division (*, /)	Less than (<)	Or
Integer division (\)	Greater than (>)	Xor
Modulus arithmetic (Mod)	Less than or equal to (<=)	Eqv
Addition and subtraction (+, −)	Greater than or equal to (>=)	Imp
String concatenation (&)		

Math Functions

Function	Calculates this
Abs Function	Absolute value
Atn Function	ArcTangent
Cos Function	Cosine
Exp Function	Exponentiation
Fix Function	Fix places
Int Function	Integer value
Log Function	Log
Rnd Function	Random number
Sgn Function	Sign
Sin Function	Sine
Sqr Function	Square root
Tan Function	Tangent

The String Handling Functions

To do this	Use this
Concatinating two strings	&, +, String.Concat, String.Join
Compare two strings.	StrComp, String.Compare, String.Equals, String.CompareTo
Convert strings.	StrConv, CStr, String.ToString
Copying strings	=, String.Copy
Convert to lowercase or uppercase.	Format, Lcase, Ucase, String.Format, String.ToUpper, String.ToLower
Converting to and from numbers	Str, Val. Format, String.Format
Create string of a repeating character.	Space, String, String.String
Create an array of strings from one string String.Split	
Find length of a string.	Len, String.Length
Format a string.	Format, String.Format
Get a substring	Mid, String.SubString
Insert a substring	String.Insert
Justify a string with padding.	LSet, Rset, String.PadLeft, PadRight
Manipulate strings.	InStr, Left, LTrim, Mid, Right, RTrim, Trim, String.Trim, String.TrimEnd, String.TrimStart
Remove text	Mid, String.Remove

Replace text	Mid, String.Replace
Set string comparison rules.	Option Compare
Search strings	InStr, String.Chars, String.IndexOf, String.IndexOfAny, String.LastIndexOf, String.LastIndexOf Any
Trim leading or trailing spaces	LTrim, RTrim, Trim, String.Trim, String.TrimEnd, String.TrimStart
Work with character codes.	Asc, AscW, Chr

The If statement

```
If condition
Then
[statements]
[ElseIf condition-n Then
[elseifstatements] ...
[Else
[elsestatements]]]]
End If
```

The Select Case Structure

```
Select Case testexpression
[Case expressionlist-n
[statements-n]] ...
[Case Else
[elsestatements]]
End Select
```

The For Loop

```
For index = start To end [Step
step]
[statements]
[Exit For]
[statements]
Next [index]
```

The Do Loop

The Do loop has two versions; you can either evaluate a condition at the beginning:

```
Do [{While | Until} condition]
[statements]
[Exit Do]
[statements]
Loop
```

or at the end:

```
Do
[statements]
```

```
[Exit Do]
[statements]
Loop [{While | Until} condition]
```

The While Loop

```
While condition
[statements]
Wend
```

The For Each Statement

```
For Each element In group
[statements]
[Exit For]
[statements]
Next [element]
```

The With Statement

```
With object
[statements]
End With
```

The Exit Statements

```
Exit Do
Exit For
Exit Function
Exit Sub
Exit Try
```

The End Statements

```
End
End Class
End Enum
End Function
End Get
End If
End Interface
End Module
End Namespace
```

```
End Property
End Select
End Set
End Structure
End Sub
End SyncLock
End Try
End While
End With
```

Declaring Subroutines

```
[ <attrlist> ] [{ Overloads |
Overrides | Overridable |
NotOverridable | MustOverride |
Shadows | Shared }]
[{ Public | Protected | Friend |
Protected Friend | Private }]
Sub name [(arglist)]
    [
statements ]
    [ Exit Sub ]
    [
statements ]
End Sub
```

Declaring Functions

```
[ <attrlist> ] [{ Overloads |
Overrides | Overridable |
NotOverridable | MustOverride |
Shadows | Shared }]
[{ Public | Protected | Friend |
Protected Friend | Private }]
Function name[(arglist)] [ As
type ]
    [ statements ]
    [ Exit Function ]
    [ statements ]
End Function
```

Showing and Hiding Forms

To show a form on the screen, you use the **Show** method, to hide it you use its **Hide** method.

Creating a Class

```
[ <attrlist> ] [ Public |
Private | Protected | Friend |
Protected Friend ]
[ Shadows ] [ MustInherit |
NotInheritable ] Class name
    [ Implements interfacename ]
        [ statements ]
End Class
```

Creating a Structure

```
[ <attrlist> ] [{ Public |
Protected | Friend |
Protected Friend | Private }]
Structure name
    [ variabledeclarations ]
    [ proceduredeclarations ]
End Structure
```

Creating an Object

```
[ <attrlist> ] [{ Public |
Protected | Friend | Protected
Friend |
Private | Static }] [ Shared ] [
Shadows ] [ ReadOnly ] Dim
[ WithEvents ] name[ (boundlist)
] [ As [ New ] type ] [ =
initexpr ]
```

When you create a new object from a class, you use the **New** keyword. If you omit the **New** keyword, you're just declaring a new object, and it's not yet created.

Overview of ADO.NET Objects

Here's a list of the most common ADO.NET objects:

* *Data Connection objects*—To start working with a database, you must have a data connection. A data adapter needs a connection to a data source to read and write data, and it uses **OleDbConnection** or **SqlConnection** objects to communicate with a data source.

(continued on Inside Back Cover...)